DREAM HOUSE

The White House as an American Home

A Kodak moment in living color with the Eisenhower family, Christmas Day 1960. The Beaux-Arts dining room, created in 1903 by McKim, Mead & White for the Theodore Roosevelt family, had been reconstructed and redecorated for Harry Truman. In 1952 B. Altman & Co., the New York department store, painted its dark, carved oak walls a muted Colonial green, replaced the baronial stone mantelpiece with slabs of dark green marble, and domesticated the vast space with neutral wall-to-wall carpeting. The vaguely colonial chairs date to 1903, and their golden damask upholstery shows the influence of Colonial Williamsburg on suburban decorating in the years after World War II. The history of the room was a summary of 20th-century White House decor, from the aristocratic aspirations of an imperial presidency to the nondescript tastes of an American war hero.

DREAM HOUSE

The White House as an American Home

Ulysses Grant Dietz and Sam Watters

History of the White House Architecture by Thomas Mellins

ACANTHUS PRESS

NEW YORK : 2009

Acanthus Press, LLC
1133 Broadway, Room 1229
New York, New York 10010
www.acanthuspress.com
212-414-0108

Library of Congress Cataloging-in-Publication Data

Dietz, Ulysses G. (Ulysses Grant), 1955-
Dream house : the White House as an American home / Ulysses Grant Dietz
and Sam Watters. History of the White House architectture / by Thomas Mellins.
p. cm.
Includes bibliographical references and index.
ISBN 978-0-926494-65-7 (hardcover)
1. White House (Washington, D.C.) 2. Architecture, Domestic--United
States. 3. Architecture--United States--History. 4. Interior
decoration--United States--History. 5. Washington (D.C.)--Buildings,
structures, etc. I. Watters, Sam, 1954- II. Mellins, Thomas. Chronological
history of the architecture of the White House. III. Title.

NA4443.W3D54 2009
728.0973--dc22
2009011705

Printed in China

CONTENTS

ACKNOWLEDGMENTS

Like the White House itself, our work has been made possible by the talents of others. The herculean scholarship of William Seale and Betty C. Monkman provided essential pathways; James Archer Abbott, historian of the Kennedy White House decoration, was generous with his knowledge of presidential interiors.

We owe thanks to James B. Garrison; Michael C. Kathrens; Marion E. Oster, Atherton Heritage Association; Janet Parks, curator of drawings, Avery Architecture and Fine Arts Library, Columbia University; Melissa McCready and Brianna Bedigian at the Baltimore Museum of Art; Barry Harwood and Ruth Janson at the Brooklyn Museum; Kathy Struss at the Dwight D. Eisenhower Presidential Library; Tom Culbertson and Gilbert Gonzalez at the Rutherford B. Hayes Presidential Center; Lynn Smith at the Herbert Hoover Presidential Library; Colleen McKnight at the Historical Society of Washington, D.C.; Maryrose Grossman at the John Fitzgerald Kennedy Library; Janice Grenci, Marylyn Ibach, Barbara Nathanson, and Ford Petros at the Library of Congress; Jacqueline Vivirito at Lorenzo New York State Historic Site; Amelia Peck at the Metropolitan Museum of Art; Lori Eurto at the Munson-Williams-Proctor Institute Museum of Art; Erin Schleigh at the Museum of Fine Arts, Boston; Daryl Bottoms and Kimberly Cardwell at the National Archives; Eleanor Gillers and Miranda Schwartz at the New York Historical Society; Anne Cassidy at the New York State Parks, Bureau of Historic Sites; Olivia Arnone and Millicent Matthews at the Newark Museum; Michele Clark at the Frederick Law Olmsted Archives; David Barquist and Holly Frisbee at the Philadelphia Museum of Art; Ellen V. Alers and Kelly A. Crawford and at the Smithsonian Institution; Janice Davis at the Harry S. Truman Library; Vicki Catozza and Ann Sindelar at the Western Reserve Historical Society Library & Archives; William G. Allman, curator of the White House; Hillary Crehan at the White House Historical Association; Derek Jensen at WhiteHouseMuseum.org; Susan Newton at Winterthur Museum and Gardens; Frank J. Aucella at the Woodrow Wilson House; Heidi Hackford at the Woodrow Wilson Presidential Library.

Finally, we thank the staff of Acanthus Press, publisher Barry Cenower, and our many friends and family who have patiently supported our efforts to contribute to the illustrious history of America's first home.

INTRODUCTION

America is a land of monuments, both natural and man-made. We designate, build, and venerate them—Plymouth Rock in Massachusetts; Yellowstone National Park in Wyoming; Grant's Tomb in New York; the La Brea Tar Pits in Los Angeles; Alcatraz Prison in San Francisco; Castillo de San Marcos in St. Augustine, Florida. Monuments—national treasures pulled out of our history as talismans—mark our progress on the road to fulfilling the promise of democracy over two centuries of hard work and ingenuity.

Among the most beloved American monuments are the places where men and women have lived: George Washington's Mount Vernon; Thomas Jefferson's Monticello; Brigham Young's Beehive House in Salt Lake City; the Unsinkable Molly Brown's mansion in Denver; Mark Twain's mansion in Hartford. These houses are treasured because they offer a voyeuristic look into the lives of the people who inhabited them. Whether rich or poor, famous or infamous, the builders of historic houses were like all of us. In diverse and inventive ways, they participated in the evolving drama of American history.

The greatest American residential monument is the White House. National and international antiquarians, novelists, and journalists have defined the president's house as a home unique and apart from any other in the nation. Today's established chronicler of the White House, William Seale, writes of being "irresistibly attracted to the ultimate house."[1] First ladies have likewise described the allure of the nation's first home. Lady Bird Johnson, beautifier of the nation's landscape, wrote: "When I walked through the rooms of the White House . . . I knew I had walked through history." Similarly, Hillary Rodham Clinton noted that not only is the White House "a repository of America's storied past, but history is being made within these walls every day."[2] To Michelle Obama, the White House is "awe inspiring," as every monument should be.[3]

Words help to build monuments, and any author of a book about the White House participates in the tradition of veneration that has made it a monument at the expense of its legacy as a home. At a time when America's place in the world is uncertain, we revere the White House as an enduring symbol of democracy's illustrious history. But we also treasure the long history, marked by invention moderated by common sense, of the American home. This book seeks to join these two streams of American culture to create a new history of our "first home," one that restores to the White House its place in the story of the American house next door.

At first the White House was unique in all America, both in scale and in aspiration. With time and the increasing prosperity of the world's richest nation, it became just another very large house. In purpose, however, the White House has always been exceptional. Part home, part office, part hotel, part national reliquary, it has had to adapt continually to the increasingly complex and public life of the American president.

The White House has accommodated its many roles by tapping into the rich culture of American architecture, landscape design, and interior decoration. The nation's finest designers have addressed not only the demands of a public residence, but the ideas of home that each presidential family has brought to 1600 Pennsylvania Avenue. The designers' solutions, usually good and sometimes exceptional, were always distinctly American. Until the Kennedy administration, when the White House became a museum with hotel amenities, changes in its design paralleled developments in American domestic design at large.

Of course the White House has never been a *typical* American home, which only makes its parallels with mainstream domestic culture more surprising. At first the White House was too big to live in properly, and today it is too famous to be just another house. But in design and conception, the president's residence was historically allowed to be another American home.

Born into a democracy, we believe in independent thinking. But when we build and decorate houses, our choices reflect an acceptance or rejection of what our culture at large believes is right. We all aspire to live in a dream house, one that expresses our personal and cultural ideals. But the perfect living room overlooking the perfect lawn eludes us. We aspire to perfection; we live with acceptance. As American citizens participating in American life, first families from the Washingtons to the Kennedys envisioned the perfect American home, ideal both for themselves as residents and for American citizens looking to the White House as a model of American taste and manners. The political and social history of the president's house has influenced the choices of first families, but this history has always accommodated the personal likes and dislikes of first families and their advisors.

Key moments in the design of the White House coincide broadly with shifts in the history of the American home. Only the earliest and the most recent incarnations of the White House seem disconnected from domestic design history, the first being the idealistic vision of the White House in 1800, the other the present status of the house as a museum-cum-hotel. The antebellum concept of the villa in a garden suburb was the first deeply American model to influence presidential design. This was followed by the mansion phase of the White House, when industrial America became rich and confident in the post–Civil War years, now known as the Gilded Age. Before income taxes and progressive politics cut into upper-class enthusiasm for display and ostentation, the White House participated in America's palace-building era. Booming suburbanization from the 1920s on—and especially after World War II—influenced how first families lived and decorated the White House, with tasteful, neutral interiors and patio-style exteriors.

This volume looks at the White House according to its evolving identity and appearance: as a country house; a villa; a mansion; a palace; a suburban home; a shrine. Each historical phase considers the house's architecture, its gardens, its interior decoration, and its furnishings. Not all aspects of the house developed consistently or at the same pace. Its house architecture ceased changing in the early decades of the 20th century, but the expansion of the executive offices on both the east and west sides has since altered the appearance of the house and garden as originally envisioned by George Washington and Thomas Jefferson. The state rooms no longer change, but interior design of the second-floor private rooms accommodate the taste of each new administration. Furniture that was fashionable in one era is used in lesser roles decades later, although most of what filled the White House during its 200-plus years has long since been lost. We begin here with an overview of the four disciplines that have made 1600 Pennsylvania Avenue both a house and a home.

HOUSE

Despite its importance as a symbol, the White House has been overlooked and underanalyzed as architecture. The preeminent architectural historian Vincent Scully neglected even to mention the White House or its first architect, James Hoban, in his landmark 1969 survey *American Architecture and Urbanism.* Although the White House's original design is still immediately apparent, over time it has undergone extensive changes that reflect an inventive American "do-it-yourself" spirit and connect the house to distinct phases in American domestic architecture.

The initial vision of the White House was as an aristocratic dream house modeled on the noble British country house, familiar to America's self-appointed gentry largely through books. It started out as a house that was not only the largest residence of any kind in the United States, but possibly the largest building of any sort in the new nation.[4] Its stylistic conservatism was echoed throughout the young nation as it updated Georgian forms in the Federal houses of the late 18th century and again with the Greek Revival in the 1830s, foreshadowed by the north and south porticoes added to the White House in the late 1820s.

As America prospered under independence, a new kind of home appeared as an American icon: the semirural villa. The villa was the dream house of a prosperous, refined democracy and a solution to the evils of urban life. Through the mid-1840s, the Greek Revival villa popped up all over the country, echoing the White House in

The White House has always been both private residence and public icon, its noble south facade synonymous with American presidential authority since 1800. In this hand-tinted lantern slide from the 1860s, visitors stroll in the president's grounds, a simple villa park with a river view, trees, and flowering vines and shrubs. On the west colonnade, a private conservatory has been recently completed. This modest glasshouse and its horticultural collection expanded to Crystal Palace splendor as America grew rich after the Civil War.

form and color. Beginning in the 1840s, the ideal villa was *not* supposed to be painted white, nor was it supposed to be classical in style. The connotations of Greek democracy suggested by classical buildings had become uncomfortable reminders of paganism for Protestant America. Romantic styles emerged as appropriate for the villa dream house, placing the physical envelope of the White House at odds with the American home. With no intention of demolishing what was already an icon, presidential families did the best they could on the inside and with the grounds to make the White House a home in line with contemporary domestic ideals.

After the Civil War the nation seemed to outgrow the genteel limitations of the villa, as new industrial wealth gave some Americans spending power the likes of which they had never known. A more luxurious dream-house model emerged, consciously separate from the homes of average Americans. The forms and floor plans expanded in size, with new rooms having specialized

functions, along with more bedrooms and more elaborate accommodations for servants. Architectural styles grew more exuberant and eclectic, loosely mimicking aristocratic models from Europe, and lavish materials were imported from abroad. The romantic, vaguely literary aesthetic of the villa gave way to a glittering imperial dream house that paralleled America's growth as an international power. Stylistically, the White House was still at odds with the new American mansion, but at last its large scale seemed appropriate for what was happening in the world around it.

In the last decades of the 19th century and the first of the 20th, a self-proclaimed American aristocracy surpassed all previous standards of residential opulence and scale. American palaces rivaled their European counterparts in size and grandeur, to the extent that the White House came to be perceived as small and inadequate to the demands placed on it. Yet at this moment, the president's house paradoxically took on renewed relevance as a model of typically American elegance. The European aristocratic roots of its design were suddenly in tune with the pretensions of America's palace builders. McKim, Mead & White's interior transformation of the White House in the first years of the 20th century brought its stylistic relevance full circle, making the White House as urbane and sophisticated as America's new palaces and simultaneously fostering a renewed interest in America's architectural past focused directly on a key exemplar of that heritage.

After World War I, suburbanization began to transform the country's image of the dream house. Although the architecture of the White House did not largely reflect this process (though aspects of the house's interiors and landscaping did), the house's iconic status encouraged the profusion of Colonial Revival suburban imitators. Porticoes were designed as the frontispieces to countless Georgian-style houses during the 1910s, 1920s, and 1930s. This stylistic trend rendered the architecture of the White House both more accessible and more revered, elevating the structure to the status of a national icon.

GARDEN

The White House gardens began in 1800 as 82 open acres extending from the northern boundary of today's Lafayette Park south to the marshy banks of the Potomac River. The residence was barely finished in 1804 when Thomas Jefferson designated five acres immediate to the White House as the president's private garden. These walled grounds, later expanded to 18 acres, reflected the development of American landscape design for more than a century before being enshrined as naturalized park in the grand American tradition of Frederick Law Olmsted and his followers.[5]

The English aristocracy of the 18th century derived its power from inherited property, so it is no wonder that American citizens shuddered when land, hard-won during the American Revolution, was allocated to a presidential estate. William Thornton, architect of the first Capitol building and commissioner for the new Federal City that in 1871 became Washington, D.C., wrote by 1797: "Gardens and extensive walks are proper appendages to the House of the People . . . Avoid palaces and the gardens of palaces. If you build a palace I will find you a king."[6] As a result of this enduring sentiment, the traditions of the English landscape style and Jeffersonian ideals of public property informed the development of the presidential grounds from a country-house pasture to an urban oasis.

The president's park has proved to be democratic in its accommodation of both public and private needs. The White House grounds were a supply yard during the Civil War and a rallying place for modern political demonstrations. A kitchen garden provided food for early administrations, and numerous animals, including sheep, cows, a possum, and a turkey, have lived at the White House. When the demand for presidential security increased after Lincoln's assassination, General Grant fully enclosed the grounds immediate to the house. Public enjoyment of the president's garden became almost exclusively visual. Today, only by observation from the south fence and through photographs does the president's garden remain open to the public.

Even though the White House garden was carefully planned by leading American designers of both public parks and private estates, their work was rarely carried out consistently. Congressional budgets, politics, security concerns, and short executive terms prevented ongoing development and timely completion.

From the earliest years, garden plans have resisted the classicism of capital city planner Pierre-Charles L'Enfant while preserving the essential symbolic relationship of the executive White House to the legislative Capitol building to the east. In 1851 America's early advocate of naturalized gardens, Andrew Jackson Downing, provided the first comprehensive landscape design for the White House and National Mall. Though never realized, landscape architects turned to Downing's plan for guidance and continuity. Later in the 19th century, the urban and national park movement gained momentum and the White House grounds themselves became a semiprivate park with trees shading a rolling lawn.

Downing's belief that every house, not just the houses of the rich, should reflect an owner's unique identity was fulfilled at the White House, where the flower gardens close to the house evolved with changing administrations. As gardening and the study of plants became acceptable occupations for women in the 19th century, the care of these gardens became the province of first ladies. Working with White House gardeners and a staff that grew in size and sophistication over the decades, presidential wives saw that the beauty and gentility they sought for the interior were made manifest on the exterior. The choices they made for the White

Children pose in the president's garden during the Easter Egg Roll, 1898. By the time Rutherford B. Hayes initiated this annual event, the original 82 acres of the president's house had become both private garden and public park. In this photograph, official White House photographer and social progressive, Frances Benjamin Johnston, captured the hope for a more integrated society in post–Civil War America, though not without quizzical onlookers.

House gardens reflected what was fashionable in American landscape design.

At the house of democratically elected presidents, it is not surprising that presidential botanical collections requiring expensive care were hidden from public view. The first White House flower gardens were closed to the public by a locked gate in a wood fence. This south garden was replaced in the 19th century by a greenhouse built on the site of today's west wing. This modest structure became a sprawling conservatory before being razed in 1902. The east and west garden terraces created then are now the elaborate parterres of the rose garden and Jacqueline Kennedy Garden, memorials to JFK's royal Camelot.

At the behest of President Franklin D. Roosevelt, Frederick Law Olmsted Jr. reviewed the conditions of the White House garden within its historical context. The resulting 1935 Olmsted plan, drawn up as America sought inspiration from its past to recover from the devastation of the Great Depression, called for preserving the historic White House landscape. This plan and related commentary have guided administrations since the FDR years. Olmsted's preservationist pride in the White House foreshadowed the Kennedy vision of the residence as a monument to America's upper-class colonial heritage.

Today the design of the White House garden does not evolve with contemporary taste as it did throughout the 19th century. Instead, it belongs to the Anglo-American White House vision that champions preservation over fashion. Though they are but a fragment of Washington's dream for capital city gardens, the presidential grounds remain iconic and unchanging. With Colonial Revival flower beds and commemorative presidential trees, the White House garden is a reassuring symbol of conservative American values—tradition, endurance, and simplicity.

INTERIORS

The earliest interiors of the White House reflected occupants' attempts to come to grips with its grand spaces by using the materials available to the elite in America's major cities. The first presidents and their wives adapted their provincial understanding of English gentry life to the unfamiliar, aristocratic scale of the house. The Madisons had only begun to accomplish this task when the house was gutted by fire in 1814. With the Monroes, Washington's impossible dream house began to be less alien, and its late classical interiors echoed the increasing sophistication and interest in French taste that began to pervade American homes in the 1820s. Andrew Jackson was the first president to fully decorate the vast interior spaces, an undertaking that represented both the maturing self-confidence of the American consumer and the rise of the nation's commercial furnisher-manufacturers. Americans learned how to shop for what was fashionable and socially expected, and presidents were no exception.

The rise of the villa in America saw a cultural shift in decorating responsibilities from the president to the first lady, in line with the evolving cult of domesticity, which charged women with making the home into a place of comfort, convenience, and beauty. Women, as the primary domestic consumers, knew where to buy the latest styles and the finest materials. Sarah Polk first transformed the White House into a modern villa with a prosperous middle-class homemaker's budget judiciously spent on the rooms of a gargantuan home.

By the time Julia Grant ensconced her family in the White House, Gilded Age social pressures demanded that the richest citizens live in dream houses considerably larger and more lavish than those of ordinary Americans. Accordingly, Mrs. Grant began the transformation of the White House from villa to mansion, with no more experience than a sharp eye for what was going on around her. While Mrs. Grant was still bound by politically imposed budgets, she made the first forays into high-style custom interiors with her East Room renovation, which was carried even further by the widowed Chester A. Arthur in the early 1880s. Arthur brought the first truly upper-class interiors into the White House with the talents of Louis Comfort Tiffany.

Teddy and Edith Roosevelt transformed the White House into a palace, acknowledging that the president's house needed to be imperial in its grandeur and function to reflect the international presidency. Their 1902 renovation by McKim, Mead & White created a division between the state floor and the second-floor private quarters that allowed the first family to live a comfortable suburban life upstairs and an official life downstairs.

In the 1920s and 1930s, the White House went through a transitional phase. The first serious movement toward decorating the house as a museum began in this period, but in a romantic, unscholarly way. Embarrassed by the anachronistic splendor of the main floor, first ladies sought ready-made goods acquired under the watchful eye of increasingly intrusive advisory groups. The first-floor interiors were dominated by department-store interpretations of America's colonial heritage, while the first families lived increasingly isolated suburban lives on a second floor designed for comfort and modern convenience. The culmination of the suburbanization of the White House was its total gutting and renovation during the Truman administration, which left it completely modernized, decorated, and furnished but rendered it just as lacking in personality as when it was first completed in 1800.

It took Jacqueline Kennedy to create the final dream house, bringing the upper-class taste of the modern American millionaire into the diluted suburban colonial interiors of the mid-20th century. Gathering upper-class advisors and elite decorators about her, Mrs. Kennedy created a paradigm that irrevocably split the house into three spaces (public, private, administrative) and established a model for its interiors that strictly limited the ability of subsequent first ladies to make further substantive changes. Under Mrs. Kennedy, the White House became something it had never been before but that most Americans now imagine it always has been.

The Blue Room.

The Blue Room, seen here in the mid-1880s, has always been the ceremonial and stylistic center of the White House. In this tinted photograph, three distinct phases of the American home coexist. The gilded French pier table by Antoine Bellangé, purchased for the room by President Monroe, is still ornamented with the ormolu "Minerva" clock and candlesticks that came to the presidential country house in 1817. The American-made gilt furniture ordered by Harriet Lane for her uncle James Buchanan's presidential villa in 1859 still fills the 40-foot-long room. Julia Grant's glittering gasolier continues to adorn the ceiling as it had since 1869, when she made her first efforts to transform the president's house into a Gilded Age mansion. And layered on top of all of this is Louis Comfort Tiffany's complex and exotic decorative treatment, ordered by Chester Arthur in 1882 to make his house as sophisticated and modern as the most opulent Fifth Avenue residence.

FURNISHINGS

Almost all evidence of its early interiors was tragically lost when the British burned the White House in 1814. The furnishings initially allotted to George Washington's dream house were probably inadequate to the task, simply because no country house of its scale had ever been furnished in America before; nor had a central government ever been charged with maintaining such a house for a democratically elected leader. From what evidence survives, it seems that the first presidential families made do with what they knew about modest American country houses. The first occupants who began to understand what the vast rooms of the president's house required to fill them were the Madisons.

From the late 1810s to the Civil War, White House furnishings evolved in a way that appears to have closely followed general patterns of consumption among increasingly affluent and style-conscious Americans up and down the eastern seaboard. The

presidents and their wives shopped for their furnishings at major retailers in the main style centers of New York, Philadelphia, and Baltimore, while also patronizing local manufacturers and retailers in the growing city of Washington. The dominance of the English classical style in the 1810s and 1820s gradually gave way to a taste for French-style furniture and objects as the concept of the villa matured in the 1830s and 1840s.

The villa decades brought with them a variety of new styles—the rococo, the Gothic, the Renaissance. The White House followed the furnishing trends that typified the emerging American villa of the pre–Civil War years, with different styles associated with different rooms. The White House's oversized 18th-century rooms didn't actually correspond with villa-sized furniture; even so, the presidents' wives in the 1840s and 1850s continued to purchase what their peers all over the country were buying, adapting it to the scale and mixed public–private function of the rooms.

Since 1900, the style of the Lincoln bed has been unpopular. Seen here in the Lincoln Bedroom in 1983, the bed is flanked by two of Andrew Jackson's 1829 Quervelle tables from the East Room. This historic furniture allows for a continued presence of the Victorian era in the modern White House.

After the Civil War, White House furnishings continued to follow trends of style and consumption that predominated all over the expanding country. As wealthier Americans bought more novel, ornate, and expensive furnishings to set themselves above average homeowners, the first ladies followed suit, mixing ready-made commercial objects with custom-ordered pieces when budgets allowed.

At the very end of the 19th century, the White House was again partly refurnished under the Theodore Roosevelts to reflect a new palatial taste, echoing the heavily European-style furnishings seen in industrialists' palaces in major cities and in resort towns. At the same time, a selective retention of old historic pieces that had survived in the house contrasted with the last wholesale dispersal of outmoded and used furnishings in 1903. As the 20th century unfolded and a more focused historic interest in the White House developed, new furnishings that reproduced past styles began to appear, paralleling a similar explosion in the use of new American-made department-store reproductions at all socioeconomic levels in U.S. suburbs. As the era of palace building faded into the era of income tax and, finally, depression, the White House furnishings grew even more like those of suburban America, dominated by the comfortable familiarity of Colonial Revival and Early American styles. This suburbanization of the White House furnishings was at odds with the rooms' lingering grandeur and culminated in the house's drastic renovation after the end of World War II.

In its final phase, the White House moved dramatically away from developments in the American home. With its transformation into a historic shrine in which the president's family lives, the emphasis for its furnishings turned quickly and irrevocably to real antiques and pieces of historic importance. While Americans in general, encouraged by museum installations, had developed a taste for antiques, mainstream American homes continued to depend on reproductions as well as new, modern-style furniture. Except for the introduction of a collection of contemporary American crafts in the 1990s, the only modern-style furnishings in the White House have been in more utilitarian contexts and have not formed part of the public image of the president's house.

NOTE TO THE READER

We have organized the six chapters that follow—Country House, Villa, Mansion, Palace, Suburban Home, and Shrine—according to a straightforward formula that we hope allows you to see clearly parallels between the White House and the type of American home explored in each section.

To place the White House in its design context, we open each chapter with houses that exemplify each chapter title. These are followed by images of key figures in the life of the White House. They are not the only presidents and first ladies discussed in the story that follows, but they are the men and women who made changes emblematic of American house history. Finally, in order to remind the reader of the ongoing importance of room size and arrangement, each chapter includes a plan of the White House at the period in question, compared with that of a contemporary private house. These plans are presented in the same scale so that the reader may compare the White House in each period with a house of comparable social ambition. For the final chapter, we have not offered such a comparison because the White House in the 1960s ceased being an American home and became a museum with a residential apartment.

1600 Pennsylvania Avenue has been home to generations of first family children. Top left: The press recounted daily the life of Benjamin "Baby" Harrison McKee who grew up at the White House during the presidency of his doting grandfather, Benjamin Harrison. With his uncle, speculator Major Russell Harrison, Baby McKee sat in a goat buggy guided by one of his sisters; photograph, circa 1891-93. Top right: Teddy Roosevelt brought four servants, six children, and a menagerie when he came to the White House in 1901. Theodore Roosevelt Jr. posed with Eli Yale, his blue macaw, in the president's conservatory before it was razed in 1902. Bottom left: Swing sets were ubiquitous on suburban lawns 75 years before Barack Obama installed one for his daughters in the White House garden. Here Franklin D. Roosevelt's granddaughters, Anna "Sistie" and Curtis "Buzzie" Dall play outside the south portico, 1933. Bottom right: In 1961, Jacqueline Kennedy strolled in the White House garden with her elegant British-style perambulator carrying John F. Kennedy Jr.

RESIDENTS OF THE WHITE HOUSE

COUNTRY HOUSE

John and Abigail Adams, 1800–1801

Thomas Jefferson, 1801–09

James and Dolley Madison, 1809–14

James and Elizabeth Monroe, 1817–25

John Quincy and Louisa Adams, 1825–29

VILLA

Andrew Jackson, 1829–37

Martin Van Buren, 1837–38

Martin and Angelica Van Buren, 1838–41

William Henry Harrison, 1841

John and Letitia Tyler, 1841–42

John and Julia Tyler, 1842–45

James and Sarah Polk, 1845–49

Zachary and Margaret Taylor, 1849–50

Millard and Abigail Fillmore, 1850–53

Franklin and Jane Pierce, 1853–57

James Buchanan and Harriet Lane, 1857–61

Abraham and Mary Lincoln, 1861–65

Andrew and Eliza Johnson, 1865–69

MANSION

Ulysses and Julia Grant, 1869–77

Rutherford and Lucy Hayes, 1877–81

James and Lucretia Garfield, 1881

Chester Arthur, 1881–85

Grover and Frances Cleveland, 1885–89, 1893–97

Benjamin and Caroline Harrison, 1889–93

William and Ida McKinley, 1897–1901

PALACE

Theodore and Edith Roosevelt, 1901–09

William and Helen Taft, 1909–13

Woodrow and Ellen Wilson, 1913–14

Woodrow and Edith Wilson, 1915–21

SUBURBAN HOME

Warren and Florence Harding, 1921–23

Calvin and Grace Coolidge, 1923–29

Herbert and Louise Hoover, 1929–33

Franklin and Eleanor Roosevelt, 1933–45

Harry and Elizabeth Truman, 1945–53

Dwight and Mamie Eisenhower, 1953–61

SHRINE

John and Jacqueline Kennedy, 1961–63

Lyndon and Lady Bird Johnson, 1963–69

Richard and Patricia Nixon, 1969–74

Gerald and Betty Ford, 1974–77

James and Rosalynn Carter, 1977–81

Ronald and Nancy Reagan, 1981–89

George H. W. and Barbara Bush, 1989–93

William and Hillary Clinton, 1993–2001

George W. and Laura Bush, 2001–09

Barack and Michelle Obama, 2009–

DREAM HOUSE

The White House
as an American Home

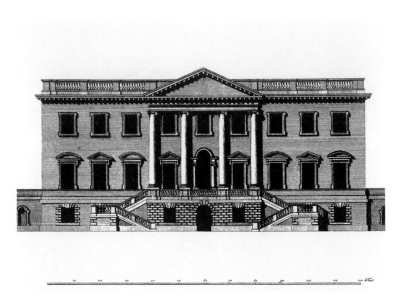

ENGLISH AND IRISH HOUSES

Top left: Kirtlington Hall, Oxford, Oxfordshire, England, 1746, by architect William Smith and landscape architect Lancelot Brown, a founder of the English landscape movement. Engravings like this from Vitruvius Brittanicus, *1739, would have guided George Washington when he planned the White House. Top right: Kildare House, now Leinster House, Dublin, Ireland, 1748, by Richard Cassels, architect. This city residence has traditionally been considered the inspiration for the White House. Bottom left: Claremont House, Esher, Surrey, England, 1774, by Henry Holland and Lancelot Brown, architect and landscape architect. Bottom right: Attingham Park, Shropshire, England, 1785, by architect George Steuart and Humphrey Repton.*

COUNTRY HOUSE
1801–1829

The building is vast and imposing; made more to lodge a sovereign who can tax his subjects at will than to be the residence of a magistrate who receives from his fellow citizens only the modest salary of 25,000 doll[ars]. This house of the president and one part of the Capitol are the only public buildings to be seen.

—Julian Ursyn Niemcewicz, Polish scholar,
poet and statesman, *Travels Through America, 1797–1807*

What were country houses for? … Essentially they were power houses—the houses of a ruling class.

—Mark Girouard, *Life in the English Country House,* 1978

LIVING LIKE LANDED GENTRY

The country house was the single most potent symbol of aristocratic power in 18th-century Britain. It represented the physical presence and financial clout of the landowner, whose wealth derived from rents received from tenant farmers. Even if he gained wealth from additional sources such as coal or manufacturing, and even if he maintained a house in London or a provincial city, the nobleman derived his public identity from his country house.

The grandest American country houses were small by English standards, but they symbolized political and social power like their English counterparts. America's chief landowners generally maintained residences on farm properties that were the source of their wealth. George Washington's Mount Vernon encompassed 8,000 acres, and Thomas Jefferson's plantation Monticello included 5,000 acres. Morrisania, the estate of Declaration of Independence signer Lewis Morris near New York, had more than 1,000 acres when the British burned its house during the Revolutionary War. In 1787 John and Abigail Adams purchased a more modest 40-acre farm, Peacefield, in Quincy, Massachusetts. Unlike these country estates, town houses were for merchants and lawyers and had only as much ground as needed to support immediate family needs.

The house of the president began as no more than a building in an imagined capital city. First conceived by Frenchman Major Pierre-Charles L'Enfant as the "President's palace," the White House from the beginning was hybrid in concept. It was literally a town house on public land, but was designed as a country estate with a terraced garden. The reason for this dichotomy is that its early creators and advisors—L'Enfant, George Washington, James Hoban, and Thomas Jefferson—wanted the president's house, in a model American city, to project the authority of a landed property. Because the new house was to be on a scale and of a sophistication unknown in America, they relied on European models for inspiration and assurance.

The design of the president's house was guided by direct experience and published accounts and images. L'Enfant was a native Frenchman who had seen the vast complex of the royal Bourbon family's Château de Versailles. The polyvalent Thomas Jefferson had experienced British and Continental houses and gardens firsthand during his years as colonial America's emissary to the French court. Hoban was Irish-born but the American-born George Washington, the sure hand in the development of the Capital City, never traveled to Europe. He was left to imagine English estates as published in widely distributed engravings and illustrated books. Through such images, Palladian Revival houses like Prior Park and Attingham Park, impressive for their aristocratic presence and scale, would have been known to the first president and his colleagues on the capital city commission. The classical architecture of such Georgian palaces and their tree-filled parks, designed by creators and theorists of the English landscape style, were the inspiration for the American president's house that rose majestically from the labor of American slaves and émigré craftsmen.

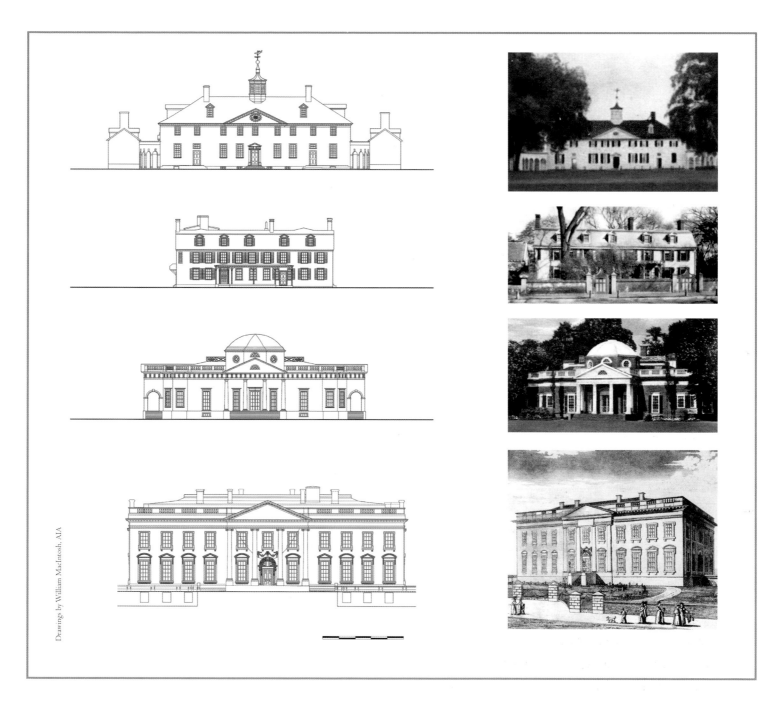

Drawings by William MacIntosh, AIA

From top to bottom: Mount Vernon, 1735–99 (7,000 square feet without piazza and basement; 94 feet long x 33 feet deep [without piazza], x 33 feet 6 inches high to ridgepole). Peacefield, 1731–1800 (6,200 square feet, first and second floors; 79 feet 9 inches long x 32 feet deep, 67 feet deep on L–wing x 27 feet high to ridgepole). Monticello, 1769–1809 (9,500 square feet without basement; 110 feet long x 87 feet 9 inches deep x 44 feet 7 inches high to top of dome oculus). President's House, 1800 (29,500 square feet, first and second floors; 168 feet long x 85 feet 6 inches deep x 50 feet 4 inches high, north side, and 60 feet high, south side, from lawn to parapet).

America's first three presidents owned country houses that were considered mansions in their time. Washington's Mount Vernon and Jefferson's Monticello were among the grandest private homes in America, and Abigail and John Adams' capacious farmhouse Peacefield was far larger than the average New Englander's home. In comparison with these private residences, Hoban's president's house loomed as America's largest residence for more than half a century, with 6,000 square feet more living space than the three other houses combined.

COUNTRY HOUSE PLANNERS
AND RESIDENTS

THE WASHINGTON FAMILY, engraving by Edward Savage after his 1796 painting. London, 1798. Washington owned four copies of this image.

General Washington's dream of a noble English country house, larger than any other in the nation, but appropriate for the world's first democratic leader, guided his choice of site and architecture for the president's house in the new Capital City of Washington.

Here the first president and his wife and her grandchildren sit at Mount Vernon, imagined by the artist as an aristocrat's estate with marble columns and a servant, possibly William Lee, in Washington's livery. Martha Washington points with her fan to the "grand avenue," now Pennsylvania Avenue, on the map of the District of Columbia, founded in 1790.

THOMAS JEFFERSON, bronze, Pierre-Jean David d'Angers, c. 1832.

The nation's third president influenced the design of the White House and from 1801–09 lived there in the manner of an English landowner. With architect Benjamin H. Latrobe, Jefferson created the first White House garden plan that defined five acres as the president's own within the 82-acre park.

Democrat James K. Polk moved this bronze statue from the Capitol to the north lawn in 1848. It remained there until Republican Ulysses S. Grant moved it back to the Capitol in 1874 where it is today. Unlike an aristocratic park with monuments to kings, the White House garden only ever had this statue of a president.

1789–97

1801–09

DOLLEY PAYNE MADISON, engraving after Gilbert Stuart, c. 1820–22.

After arriving in the Capital City in 1809, Dolley Madison, with Benjamin H. Latrobe, took the shabby White House left by Thomas Jefferson and transformed it into a stylish and colorful country seat befitting the nation's president. Inspired by English models, the Madison White House reflected elite American taste, before it was burned by the British in 1812.

JAMES MONROE, engraving after Gilbert Stuart, c. 1820–22

In 1817, President Monroe filled the rebuilt White House with glittering French objects and luxurious textiles. He was the first president who seemed to understand that the president's house needed furnishings finer and grander than those found in other American country houses. He persuaded the Congress to provide funds for his costly imports.

For the grounds devastated by the War of 1812, the president commissioned a landscape plan from one of the first American-born architects, Charles Bulfinch. Monroe hired the first White House gardener to carry out anticipated improvements.

1809–17

1817–25

AN ENGLISH COUNTRY HOUSE

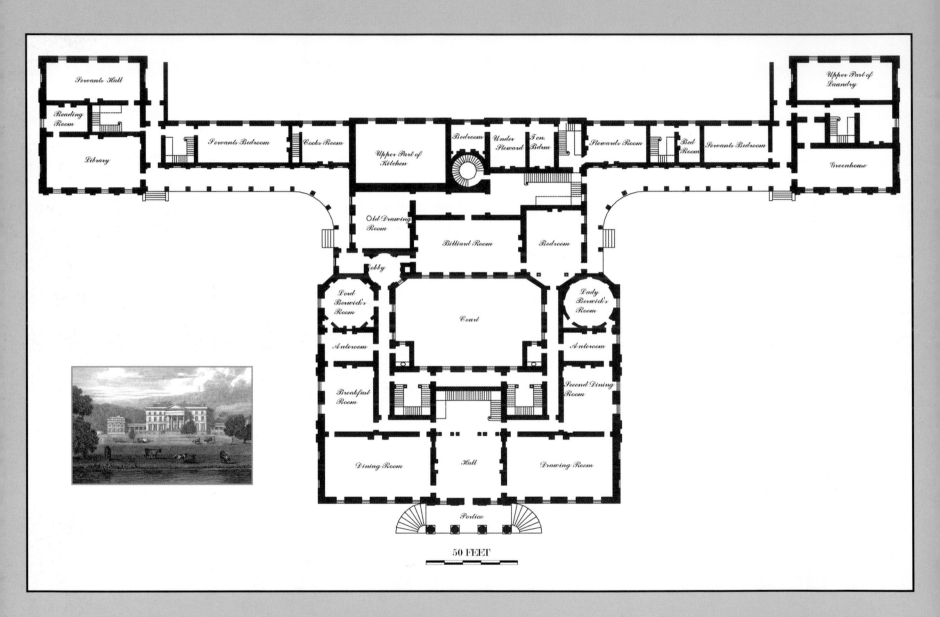

Servants Hall

Reading Room

Library

Servants Bedroom

Cooks Room

Upper Part of Kitchen

Bedroom

Under Steward

Ten. Bdrm.

Stewards Room

Bed Room

Servants Bedroom

Upper Part of Laundry

Greenhouse

Old Drawing Room

Billiard Room

Bedroom

Lobby

Lord Berwick's Room

Lady Berwick's Room

Court

Anteroom

Anteroom

Breakfast Room

Second Dining Room

Dining Room

Hall

Drawing Room

Portico

50 FEET

ATTINGHAM PARK, 1785

Entrance façade (inset) and first-floor plan, Scots architect George Steuart, 1783–85, for 1st Lord Berwick, heir to a merchant fortune. The mid-Georgian house overlooked the Tern River in grounds designed by Humprey Repton. Initially the landscape architect was disappointed with Attingham's setting and commented in the project's 1797 Red Book that it was "impossible to annex ideas of grandeur and magnificence to a mansion which appears to have little extent of park belonging to it." By siting the White House on a terrace with a view to the Potomac River, George Washington and Major L'Enfant assured that the president's park was appropriate to a house with grand ambitions.

THE PRESIDENT'S PALACE
AS A COUNTRY HOUSE

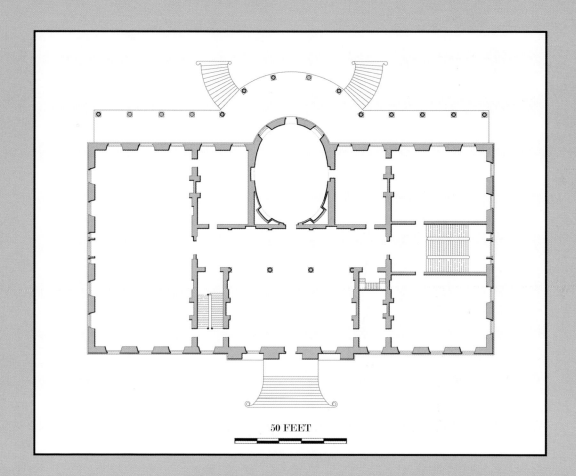

WHITE HOUSE, 1800

First-floor plan, drawing after James Hoban's 1793 design. The house was built as an Irish-born architect and American-born president envisioned. While more simply laid out than a comparable English nobleman's house, Attingham Park, the White House aspired to similar nobility in the dimensions and height of its rooms. In both houses the state rooms were arranged in processional suites. At the president's house, the main suite started with the oval "saloon" (today the Blue Room) and ended in the largest room to the west (today the State Dining Room), befitting the public nature of the building. The rooms of Attingham's first floor, with 24,600 square feet, almost as large as the two floors of the White House combined, moved in a reverse procession, starting with the largest, more public rooms and terminating in intimate private spaces. Thomas Jefferson partially realized terrace wings on the east and west sides of the president's house, which extended the first-floor rooms.

"George Town and Federal City, or City of Washington," an aquatint by T. Cartwright after George Bleck of Philadelphia, 1801. With river views and open fields, the new city was ideal for a presidential estate.

HOUSE

The White House was dramatically distinguished from its American contemporaries, including Mount Vernon, by its enormous size and its materials. Perhaps its magnitude reflected the ambitiousness of the new government or implied the power the president would wield. Regardless, the house's size confounded its early occupants, who simply lacked experience of such vast surroundings. Its exterior sandstone walls also distinguished it from most American residences of the time, which used wood and brick, less expensive and more readily accessible materials. In concept, the White House's oval rooms and grand hall echoed those of Gore Place, 1797–1804, in Waltham, Massachusetts, but with its smaller scale and brick exterior, Gore Place was far less Olympian than the White House.

Begun in 1792 and first occupied in 1800, the White House was George Washington's dream house, although he did not live to see it completed. In its day, it was not only the nation's largest house, but also, for a while, its largest public building. Initially, the first family's domestic and governmental activities did not require so much space. Later, however, as America grew richer and the government expanded, the White House, from its inception both a residence and a workplace, was deemed too small. In contrast to the long-standing traditions established and followed by British and European monarchs, what constitutes appropriate protocol for the U.S. president has been defined over time via incrementally realized architectural changes. These gradual alterations became a

Gore Place, the residence of Christopher Gore in Waltham, Massachusetts, 1808. Planned by Rebecca Gore for her lawyer husband, this house was influenced by French estates and English country houses. Gore Place was contemporary with the White House but comparatively modest in scale.

hallmark of much of the White House's first century. Beyond evolving in step with the nation, they reflected the shifting winds of architectural fashion and a do-it-yourself approach to domestic life in a house-proud nation; they also expressed the lack of any consistent vision of how the chief executive should live or how the house should function on a symbolic level.

Prior to the completion of the planned city of Washington, D.C., there had been two purpose-built presidential residences, one in New York and the other in Philadelphia, neither of which was lived in by George Washington.[1] In 1790 Congress, then located in New York City, ratified the Residence Act, which called for the construction of a new capital city at the confluence of the Potomac and Anacostia rivers. The legislation provided for an official residence for the chief executive. As envisioned by the city's principal planner, French-born Major Pierre-Charles L'Enfant, a French artist and engineer who had fought on the American side in the Revolutionary War, the president's house was to be grand, far surpassing its predecessors in size.

L'Enfant envisaged Washington, D.C.'s plan as analogous to the new nation's innovative form of government, distinguished in part by its system of checks and balances. At the heart of the U.S. Constitution lay the separation of governmental power into executive, legislative, and judicial branches. At the time, the houses of England's Parliament were not accommodated in a discrete building, and the French government shared space with the king in the Palace of Versailles. L'Enfant called for separate buildings for the U.S. president and

the Congress, to be connected by a diagonal avenue, one of many grand boulevards overlaying a regular street grid.

By 1792, the Capital City Commission had dismissed L'Enfant. Although George Washington ensured that the proposed city plans were largely realized, L'Enfant's plans for individual buildings, including a national university, a national church, and what he identified as the presidential "palace," were abandoned. Excavations already executed for the official residence's cellars revealed, however, L'Enfant's ambitious vision: the president's house was to be 700 feet long. [see page 43]

Nearly two years after passage of the Residence Act, plans had not been completed for any of the capital's public buildings. To jump-start the process, Thomas Jefferson proposed national design competitions for the presidential residence and a building to house Congress. L'Enfant's referral to the president's house as a "palace" incited public opposition, on the grounds that the designation was inappropriate in a democracy. This objection motivated Congress to officially name the structure the Executive Mansion.

A public call for designs for the house was issued on April 3, 1792. By that time, Washington had begun to search for a competent builder and, at the recommendation of his friend Henry Laurens, in Charleston, South Carolina, met with James Hoban, who had immigrated to America from his native Ireland in 1781. Hoban had apprenticed to the architect Thomas Ivory, who played a significant role in the 18th-century development of Dublin, and he had extensive professional experience in both Ireland and

Drawn from Mr. Allens Road in the Year 1750.

PRIOR PARK the Seat of Ralph Allen Esqr. near Bath. PRIO

Printed for John Bowles ── at the Black Horse in Cornhill.

Parc la Residence de Raoul Allen Ecuyer pres le Bath.

Ant: Walker Sculp!

Prior Park, by architect John Wood and landscape architects Lancelot Brown and Alexander Pope; engraving by Anthony Walker, published by John Bowles, London, 1750. As at Attingham Park, this Georgian estate with its early picturesque garden was what George Washington envisioned as a noble country house and garden.

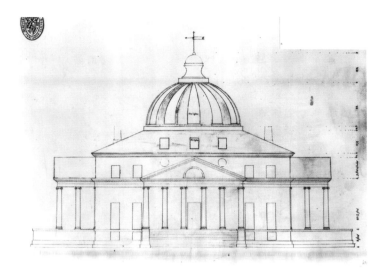

Rejected design for the president's house, by Thomas Jefferson, c. 1792, based on Andrea Palladio's Italian 16th-century Villa Rotonda.

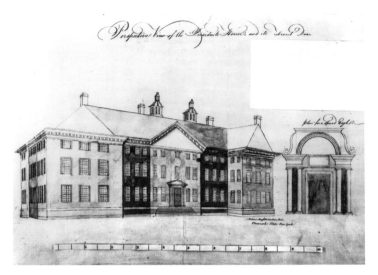

Rejected design for the president's house, by architect Andrew Mayfield Carshore, c. 1792. Architecturally, this proposal was a century out of date.

America; in 1789 Hoban had completed the South Carolina State Capitol. Washington authorized Hoban to visit the building site and begin to sketch. The president subsequently reviewed competition submissions before they went to the Capital City Commission. In a letter to Thomas Jefferson, Washington noted, "If none more elegant than these should appear . . . the exhibition will be a dull one indeed."[2]

Jefferson intended to align American architecture aesthetically with that of the ancient world to establish the new nation as rightful heir to democratic Greece and republican Rome. He looked at ancient precedents chiefly through the lens of Renaissance genius. In designs for his own house, Monticello, and the University of Virginia, which he established as the world's first secular university, Jefferson was inspired by Andrea Palladio's *Four Books of Architecture.* Jefferson's architectural searches, which also drew upon Charles-Louis Clerisseau's *Antiquités du Midi de la France,* were intended not only to forge a broadly expressed national identity, but also specifically to liberate American architecture from contemporary English taste. Following a visit to England in 1785, Jefferson wrote, "Their architecture is in the most wretched style I ever saw, not meaning to except America, where it is bad, nor here in Virginia, where it is worse than in any other part of America I have seen."[3] Even Jefferson's earliest version of Monticello, conventional in comparison to his later work on the house, pushed the reigning Georgian vocabulary in new directions and impressed visitors, including the Marquis de Chastellux, who stated in 1782, "Mr. Jefferson is the first American who has consulted the fine arts to know how he should shelter himself from the weather."[4]

In a letter to L'Enfant in 1791, Jefferson described his architectural vision for both the Capitol and the president's house, clearly delineating different stylistic approaches to each of the new buildings: "Whenever it

is proposed to prepare plans for the Capitol, I should prefer the adoption of some one of the models of antiquity, which have had the approbation of thousands of years; and for the President's House, I should prefer the celebrated fronts of modern buildings, which have received the approbation of all good judges."[5] Jefferson drew various plans for the president's house, submitting one, identified only by the pseudonym "A. Z.," to the public competition. Following the notion of basing a design on one of "the celebrated fronts of modern buildings," Jefferson's scheme strongly evoked Palladio's Villa Rotunda (1571), which by that time had been imitated throughout Europe. The design called for a square building, surmounted by a dome and incorporating four porticos, one on each side. Jefferson had also drawn a scheme (not submitted to the competition) synthesizing elements from three French buildings, all of which he had suggested to L'Enfant as design sources: the Galérie du Louvre, the Garde-Meuble, and the Hôtel de Salm.

Jefferson's recommendations for the president's house were not followed and in fact would not have made much sense to George Washington. Washington, unlike Jefferson, had never traveled abroad, and probably the most opulent house he had ever seen was the red-brick, Georgian-style Governor's Palace in Williamsburg, Virginia, begun in 1704. On July 16, 1792, Washington, drawn to British and Irish precedent, officially selected a neoclassical scheme by Hoban that strongly evoked Leinster House, the Duke of Leinster's well-known Dublin residence, designed by Richard Cassels[6] and later remodeled by James Wyatt around 1780. Leinster House was partially open to the public, and Hoban had visited it when a student at the drawing school of the Royal Dublin Society. As the architectural historian Fiske Kimball has pointed out, however, Hoban's design also strongly resembled a "Design for a Gentleman's

ORIGINAL DESIGN FOR THE WHITE HOUSE, BY JAMES HOBAN, 1792.
From the collection of Mr. Glenn Brown, F. A. I. A.

Original design for the president's house, by Irish-born architect James Hoban, 1792.

House" by James Gibbs, a student of Christopher Wren. The design had been reproduced in Gibbs's classic *A Book of Architecture*, published in 1728 and widely known by members of the Royal Dublin Society and builders in America.[7] The exact roots of Hoban's design are ultimately unimportant. What matters is that the house was designed after the manner of an aristocratic English country house.

Hoban's first elevations of the president's house have not survived. Based on an early iteration and an original section, however, Hoban's intentions can be largely inferred. The three-story house, sited on an open field sloping down to the Potomac River, was to have a simple rectilinear massing and be set atop an exposed basement. On its northern facade, resembling Leinster House, the lower level presented a rusticated central section that served as the base of four Ionic columns. The upper floors were to have smooth walls. Visually prominent pilasters, as well as stone carvings, were to embellish the scheme. In contrast to the Irish house, the short side of which incorporated shallow bays, the proposed president's house was to have flat ends and a southern facade distinguished by a bold three-story bay and a long porch. The porch brought a quintessentially American element to the overall composition and evoked George Washington's own house, Mount Vernon.[8] The porch also made the southern facade seem decidedly more accessible in its domesticity, contrasting with the more imposing and palatial northern facade.

Collectively, the two facades seemed to express a national ambivalence toward how the president should live.

Inside, recalling Leinster House, Hoban's plan called for a large entrance hall that provided access to a transverse hallway that in turn led to the principal rooms. In its location, the East Room, to be used for state receptions, resembled the dining room at Leinster House. The East Room also echoed, on a much larger scale, the so-called New Room that Washington had added to Mount Vernon in the early 1780s, in its spatial relation to the rest of the house and its extra-high ceilings. Overall, the proposed plan was simpler than that of Leinster House, containing fewer rooms than similar houses in England and Ireland.

Hoban, who had no known professional design collaborator, conferred often with Washington during the design process, and Washington made sure that the Capital City Commission did not significantly intervene. Though Washington is said to have often remarked on his own lack of architectural knowledge and expertise, his claims were in part contradicted by his direct involvement in the design and construction of Mount Vernon, and he played a large role in the development and execution of Hoban's design. After seeing an initial scheme, Washington, reflecting his ambitions for the new nation, immediately demanded that the house, approximately one-fourth the size of the structure begun by L'Enfant, be enlarged by 20 percent. He also ordered its embellishment with robustly carved stone trim.

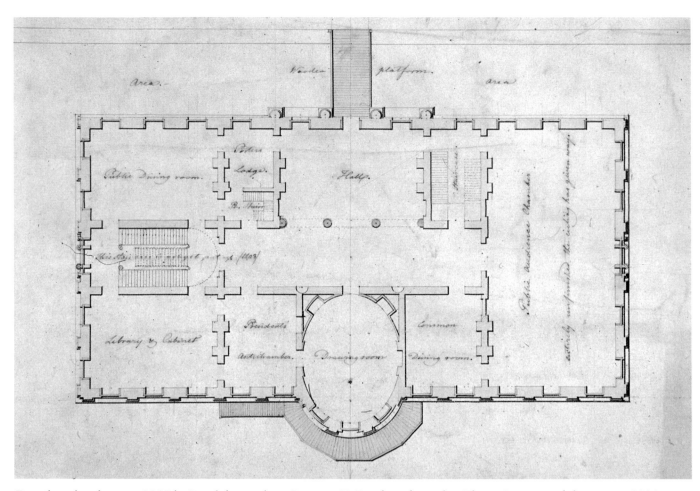

First-floor plan, drawn in 1807 by British-born architect Benjamin H. Latrobe, reflecting how Thomas Jefferson used the rooms in 1803.

The fact that the house, even as enlarged by Washington, was a fraction of the size proposed by L'Enfant in his master plan for the capital, raised the question of siting. The commissioners overseeing the capital's design allowed Washington the decision of where to place the house. He in turn visited the site and determined that the house should occupy the northern edge of the plot selected by L'Enfant; in so deciding, Washington oriented the house toward the public square to the north, not Pennsylvania Avenue, and thus significantly deviated from L'Enfant's scheme by moving the house out of a line of vision commencing at the Capitol.

Washington wanted the house, and all major public buildings in the new capital, to be made of stone, arguing that in this way they would equal the civic buildings of Europe. At Mount Vernon, Washington accommodated economic limitations by milling readily available wood to look like stone, even adding sand to the white paint to evoke stone's texture. These measures serve as a reminder that in America, even the richest citizens lived on a scale far below that of English aristocrats.

The commissioners were uncertain that the nearby Aquia Creek quarry could provide enough sandstone to complete both the president's house and the Capitol. In 1793, aware of Washington's desire to avoid the use of red brick, used at the colonial capitol of Virginia and so strongly associated with English Colonial architecture, the commissioners suggested a reduction in the house's size. Washington agreed, and the lower level was eliminated. In addition to reducing cost, this change distinguished the design from a more typically English Georgian composition. To visually enhance the north facade, four columns were to support a finely articulated pediment, incorporating carved-stone depictions of an eagle surrounded by rays of sunlight. (In contrast with other changes, the addition of a prominent pediment over the main entrance further strengthened the resemblance to Leinster House.) On the revised south facade, the basement was to be exposed and fully rusticated. The extensive back porch indicated on the original plan was to be eliminated. Inside, basement-level groin vaulting was to be finished in brick, not stone, and wood was to replace marble as flooring in the house's main rooms.

The house was realized largely according to the revised plan. Built of local sandstone, it was defined by its large size and monumental scale, both in terms of its overall dimensions and the manner in which the facades were articulated. The president's house measured 168 feet along its dominant north and south facades, ran 85 feet to the east and west,

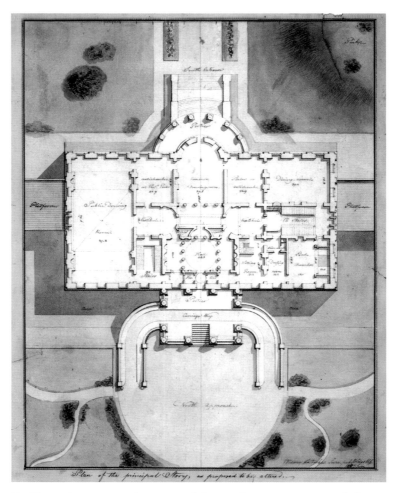

For Thomas Jefferson, Latrobe reconceived the first floor as a series of interlocking rooms needed for an evolving presidency. Drawn in 1807, the plan was never realized. Elevations for the south and north porticos were drawn the same year.

and rose on its northern facade 45 feet from the ground to the roof eaves. No other American house surpassed its size until after the Civil War, when the new rich of the Gilded Age started a palace-building trend that ended only with World War I.

Departing from dominant English Georgian precedent in colonial America, the house incorporated large-scale windows that were visually emphasized by dramatic moldings, and, along the north facade, an alternating pattern of rounded and angular hoods. The house's elaborate stone carvings were also exaggerated in scale, serving to balance the building's mass with commensurate surface detail and interest. In this regard, the White House recalled Jefferson's use of scale and exaggeration at Monticello, with a characteristically American amplification of detail to match the enormity of the landscape.[9]

The original floor plan of the White House changed very little between the Adamses' era and the brutal "restoration" performed under President Theodore Roosevelt at the turn of the 20th century. The fact is, most homes lived in by prosperous Americans in 1800 would have comfortably

fit inside the vast space of the East Room, which measured 38 feet by 78 feet and 22 feet high. This fact, as much as financial issues, probably explains why the room was not properly finished until President Jackson's term of office.

The two parlors that eventually became known as the Red and Green rooms were 22 feet, 6 inches wide by 28 feet, 3 inches long, and 18 feet high. The oval room now called the Blue Room was 30 by 40 feet—undoubtedly the largest oval room in America.[10] In the high Gilded Age of the 1880s, critics referred to these rooms as small, yet these spaces—the smallest of the state rooms in the White House—were as big as the largest rooms in the grandest houses of 18th-century America. For example, the great central hall at Stratford, birthplace of Robert E. Lee, measures 28 feet, 6 inches square. The grandest private room in all of colonial Virginia was only slightly larger than the "common parlor" of Jefferson's White House. Similarly, the largest rooms in South Carolina's Drayton Hall—considered the greatest Palladian house built in America—were 23 feet, 6 inches wide by 29 feet, 9 inches long, or just a hair larger than the "small" Red and

Green rooms at the White House. Finally, the Large Dining Room, or "New Room," built by George Washington at Mount Vernon in the 1780s, was among the grandest rooms of its day in all of Federal America. It is often compared with the East Room, owing to its position and its extra-high ceiling. It measures nearly 23 feet wide and almost 30 feet long, making it virtually the same size as the Red and Green rooms at the new White House. In its scale alone, and despite the reduction of L'Enfant's original palatial scheme, the White House was a dream house of a type previously unimagined in the new United States.[11]

The brief residence of John and Abigail Adams in the president's house was less than dreamlike, although Mrs. Adams seemed to appreciate the country-house nobility of the design: "The house is upon a grand and superb scale, requiring about thirty servants to attend and keep the apartments in proper order . . . To Assist us in this great castle, and render less attendance necessary, bells are wholly wanting, not one single one being hung through the whole house, and promises are all you can obtain."[12] The structure was still unfinished, and Mrs. Adams adjusted to daily life amid damp plaster walls and smoking fireplaces, noting, famously, in a letter to her daughter, "We have not the least fence, yard or other conveniences without, and the great unfinished audience-room I make a drying-room of, to hang up the clothes in."[13] It was clearly an overwhelming experience, even for the pragmatic and even-tempered Mrs. Adams.

Within a month of the Adamses' arrival, Thomas Jefferson had been elected president; following Jefferson's inauguration, changes affecting the architecture of the president's house came swiftly. Jefferson replaced the Capital City Commission with a public-buildings surveyor who was directly accountable to the president and gave this job to English-born architect and artist Benjamin Henry Latrobe, who was also charged with completing the still-unfinished Capitol, as well as expanding and altering the president's house. Architectural historian Talbot Hamlin has identified Latrobe as being, "more than any other one man . . . the creator in America of the architectural profession, as well as the instigator of a new kind of architecture," bringing "to the country a new vision of the dignity of classic simplicity."[14] Hamlin also noted that in contrast to Hoban, whose design for the house "was purely in the 18th-century manner," Latrobe had been schooled "in the more efficient planning of the classic revival."[15]

Jefferson's selection of Latrobe to work on the president's house was thus not surprising, particularly given that the two men shared a dislike for Hoban's design. Latrobe dismissed the architecture of the White House, and of the Capitol, as well, making the rather catty statement that "General Washington knew how to give liberty to his country but was wholly ignorant of art. It is therefore not to be wondered, that the design of a physician, who was very ignorant of architecture was adopted for the Capitol and of a carpenter for the President's House. The latter is not even original, but a mutilated copy of a badly designed building near Dublin."[16]

Jefferson, a Republican, emphasized the president's house's role as the home of a democratically elected leader over its function as a site for official ceremony. Discontinuing large receptions such as those favored by Adams, a Federalist, Jefferson used his predecessor's "levée" room as a private library and office. He also returned to using the north facade as the principal entry, as Hoban had intended, in contrast with Adams, who had designated the south entrance, reached via a temporary wooden bridge, for that purpose. In the large dining room, Jefferson installed a concealed, rotating server, such as he had at Monticello; this feature rendered servants less visible, a phenomenon he had noticed and admired in Paris. (Jefferson and selected guests served food themselves.) Jefferson hired Latrobe to complete still-unfinished aspects of Hoban's scheme, including the principal staircase. Latrobe rejected Hoban's design, which called for a freestanding flight to reach a landing and then divide into two, instead creating a pair of arc-shaped stairs that converged on a landing where a short, straight flight began. Latrobe's design opened up the house's transverse hallway and, by virtue of being less easily accessible from the main entrance used by the public, gave the president's second-floor living quarters greater privacy—a quality Jefferson valued. Indeed, the staircase reveals the intrinsic contradictions resulting from the house's dual role as public and private place: a grandly scaled and articulated staircase was appropriate, and indeed expected, in a building dedicated to official ceremony, but a placement to the side was more suited to family life, paralleling staircase location in English country houses, where very few visitors were ever invited to the private second-floor living quarters.

This original clear division in the president's house between public and private spaces was later interrupted when executive offices evolved upstairs in the 19th century, only to be reaffirmed by McKim, Mead & White in 1902.

Working with Jefferson, Latrobe proposed two wings connecting the house to the Treasury Building on the east, and the War and Navy Building on the west. Jefferson had also drawn designs not only for the wings, but also for stables, a coach house and saddle room, an icehouse, a meat house, and even a henhouse. The wings, holding service areas and fireproof record-storage rooms, were largely submerged below grade on the northern facade, presenting only rows of lunette windows. To the south, the wings were fully exposed and bordered by colonnades that incorporated double doors topped by the same type of half-round lunette windows found on the other side of the house. The flat roofs of the wings served as terraces. The partially realized scheme recalled Jefferson's

Proposed elevation of the south portico by Benjamin H. Latrobe, 1807. The design strongly resembles changes made in the 1820s. The walk from the south portico was included in the first garden plan for the White House by Latrobe and Thomas Jefferson.

Proposed alterations showing north and south porticoes, by Benjamin H. Latrobe, 1807. These changes foreshadow what was built under President Jackson.

"A View of the President's House in the City of Washington after the Conflagration of the 24th August 1814," aquatint by William Strickland after George Munger, c. 1814. The first stands of trees remained after the British soldiers burned the 14-year-old residence.

work at Monticello: the wings' horizontality contrasted with the vertical central block, the additions were recessed into a sloping site, and the open-air terraces mediated between indoors and outdoors. These additions echoed plantation designs of the colonial South as well as much grander lateral extensions found on classical-style English country houses of the late 18th century. The extensions were also intended to offer easy communication between the president and the government, a plan that underscored the house's role as a workplace and anticipated the more ambitious east and west wings of a later century.

Grand tripartite archways punctuating each wing were to have added a strong note of country-house ceremony, each archway containing quarters for a gatekeeper and accommodating roadways connecting the northern and southern parts of the extensive grounds. Latrobe, not known for his tact, was critical of some of Jefferson's artistic contributions, stating, "I am sorry I am cramped in this design by his [Jefferson's] prejudices in favor of the old French books, out of which he fishes everything—but it is a small sacrifice to my personal attachment to him to humour him, and the less so, because the style of the colonnade he proposes is exactly consistent with Hoban's pile—a litter of wings worthy of the great sow it surrounds, and of the Irish boar, the father."[17]

In 1807, Latrobe and Jefferson proposed a radical reworking of the house's arrangement. In the large entrance hall, which Latrobe felt rendered the house a "Polypus [*sic*]—all mouth," they called for the replacement of two fireplaces with niches and column screens, and the replacement of the oval-shaped drawing room's north wall with a third column screen.[18] The house's oval drawing room, which may have seemed dated to Latrobe, was to be modified with new entrances, and the large East Room was to be divided into five contiguous spaces, defined by the treatment of the east wall and ceiling. The kitchen was to be moved from its basement location below the entrance hall, where noise and odors could travel to interfere with official greetings, to a position directly below a relocated dining room. Latrobe proposed creating a first-floor bedroom suite—similar to the state bedroom suites that were a standard part of English noble houses—that would be more easily accessible to servants, whose quarters were in the basement. It was probably Jefferson's idea to furnish the new bedroom with the type of French-inspired alcove bed he favored. Efforts to realize Latrobe and Jefferson's proposed interior alterations seem to have been abandoned by the spring of 1808; none of the changes were realized.

By 1809, Latrobe had completed the extension of an existing six-and-a-half-foot-high stone wall to fully enclose the White House grounds; the wall

The president's house as it was rebuilt under presidents Madison and Monroe, 1815–18. The State and Treasury buildings on the east and the War and Navy departments on the west were on land that had first been part of the president's park. The house was both home and government office. Watercolor by the Baroness Hyde de Neuville, wife of the French ambassador to the United States under Louis XVIII (1816–22), sketched in 1820, watercolor 1821.

was punctuated by an arch at the end of Pennsylvania Avenue. Dr. William Thornton, who had served as the original architect of the Capitol and who had been the object of Latrobe's criticism, lambasted the project, charging that "instead of being adapted to the termination of a grand Avenue, and leading to the Gardens of a palace, [it] is scarcely fit for the entrance of a Stable Yard. Though in humble imitation of a triumphal Arch, it looks so naked, and disproportioned, that it is more like a monument than a Gateway: but no man now or hereafter will ever mistake it for a monument of taste."[19]

On August 25, 1814, with the nation under James Madison's leadership and at war with England, British troops occupied the White House and set it on fire. Aided by his wife, Dolley (who famously had evacuated the house only after securing the safety of Gilbert Stuart's 1796 portrait of George Washington), President Madison subsequently hired Latrobe to supervise the rebuilding of the house. At that time, in an effort to mask marks left on the stone facades by the fire, the structure was whitewashed, giving rise to its popular appellation, the White House. The residence's official name, the Executive Mansion, was not formally changed to the White House until 1902. Latrobe called for adding porticoes to the north and south elevations and, in a reflection of prevailing British taste, sought

once again to rearrange the plan with twice as many rooms as had previously existed. Latrobe did not complete the task and was replaced by Hoban, who, following Madison's desire to establish a sense of equilibrium following the conclusion of the War of 1812, meticulously rebuilt the house as he had first designed it. It rose phoenix-like, sparkling white, a sacred building less than two decades old.

In 1824 Hoban used Latrobe's detailed drawings to build a two-story Ionic portico outside the oval bay of the south front. Made of Seneca sandstone and accessible from the White House gardens by means of a double stairway, the porch opened into the three state parlors. Hoban also realized Latrobe's plan for a portico on the house's north facade. Begun in 1829 and completed the following year, it served as a porte cochere and echoed the central portion of the original facade. To Fiske Kimball, writing in 1919, the additions gave the White House "much of the monumental dignity which still makes it supreme among American houses."[20] These two monumental porches transformed the house from a slightly dated 18th-century country house into a very modern Greek Revival villa. The columned portico became an iconic feature of American houses, large and small, for the next quarter century.

Woodlands, the Philadelphia residence above the Schuylkill River of horticulturalist William Hamilton, built c. 1789, had a 600-acre park in the English landscape style. Colonial house owners thought that naturalized parks were more appropriate to American estates than formal gardens, like the one planned for the president's house by Major Pierre-Charles L'Enfant. Thomas Jefferson so admired Hamilton that he invited him in 1807 to advise on the garden at Monticello. Colored engraving by William Birch, self-published, Springland, Pennsylvania, 1808.

GARDEN

When George Washington and the capital city commissioners considered the land set aside for the president's house and garden, they faced a dilemma. On the one hand, the final 82 acres belonged to the citizenry and any landscape plan needed to address the public good. On the other, a person of the president's stature was expected to live in a house with private grounds.

At a time when America was in transition socially and politically, landed properties remained comforting and accepted symbols of status and rank to colonists who had only recently been western Europeans. As historian Catherine Allgor has observed, America "unfolded within a culture of denial—one that simultaneously rejected monarchical forms, embracing simplicity and republican virtue, all the while longing for the legitimacy of a monarchy."[21] The challenge for Pierre-Charles L'Enfant was to provide a garden that in scale and design signified the authority of the American president as well as the democratic values of public ownership.

Like the nation itself, early 19th-century American garden design was in transition as baroque formalism gave way to English romanticism. American estates, laid out to provide food as well as pleasure, were organized following the French tradition of the *ferme ornée,* "the ornamental farm." Roundabout roads and allées linked surrounding woodlands to flower gardens close to manor houses and their dependencies. As seen at Washington's Mount Vernon and Jefferson's Monticello, site was a determining factor in locating the colonial house. Views from high riverbanks and hilltops were natural features integral to enjoyment of the domestic garden.

Reflecting his generation's conception of the ideal country life, William R. Birch, a distinguished artist who lived in Philadelphia and had Thomas Jefferson as a patron, wrote in 1808, "The comforts and advantages of a Country Resident, after Domestic accommodations are consulted,

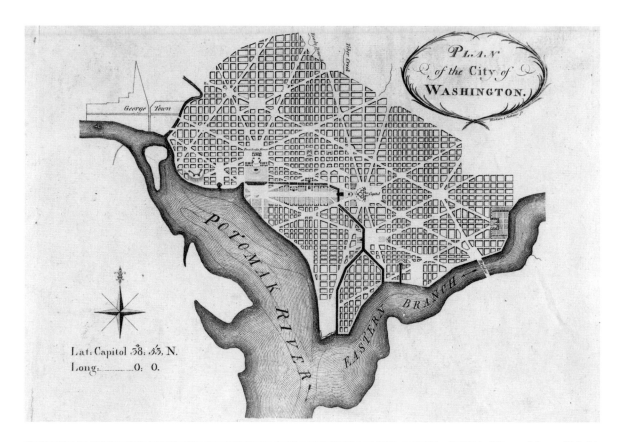

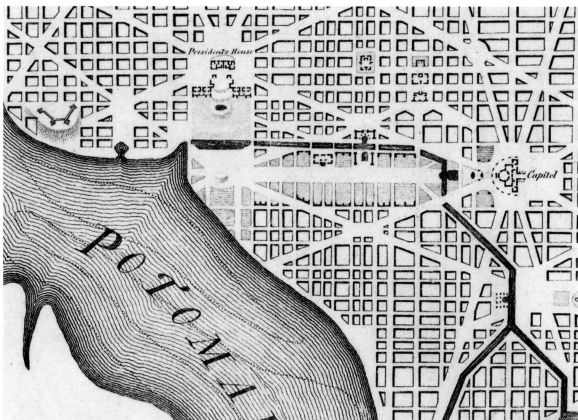

Top: Plan for the city of Washington by Major Pierre-Charles L'Enfant, first published version, engraving, Philadelphia, 1792. The garden at Versailles and European city plans influenced the design of America's new capital. Bottom detail: For the president's park, L'Enfant envisioned a statue of George Washington in a terraced garden, with the city's Tiber River in a canal running through the White House grounds. The president's house was to be four times the size it was actually built.

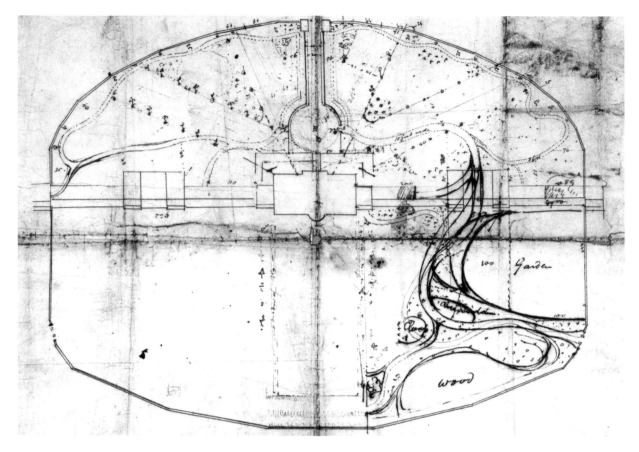

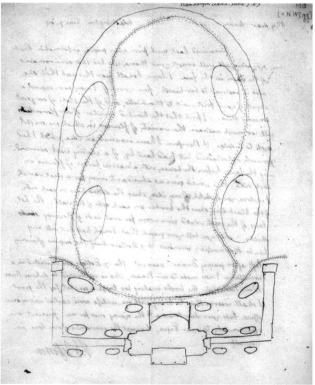

Top: The first plan for the president's garden, attributed to Thomas Jefferson and Benjamin H. Latrobe, late 1806–early 1807, reflected a transitional period in American garden design, from the formal to the natural. Alleys of trees and an axial walk from the south portico were in a park; a serpentine walk defined a flower garden at the east entrance. Bottom: Thomas Jefferson sketched a plan of his garden at Monticello in 1807, the same year he and Benjamin H. Latrobe conceived a garden for the White House. Both plans included a flower garden and pathways. Jefferson, influenced by picturesque theory, eliminated from his garden formal elements he had considered in the 1770s.

Top: When Thomas Jefferson visited Stowe, Buckinghamshire, England, in 1786, he thought its 1767 Corinthian arch had a "very useless appearance" because of its solitary location deep in the estate's park. Bottom: By building Benjamin H. Latrobe's arch as the east entrance to president's park, Thomas Jefferson made certain it was not "useless." Drawing by Baroness Hyde de Neuville, 1820.

consist more in the beauty of the situation, than in the massy magnitude of the edifice . . . . The man of taste will select his situation with skill, and add elegance and animation to the best choice. In the United States the face of nature is so variegated. Nature has been so sportive, and the means so easy of acquiring positions fit to gratify the most refined and rural enjoyment, that labour and expenditure of Art is not so great as in Countries less favoured."[22]

Birch illustrated his essay with engravings of the estates of America's landed gentry and included Woodlands, the Schuylkill River property of William Hamilton, an influential plant collector and landscape designer. Hamilton's 1780s house was one of the nation's first Federal period buildings and was surrounded by 600 acres landscaped in the fashionable style of English designer Humphrey Repton. A greenhouse and a hothouse reflected the rise in botanical studies in the 18th century.[23] For its first 50 years, the White House landscape itself showed the importance of Anglo romanticism and plant collecting to presidents and their gardeners.

The executive garden as envisioned by Major L'Enfant was commensurate in scale and ambition with America's largest estates. He called for a park on the level north side of a natural ridge, Wicomico Terrace, the site of his president's palace. South of the house, gardens stepped down to the shores of the Potomac River, where a monument to George Washington aligned with the house. Without walls and fences, L'Enfant's presidential park was at once appropriately formal and democratically open to the public.

L'Enfant's plan preserved a sweeping river, mountain, and forest view. For Jefferson and his generation, it was essential for a true American garden to retain a relationship to untouched nature. Gardening, wrote Jefferson, was "peculiarly worth the attention of an American because it is the country of all others where the noblest gardens may be made without expense. We have only to cut out the superabundant plants."[24] The American landscape, with its inherently sublime and beautiful qualities, did not require the embellishments of what Ralph Waldo Emerson called the "over-cultivated garden of England."[25]

The plan L'Enfant proposed for the presidential grounds was immediately problematic to the city commissioners. It may have provided for public access to the White House, but its grandeur suggested an aristocrat's estate. In February 1792, David Stuart, George Washington's personal doctor and voice on the commission, wrote the president:

"I beg leave to suggest that the intended appropriation of ground about the President's house, appears to me to be much too extensive . . . . It may suit the genius of a Despotic government to create an immense and gloomy wilderness in the midst of a thriving City, and I fear the Major has borrowed from thence; but I cannot think it suitable in our situation."[26]

City officials proposed subdividing what they called the President's Square. In 1796, shortly before his death, Washington authorized the allocation of land east and west of the president's house for public offices. The remaining 82 acres survived public criticism and became the grounds of the White House.

In January 1800, shortly before John Adams arrived in Washington to take up office, his secretary of the navy and a prominent Georgetown landholder, Benjamin Stoddert, wrote the capital commissioners. He conveyed to them that Mrs. Adams and the president, a gardener and farmer, wished for a garden to be planted on the north side of the newly built president's house.[27] A suggested model for this garden was political insider William Bingham's Philadelphia property, where shrubs, flowers, and trees were interconnected by paths. Defined by a fence, the White House grounds, wrote Stoddert, "should not be leveled, but Trees should be planted at once, so as to make an agreeable place to walk in, even in the summer."[28] Whether these grounds were to be for both the president and the public is not known, but like others of the Colonial era, they were intended for socializing and conversing along shaded walkways.

Although land was cleared for a White House vegetable garden, the duration of the Adams administration was too short for improvements to the president's grounds. They remained undeveloped, littered with building materials and occupied by structures built for construction workers. Potholes and stumps of established trees felled for firewood limited ready access to the house. A botanical garden proposed by George Washington remained unrealized, as did most of L'Enfant's grand plan for the capital city grounds. Despite these conditions, Abigail Adams responded to the beauty of the White House site in words that echo with sentiments of the natural-landscape movement. From the capital, she wrote her sister:

"As I expected to find it a new country, with Houses scattered over a space of ten miles, and trees & stumps in plenty with a castle of a House— so I found it—The Presidents [sic] house is in a beautiful situation in front of which is the Potomac with a view of Alexandr[i]a. The country around is romantic but a wild, a wilderness at present."[29]

On March 4, 1801, Adams and his wife left Washington and the administration of Thomas Jefferson began. The third president was the embodiment of the new Republican. He had the political ideals of an 18th-century revolutionary and the reverence for classical culture of an American aristocrat. He was versed in contemporary landscape theory and toured the estate gardens of England with John Adams in 1786.[30] A gentleman farmer of the Enlightenment, Jefferson sought the expansion of scientific knowledge. Looking to the wide-ranging accomplishments of Sir Joseph Banks, the scientific advisor to the British crown, Jefferson arranged the 1804 expedition of his personal secretary Captain Meriwether Lewis and William Clark.[31]

North facade, still without its portico, in a circa 1826 engraving, during John Quincy Adams' administration. James Monroe's curving wall defined the president's garden opposite the public's Lafayette Park.

When explorer Lieutenant Zebulon M. Pike brought two grizzly bear cubs from the far West, the president placed them in a cage on the north lawn for an admiring crowd. They were a symbol of the rich, untapped wilderness that had inspired the early colonists to pursue independence.

The improvements Jefferson made to the White House grounds enhanced and clarified the democratic symbolism of L'Enfant's triangular plan of Pennsylvania Avenue, the congressional mall, and the president's grounds. Concerned that the White House grounds of L'Enfant's design were too expansive for a democratic president, he enclosed five acres around the house with a modest split-rail fence, intending to replace it with a masonry wall. This fence largely defined the still-extant division between the president's private garden and the public park. Finding in the history of ancient Rome the origins of democracy, Jefferson planted along Pennsylvania Avenue double rows of Lombardy poplars, associated with liberty.[32]

Where the avenue terminated at the White House garden, Jefferson built a monumental brick-and-stone arch at the entrance. Such arches, originally derived from the Roman victory arch, were prominent features of English residential parks, where they framed vistas and established symbolic connections between estate buildings and landscape features. Jefferson's arch, captured in a rare pencil sketch in 1820 by a visitor to Washington, the Baroness Hyde de Neuville, functioned similarly. On axis with the Capitol Building, the arch made clear to all congressional visitors that they were entering the domain of the nation's president.

Jefferson and architect Benjamin Latrobe shared an interest in the study of plants and believed that naturalized landscape designs, responsive to local conditions and incorporating New World flora, would lead to authentic American gardens reflecting, in Latrobe's words, "the benevolence of nature" versus the intrusive "ingenuity of man." Together the president and his architect drew up a landscape plan for the White House grounds. In overall aspect, it was an Anglo-American park with formal and natural elements. A surviving unsigned drawing from Latrobe's office, dated to late 1806 or early 1807, divided the grounds into "garden," "clump," "wood," and "park." These were features of Colonial gardens, including the president's own at Monticello.[33]

The public entrance to the Jefferson White House was on the north side, planted with chestnut, linden, sycamore, and poplar trees, some in alleys extending the radial plan of L'Enfant. The level ground outside the north fence became a public common. The south grounds were reserved for the president's use. A flower garden, created after Jefferson left office, was in the bend of a picturesque, meandering gravel drive that led from the east entrance to the north door. The drive was screened with rhododendrons brought from the mountains west of Washington. The grounds west of this garden were left open to preserve the pastoral view down to the Potomac. Terraces, never built, were to have stepped down to an eight-foot-high stone wall completed along the southern perimeter of the garden.[34] In the tradition of a country house, the land beyond the south fence was open pasture.

South garden during John Quincy Adams' administration, in an 1826 watercolor by British diplomat Anthony St. John Baker. Though Major L'Enfant had envisioned a palace overlooking formal terraces down to a statue of George Washington at the Potomac River, Thomas Jefferson built a stone wall to define a five-acre garden appropriate to the house of a democratically-elected president.

The capital, Jefferson wrote in 1802, "may be considered as a pleasant country-residence, with a number of neat little villages scattered around within the distance of a mile and a half, and furnishing a plain and substantial good society."[35] The White House became the manor house to the capital city. From the first-floor terraces, extensions of the president's grounds, guests had a private view of the river panorama. By 1818, Arlington House in Virginia, with its imposing classical portico, could be seen sitting in the hills. It was a view that evoked the world of Claude Lorrain, the 18th-century painter whose Elysian landscapes inspired writers and landscape designers of the English picturesque movement. Engravings of the Frenchman's paintings had been imported from Europe and decorated the sitting rooms of Colonial houses.

With Latrobe, Jefferson's successor James Madison continued to plant according to Jefferson's plan. After the War of 1812, the White House grounds were once again a construction site. President Monroe, a Virginia plantation owner and former minister to France, purchased landscape plans from the prominent New England architect Charles Bulfinch to restore the

White House garden.[36] To implement these plans, now lost, the president hired the first White House gardener, Charles Bizet. An experienced plantsman, he had worked at Montpelier, the estate of James and Dolley Payne Madison. Bizet oversaw the regrading of the president's grounds and the planting of young seedling trees. He and his workmen constructed a stone fence with iron gates north of the house, following Jefferson's plan.

To be an American gardener was to enjoy the ecological riches of the new republic and to benefit from the scientific advances of modern agricultural practices. While landscape design as a profession evolved slowly, horticulture established itself as an amateur pursuit. To plant was to participate in the national betterment of America. John Quincy Adams, the son of John and Abigail Adams, was an active gardener from a family of horticulturists and farmers, a proponent of scientific exploration, and an early advocate for reforesting America after it had been plundered by the English. A 1788 graduate of Harvard, he read the influential garden writings of the time, including the landscape treatise of John Claudius Loudon, *An Encyclopedia of Gardening* (1822), and *North American Sylva* (1818), by French botanist

Arlington House, designed by English architect George Hadfield and built for George Washington's adopted grandson, was visible from the president's residence. The classical revival architecture of both houses exemplified the symbolic importance of antiquity to American democratic society. Watercolor by Anthony St. John Baker, 1826.

François-André Michaux. Adams actively participated in the exchange of plants, which rapidly expanded when trade was freed from British control.

Adams hired the talented second White House gardener John Ousley, who held the position for 30 years. With the president himself sometimes digging and planting, Ousley created beside the east entrance gate the ornamental flower garden imagined by Jefferson. The area was surrounded by a wood fence and planted with beds of flowers and herbs interwoven with meandering paths. Ousley built protective cold frames to shelter fledgling seedlings.

Like other rural estates, America's grandest house would be complete only when its garden and pathways were shaded by towering elms and oaks. To this end, Adams initiated what is today a defining tradition of the White House grounds, the planting of American trees emblematic of national pride.

As seen in watercolors by a British diplomat, the White House by 1826 was becoming an imposing presence in a landscape of muddy roads and wood-framed lodgings.[37] On the south side, a stone fence divided leveled grounds from a field where cows and sheep grazed. Inside the wall a fledgling forest was taking root.

In 1827, two years before leaving office, Adams looked out his south-facing office window and marveled at his private fenced garden. It must have given the much-maligned president a sense of national progress, of having participated in the slow realization of a suitable presidential estate.

"In this small garden," he wrote, "of less than two acres, there are forest and fruit-trees, shrubs, hedges, esculent vegetables, kitchen and medicinal herbs, hot-house plants, flowers, and weeds, to the amount, I conjecture, of at least one thousand. One half of them perhaps are common weeds, most of which have none but the botanical name."[38]

Adams' words do not reflect the viewpoint of an English squire surveying his great country park, but rather the sentiments of a new kind of American—the villa dweller—surveying his suburban domain. Thus, as the 1830s began, the White House gardens entered their next phase.

GEORGE WASHINGTON, *painted by Gilbert Stuart, 1796. In the first work of art purchased for the White House, Washington, like the house he envisioned for the president, appears both modest and noble.*

INTERIORS

By English standards, the White House was a moderate-size country house, one that might have been home to a minor country aristocrat in a Jane Austen novel. While more simply laid out than a comparable English nobleman's house such as Attingham Park, the White House aspired to similar nobility in the dimensions and height of its rooms. The state rooms at Attingham consisted of two suites running in opposite directions, beginning with the two largest public rooms and opening into a series of smaller rooms for Lord Berwick on one side and for his wife on the other. The main-floor rooms in the White House were originally conceived in a similar processional way, each room leading to the next—the central oval drawing room led to the right into what is now the Red Room, and then into the large room beyond; while in the other direction what is now the Green Room opened into the East Room. In both Attingham and the White House, service areas were located in the raised basement of the main block. Thomas Jefferson even imagined extensive service wings to the east and west of the White House, parallel to Attingham's sprawling extensions, although these weren't fully realized until the 20th century.

The White House was far grander than any house George Washington and his generation of Americans had ever lived in or even seen. Much has been made of the parallels between Mount Vernon and the White House; Mount Vernon is like a doll's house in comparison. The rooms at Mount Vernon are cozy and human in scale—including the large multipurpose New Room added in the 1780s, a space that seems to foreshadow the White

Oval drawing room in Willow Brook, Baltimore, 1799, showing ready-made composition decoration on the cornice and mantelpiece. This room, built for an upper-class Marylander, reflects what the president's oval drawing room might have looked like during John Adams' administration.

Drawing room in Lorenzo, the 1808 house in Cazenovia, New York, built for wealthy landowner John Lincklaen. Ready-made composition decoration rendered the interiors of this isolated country residence as fashionable as the president's house.

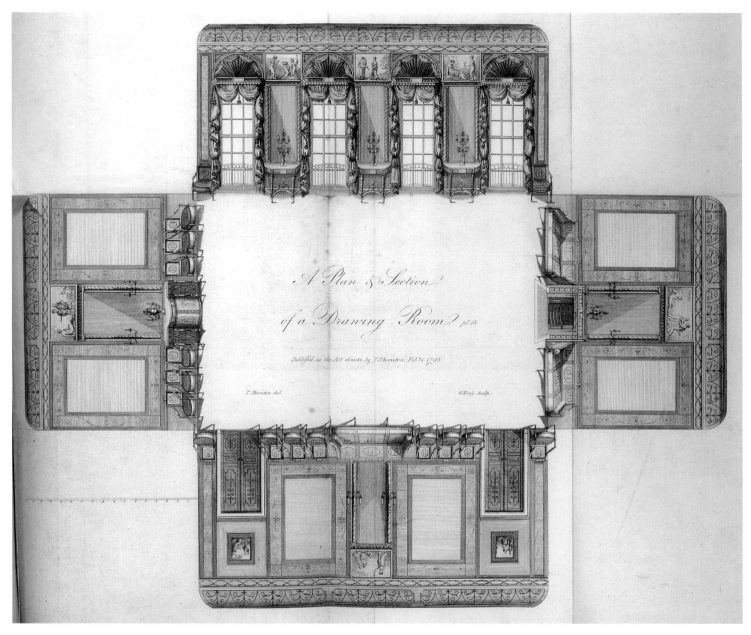

Drawing room in Thomas Sheraton's Cabinet-Maker and Upholsterer's Drawing-Book, *published in 1793. The rectangular parlors in the president's house would have been decorated according to English precedents such as this.*

House's East Room.[39] The fact that Mount Vernon's biggest public room was the same size as the White House's smallest public rooms (the parlors that became the Red and Green rooms) gives some sense of the contrast.

Not even the grandest colonial families had ever tried to decorate a place so large, which explains why no president was really comfortable dealing with the East Room until Andrew Jackson finally finished it in the 1820s. The idea of "home" that became so crucial to first families later in the century had not yet taken root in the American psyche. The Madisons carried on the 18th-century tradition of seeing the rooms as more of a rationalized stage set, filled with appropriate props, upon which they played their roles.

By 1800, standardized decorative elements had become common in the houses of the American elite through the development of precast composition ornament that imitated carved classical motifs. Such applied ornament used a principle similar to that of the applied figures on Josiah Wedgwood's two-colored jasperware ceramics, perfected in the late 18th century.[40] George Andrews, a Baltimore merchant, supplied the initial decorations for 17 doorframes on the main floor and 10 mantelpieces.[41] The availability of ready-made stylishness helped control costs and sped up the completion of the president's house.

We do not know the exact appearance of the earliest decorative features of the White House, because the fire of 1814 left the house an empty shell.

ABIGAIL ADAMS, *engraving after Gilbert Stuart, 1800–12. Mrs. Adams sits in a plain armchair like one she would have used at the president's house.*

However, surviving contemporary interiors suggest the appearance of the presidential interiors. The 1798 Octagon House in Washington City, designed by William Thornton for John Tayloe III of Virginia, retains doorframes, mantels, and cornices with ornaments supplied by George Andrews. Similar kinds of decoration appear as far afield as in the drawing room at Lorenzo, built in 1807 for land speculator John Lincklaen in the tiny rural hamlet of Cazenovia, New York.

A striking parallel is seen in the oval room designed for Willow Brook, Thorowgood Smith's 1799 rural retreat near Baltimore.[42] Although a good deal smaller than the White House oval drawing room, the Willow Brook room's assortment of cast classical decoration gives a sense of how the White House oval room might have originally looked.

For the White House oval drawing room, the centerpiece of a suite of reception rooms grander than any in the nation, a modern neoclassical scheme would have been derived, like most elite urban interiors in America, from published English designs, such as those of Thomas Sheraton.[43] Everything in the room would have been symmetrical, the upholstery matching the window curtains, the furniture arranged around the room's perimeter, following prevailing English custom. The rectangular parlors at either side of the oval room were intended for less formal social activities and like such secondary spaces in English country houses, would have harmonized with the oval room. Simplified English models were the standard.

Abigail Adams established the upstairs oval room as a private ladies' sitting room. This precedent, which has continued to the present day, acknowledged that the downstairs rooms were too forbidding for normal living requirements, the quasi-public status of the house not being suitable for private family life.

Thomas Jefferson oversaw the basic completion of the house that George Washington had approved and in which John and Abigail Adams had briefly lived. He approached the White House as he did Monticello, his plantation in the hills outside of Charlottesville, Virginia. He used the vast entrance hall of Hoban's design as a gallery of recent inventions and scientific discoveries. From Latrobe's 1807 plan of the house, we can see that the Republican president lived as an English nobleman might have in his country house a generation or two earlier, with a suite of rooms defined by their public and private uses.[44] The oval room was a public drawing room, akin to the "saloon" in an early 18th-century English noble house. The space now known as the Red Room was an antechamber—a semiprivate buffer between Jefferson and the public; what later became the

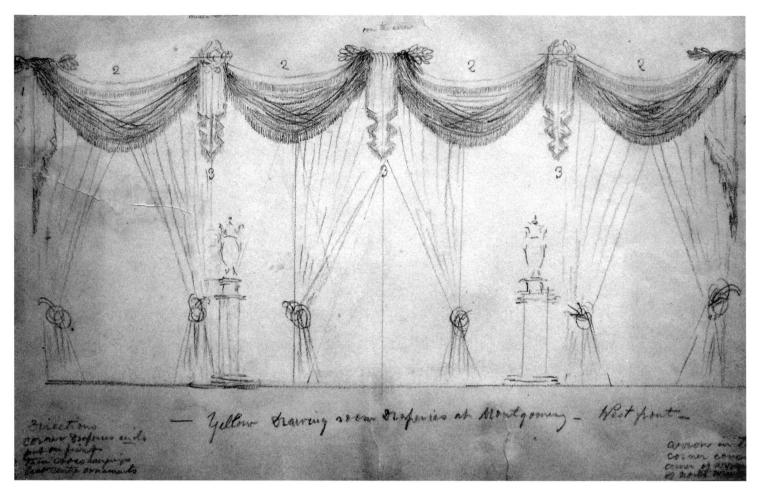

Continuous drawing-room draperies for Montgomery Place, in Annandale-on-Hudson, New York. This c. 1810 drawing by Janet Livingston Montgomery is said to have been based on Dolley Madison's parlor draperies in the president's house.

State Dining Room was used as his library and cabinet. The term *cabinet* referred in this period to the most private, personal space in an aristocrat's home. The men who made up Jefferson's governmental cabinet, accordingly, had the most direct and intimate access to their leader.

By the time of Jefferson, rooms set aside exclusively for dining had become a regular feature of American homes. Right up through the revolution, dining furniture was typically portable (using drop-leaf tables), with meals eaten wherever was most convenient. By the Federal era, better houses typically had a room set aside solely for meals.

At the White House, the dual public–private purpose of the house was evident in the dedication of two rooms for eating. The future Green Room was designated a "common" (i.e., everyday) dining room, and what would become the Family Dining Room was the "public" (i.e., state) dining room. It is worth pointing out that in the common dining room, Jefferson used a painted canvas floorcloth, whereas the public dining room, where he gave official dinners, had wall-to-wall carpeting. Although one thinks of this as a modern concept, fitted carpets were routinely installed in houses by the end of the 18th century. Floorcloths, a distant ancestor to

linoleum flooring, were a less expensive alternative to carpet, which still had to be imported. Chintz (printed cotton) curtains were hung in Jefferson's everyday dining room, whereas white dimity (a heavy woven cotton) covered the windows in the state dining room. Dimity was a fine textile, but it was an informal sort of fabric for such a huge room and not what one would have found in an English nobleman's country house. Its use probably reflected resistance to unnecessary luxury in the president's house, as well as in similar, more modest dining rooms across the country.

In March 1809, James and Dolley Madison moved into the White House, and they continued to work with Benjamin Henry Latrobe. Like most elite American women of her day, Mrs. Madison decorated the primary reception rooms in the prevailing classical style that represented the nation's commitment to the democratic ideals of ancient Greece. Mrs. Madison established for herself a "best" parlor (now the Red Room). This same room continued as the primary sitting room on the main floor into the 20th century. Dolley Madison's best parlor featured swags of sunflower-yellow drapery hung over wall-mounted rods, a style known as Grecian and inspired by contemporary English Regency treatments.[45] With matching silk satin upholstery, the room was no doubt dazzling in its modern brilliance and luxury. The only surviving image of Mrs. Madison's window treatment is a drawing by Janet Livingston Montgomery (1743–1828), widow of American Revolutionary War hero General Richard Montgomery (1736–1775), who apparently tried to replicate the effect at her country house, Montgomery Place, in Annandale-on-Hudson, New York.

The Madisons used the White House in a more flexible and modern way than Jefferson had, creating from the three parlors and the State Dining Room an enfilade of public spaces that echoed the suites of "parade rooms" in contemporary English noble houses. They moved the office spaces across the hall to Jefferson's public dining room, turning his cabinet room and library into the State Dining Room. These connected rooms could be used individually for smaller occasions or thrown open for large crowds. Both the oval room and the parlor got new marble mantelpieces, replacing the plaster-ornamented wooden ones that had, up to this time, been adequate. Wooden mantelpieces with marble facings had been the rule in elegant American rooms, but with the Grecian style and increasing American prosperity, marble mantels became increasingly de rigueur. The new State Dining Room retained the furniture that Jefferson had used and, presumably, its wooden mantelpiece. A massive life-size portrait of Washington by Gilbert Stuart was hung over the fireplace, and ingrain carpeting—a colorful flat-weave covering that was cheaper and more durable than other carpets—was installed. Exceptional only for its great size and the Stuart portrait, this space was decorated much like any other genteel dining room of its day.

Benjamin Latrobe created the first fully conceived decorative scheme for the president's house in the oval room, the only such special interior in the house. Although it would not have been out of the ordinary in the context of English houses, Latrobe's oval-room scheme was probably unique in the United States. A huge and very expensive plate-glass mirror was positioned over the mantelpiece, adding to the reflected light from the mirrored recesses flanking the door to the main hall. Brilliant red velvet draperies at the windows matched the furniture upholstery and would have created an effect far more opulent than was typical even in upper-class houses of the time. However, it is important to keep in mind that even elite American interiors would have been only middling in comparison with those in great English houses. While Americans seem to have swooned over the room's glamour, a Scottish nobleman referred to it in 1813 as "plainly but handsomely furnished."[46] Although plain and handsome was seen by the American people as appropriate for the White House, it was probably not the reaction Latrobe was looking for.

The Madison decorations were destroyed during the 1814 burning of the mansion. When the Monroes oversaw the rebuilding and refurnishing of the burned-out structure, they brought a French accent to its decoration. The Monroes' taste was not unique but reflected an overall shift taking place across America at the time. The English hegemony in American decorative arts was waning—no doubt helped by American anger against the warlike British. French style was in the ascendancy and by the 1840s dominated American taste.[47]

President Monroe, not his wife, was chiefly involved in ordering the new furnishings. His role followed the established pattern in place since colonial days, in which men were the primary decision makers relative to furnishing houses. It was only with the rise of the cult of domesticity in the 1840s, and with it the shifting of home decoration into the woman's sphere, that presidents' wives became the primary instigators in choosing White House furnishings.

With Monroe's decoration, the White House began to live up to the grandeur of its architecture. The rebuilt interiors were more monumental than the original, with doorframes, cornices, and other architectural devices of the burgeoning Greek Revival style initially promoted in the United States by designers such as Latrobe. Doors were framed with deep, broad casings, joined by ornately carved corner blocks. George Andrews and his son continued to supply cast-plaster architectural ornament for the rooms. The East Room, for the first time, finally received some plaster decoration and a coat of white plaster over its brick walls. French wallpapers were put up in the second-floor rooms, with coordinated paper borders, all in accordance with the growing American taste for anything French.

The wooden mantelpieces used in the Federal White House were no longer adequately grand, and 21 white carved-marble mantels were ordered from Italy. The best of these mantels were placed in all four rooms of the state suite and are still closely associated in the public's mind with the three main reception rooms. Similar white marble mantels were appearing in every major city from Boston to Charleston.[48]

The new decoration of the oval "saloon," or drawing room, was more imperial than the Madisons' red velvet, with red silk brocade curtains in a two-tone gold design of laurel wreaths and a custom-made Aubusson carpet on the floor. Although carpeting was commonplace in better homes by this time, French carpets from the Aubusson factory remained a luxurious exception. Red flocked wallpaper with gilt borders provided a strong visual foil for the gilt window cornices carved with large spread-winged eagles. The Stuart portrait of Washington had been returned from the State Dining Room. This was an intentionally imposing interior, imagined as the closest thing Americans would have to a royal presence chamber, and thus probably intended to be unlike any other room in the country. Mrs. Madison's parlor continued to be decorated in yellow under the Monroes. However, the Monroes began to call the Green Room by that name after its color scheme, and it stuck. The East Room also got its name under the Monroes, since it took up the eastern third of the main floor.

FURNISHINGS

The first artwork purchased specifically for the White House, in 1800, was Gilbert Stuart's full-length portrait of Washington as president.[49] In some ways it is exactly the sort of portrait an English nobleman would have added to the gallery of ancestors upon inheriting his country house. In other ways it embodies the inherent conflict that affected the furnishing of the White House for the next 150 years.

Originally hung in the president's drawing room, which became the Blue Room in 1837, the portrait is a deft combination of the imperial and the plain. All in black, Washington is shown as gentlemanly, even noble, but *not* kingly. His velvet suit marks his status, and the sword in his hand alludes to his past position as general and then current one as commander in chief. Except for the sword, Washington could be a wealthy Episcopal priest or a prosperous physician. Compared with other portraits of prominent American men of his period, it is a picture of modesty.[50] The only grand gesture in the painting is the carved and gilt furniture. Such splendid furniture would have existed in an English house of this size and grandeur, but never at the White House itself; it is a flight of fancy added by the artist.

John and Abigail Adams moved into an unfinished house in 1800 that must have been simultaneously terrifying and irritating. As prosperous but not grand Yankees, they had no instinct for furnishing a house of such palatial proportions.[51] The only furniture they brought to Washington was cartloads of used goods selected by Mrs. Adams and shipped to the new capital from the president's house in Philadelphia. This included a suite of red damask upholstered furniture consisting of 36 chairs and three settees. Ultimately, much of this made its way into the upstairs oval room—designated a ladies' drawing room by Mrs. Adams—including chairs, two card tables, and two sofas.[52] All of this plain mahogany furniture would have been fine for an American country house of the modest scale known to Adams and his peers. For the White House it was inadequate.

The Adamses' "china," of white-bodied porcelain, was imported, as porcelain had not yet been produced with any commercial success in North America.[53] It was far plainer than English squires would have used in their country houses. The Adamses also used queensware, a cream-bodied earthenware popularized for middle-class consumers by Wedgwood and other Staffordshire potteries.

Clues about household silver used by John and Abigail suggest that they had what other prominent Americans owned at the time. Colonial America held the English belief that a man's standing was reflected in the quantity

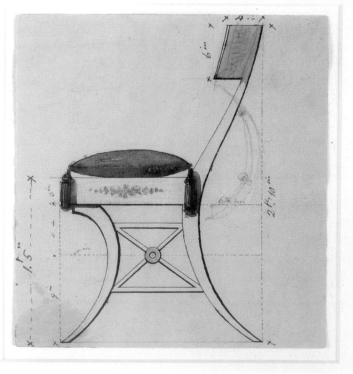

Design for klismos-form chair, by Benjamin H. Latrobe for James Madison, 1809. Although painted furniture was commonplace in upscale dwellings, Latrobe's designs for the oval room were more glamorous than anything previously known in the United States.

THE TEA PARTY, *by Henry Sargent, c. 1824. This painting offers a rare glimpse of the early use of circular, French-style center tables in American parlors.*

Types of objects used in the president's house in the early 1800s. Top left and center: Silver sugar urn and cream jug, crafted by John Vernon, New York, c. 1790. American-made silver tea accessories like these symbolized gentility and affluence. Such items were listed in the inventory of the John Adams White House. Top right: Painted fancy chair, unknown maker, Baltimore, c. 1800. Painted chairs were ubiquitous in stylish Federal homes. John Adams and Thomas Jefferson used similar chairs at the White House. Bottom left: Wedgwood Queensware dinner plate with painted border, c. 1800. English-made creamware was listed in the inventory of the Adams White House and would have been like this plate. Bottom right: Silver soup tureen, by Hugh Wishart, New York, c. 1800. Although he decried aristocratic pretension, Thomas Jefferson ordered a large tureen for the White House from a local silversmith. This one suggests what Jefferson's tureen might have looked like.

Top left: Marble-topped mahogany center table, France, c. 1817, Monroe administration. This piece, brought from France by the Monroes, reflects the sort of center tables that were being created by American furniture makers and used in elite American parlors in the 1810s and 1820s. Top right: Ormolu clock with figure of George Washington, by Jean-Baptiste Dubuc, Paris, c. 1810. The popularity of these expensive figural clocks among well-to-do Americans is evidence of the interest in French ormolu objects outside the White House. Center left: Detail of the ormolu plateau by Jean-François Denière and François Matelin, Paris, 1817, from the Monroe administration. With its figural candelabra and festoons of grapevines, this plateau was such a splendid object that it continued to impress first ladies long after it had gone out of style. Center right: These 1817 French ormolu candlesticks, flanking the Minerva clock, were purchased for the Monroe administration. Bottom left: Minerva clock and candelabra, France, 1817, purchased for the Monroe administration. The gilded bronze decorations acquired for the White House were probably grander than any such things in America at the time. The state rooms in the president's house were supposed to be exceptional, and the Monroes sought to fill the rooms with exceptional things. Bottom right: Ormolu Hannibal clock, France, 1817, Monroe administration.

Left: Tureen, Jacques-Henri Fauconnier, Paris, 1817, from the Monroe service. Few Americans, even wealthy ones, ever would have seen silver of such grandeur. Right: Wine cooler, Jean-Baptiste-Claude Odiot, Paris, 1817, from the Monroe service for the State Dining Room. American silversmiths did not make such opulent objects.

of solid silver he could present at his table.[54] The early presidents carried on this tradition as best they could, but silver in America was scant relative to that in England at the time. Basic utensils such as punch ladles, teaspoons and tablespoons, and "cream and sugar urns," listed in inventories of the Adams White House, were all readily available to the wealthy by the 1790s, both in New York and in Philadelphia. Plated tea urns, candlesticks, and candelabra branches present in the Adams White House also reflected the common practice of importing such English goods through New York or Philadelphia silver shops.[55]

Although Jefferson criticized George Washington for being an aristocrat, he himself knew how to live like one, and he added silver soup tureens to the White House collection from a Washington-based silversmith named John LeTellier for a whopping $479.35, or $6,851 in 2007 dollars.[56] Silver tureens would have been standard in English noble houses but were extremely rare in America and represented a luxury suitable for the president's table.[57]

Black-and-gold-painted chairs were used in both Jefferson's office (now the State Dining Room) and his private dining room (now the Green Room). These were bought by the Adamses and suggest the enormous popularity of such painted furniture in American country houses in the classical period.[58]

Dolley and James Madison seem to have embraced the English country-house model as fully as Jefferson did. The appearance of a pianoforte and a guitar in Mrs. Madison's yellow parlor (now the Red Room) marks the appearance of the first identifiably female objects in the public rooms of the White House. It was generally accepted that amateur skill at playing musical instruments was an asset for a woman. The

pianoforte was also, from the start of the 19th century in America, a hugely potent symbol of social status, because of its inherent cost and the expense of learning to play. The fact that Mrs. Madison put a piano in her parlor thus not only marked it as a woman's room, but also underscored her status as educated and affluent.[59] The piano is also a very domestic object, iconic of home and family life, and seems to have been an attempt to counter the public nature of the state parlors. Mrs. Rutherford B. Hayes kept an upright piano in the Red Room in the late 1870s, and Mrs. Taft ordered a white piano for the Blue Room and tried to call it the Music Room. Harry Truman was the first man in the White House to express a passion for playing the piano.[60]

The Madisons added a suite of painted classical-style furniture designed by Benjamin Latrobe as part of his glamorous redecoration of the oval room. The Baltimore firm of John and Hugh Finlay made a total of 36 grained, painted, and parcel-gilt chairs accompanied by two nine-foot-long sofas and four smaller settees, all designed after classical models.[61] Such theatrical painted furniture was particularly popular in the homes of wealthy Baltimoreans and Philadelphians but would likely have seemed middle-class in the eyes of an English aristocrat.[62]

With the administration of James Monroe, for the first time both the president and Congress seemed to understand that the White House should be furnished with objects that were appropriately grand as well as of sufficient quality and durability to last for future generations. Monroe, unlike Washington, had seen aristocratic theatricality firsthand, having attended Napoleon's self-coronation as emperor. He broke the custom of using standard American furnishings and local manufacturers for the

Pair of porcelain urns, France, 1817, Monroe administration. Such elegant vases with scenes of France were the envy of American house owners.

White House in an effort to help the state rooms live up to the grandeur of their architecture. He wanted the White House, inside and out, to be exceptional, different from other American houses.

For the first time in its short existence, the house under the Monroes struck the perfect balance between "resplendency and simplicity" that suited General Washington's dream house. The centerpiece of the oval room was the 53-piece suite of carved, gilded, red-and-gold, upholstered furniture, including a mirrored pier table and two nine-foot-long sofas by Parisian cabinetmaker Pierre-Antoine Bellangé (1758–1827).[63] By 1817, sofas were only just becoming standard fixtures in American parlors, and the two huge gilded Bellangé sofas might well have been the finest and grandest ones in the country. There were side chairs, armchairs, stools, and a special pair of closed armchairs for President and Mrs. Monroe. Unlike the dainty country-house elegance of the Latrobe–Finlay furniture that preceded it, the Bellangé furniture had an architectural quality that suited both the scale of the room and the rank of the president. Less magnificent than contemporary gilded furniture made for either the French or the English monarchs, it was glamorous enough to reflect the power of the presidency.[64] If any other households in America boasted such opulent furniture, they were few and far between at this period. [see pages 15 and 134]

The massing of glittering gilded furniture as in the oval room was carried on through all the state rooms with more French objects. The Monroes brought in large ormolu candelabra and candlesticks, as well as massive ormolu clocks featuring the Roman goddess Minerva and the Roman general Hannibal. Produced by Parisian ormolu specialists Pierre-Philippe

Thomire, Louis Moinet Sr., and the firm of Jean-François Denière and François Matelin, these pieces were worthy of the grandest English country house and far grander than anything most Americans knew.

The French ormolu marks the beginning of a trend—of using imported French mantel garnitures—that continued through the end of the 19th century in affluent American homes.[65] A smaller kind of ormolu clock featuring George Washington was produced in Paris for the American market at this period and represents the kind of French ormolu that would have been found in fancier American homes. Although the White House collection currently includes one of these clocks, it was given only in the 20th century.

The Monroe rooms also contained a round French mahogany table with gilt mounts and a white marble top. The marble-topped table, which would have been placed at the center of the Monroes' parlor, was the precursor of the center table of America's Victorian parlors, tables that by the 1820s were familiar in elite American parlors.[66] A very similar table appears in a Boston interior in the early 1820s, in Henry Sargent's remarkable painting *The Tea Party.* Although some American cabinetmakers could produce such French-style furniture by this time, the furniture in Sargent's painting might actually be French.[67]

At this same historical moment, French porcelain was beginning its rise to dominance in the American market. The two pairs of enameled porcelain vases ordered by the Monroes in 1817 for the two rectangular parlors were harbingers of a tidal wave of ornately gilded and enameled vases of Sèvres type, imported from Europe, that continued to pour into the homes of America's elite for the next century. In 1817 the American

Top left: Cut-glass punch bowl, Pittsburgh, 1815–20. American cut glass was one of the few luxury tablewares to compete successfully with foreign imports, because it equaled the quality of English or French glass at a comparable cost. Top right: Ormolu fruit baskets, Jean-François Denière et François Matelin, Paris, 1817, from the Monroe service. The ormolu table decorations purchased by the Monroes were every bit as grand as the furnishings of any great English country house but more splendid than anything in the United States. Bottom left: Dessert plate, Dagoty et Honoré, Paris, 1817, from the Monroe service. French porcelain dessert services were rare in America in 1817 but later became standard accoutrements, affordable for newly prosperous households. Bottom right: Ormolu tripod stands, Jean-François Denière et François Matelin, Paris, 1817, from the Monroe service. With c. 1880 ormolu candelabrum.

ceramics market was still dominated by English pottery and porcelain, but by the 1830s, the rising popularity of French porcelains inspired a New York china merchant, David Haviland, to move to Limoges in France and start up a porcelain empire that still bears his name.[68]

Continuing to break precedent by using aristocratic-quality French goods rather than locally made silver, the Monroes sold the White House silver wine coolers by Parisian silversmith Jean-Baptiste-Claude Odiot from their own collection and purchased large silver tureens made in the workshop of Jacques-Henri Fauconnier. Far more opulent than most

American silver of their time, these pieces are relatively plain in terms of aristocratic French or English silver of the period.[69] The austere inscription that began to appear on White House silver under President Monroe— "President's House"—is fittingly modest, reminding each succeeding president that he is only the temporary steward of all this elegance.

The Monroes' dessert service, all that survives of a large quantity of French porcelain ordered from Dagoty and Honoré's Paris china shop in 1817, is an important harbinger of American domestic taste. The service itself, with its distinctive purple-red brim and grisaille trophies

Left: Gilded armchair, Pierre-Antoine Bellangé, Paris, 1817, purchased for the Monroe administration. A massive gilded French suite for the huge oval drawing room set an aristocratic tone unlike that of any other home in America. Right: Mahogany armchair, William King, Washington, D.C., 1818, for the Monroe East Room. Although the Monroes did not finish the East Room, they did acquire elegant furniture to make it functional. The King chairs and sofas reflected American taste more closely than did the French Bellangé furniture in the oval room.

representing war, agriculture, commerce, art, and science, is more opulently decorated than was the general fashion in the United States this early in the 19th century. The growing American taste for French porcelain among the increasingly prosperous merchant class tended to focus on plain white with simple gold banding and, somewhat later, with wide bands of a single solid color. Ornate painted decoration on dessert or tea services also grew popular later on, both on American-made and imported porcelains, but the more elaborate decoration schemes such as on the Monroe service were not yet established in this country.

The most splendid of the equipment in the Monroe dining room was the panoply of gilt bronze decorations by Denière and Matelin, including a 14-foot-long mirrored plateau, with 16 candleholders modeled as classically draped women, three gilt bronze baskets held up by triads of classical women, and a pair of gilded bronze tripod stands. The fact that this group of ormolu objects survived all the purges of the ensuing century demonstrates its ongoing power to impress both occupants and visitors of the White House, right through the Gilded Age.

The Monroes ordered some American-made furniture for the White House, and the presidential glassware was made by the Pittsburgh glasshouse of Bakewell, Page & Bakewell. We can imagine what it looked like based on other Pittsburgh cut glass of this era. In 1818, William King Jr. of Georgetown made a 28-piece suite of mahogany seating furniture for the partly finished East Room, and these items survived until Julia Grant had them replaced with more fashionable ones in 1874. The 24 mahogany armchairs and four sofas, clearly inspired by the Bellangé furniture, were masterful adaptations of a French form to the prevailing English taste that still dominated American homes in 1818. The King furniture better represents what was in American country-house parlors of the 1810s and 1820s than does the Bellangé furniture. [see page 93]

As the age of George Washington's dream house came to an end, the capital city was far less isolated and rural than it had been when John and Abigail Adams arrived in 1800. The White House was still an anomaly in the American landscape because of its size, but its psychological connection to English country houses had faded, and it was increasingly revered as a symbol of America's resilience. By this time Americans had begun to develop another vision for the way they should live, and this new dream house would once again be at odds with the president's house.

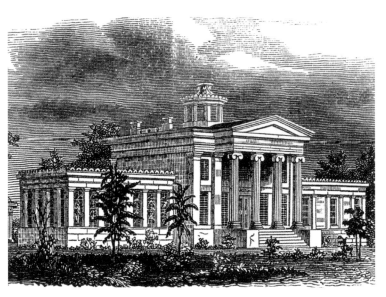

AMERICAN VILLAS

Top left: J. W. Perry house, with conservatory, in Brooklyn, New York, 1831, by architect James H. Dakin. Top right: Wodenethe, the residence of landscape theorist, horticulturist, and friend of A. J. Downing, Henry Winthrop Sargent, 1841, in Fishkill Landing, New York. Bottom left: Wellesley, the residence of Horatio H. Hunnewell, wealthy financier and influential horticulturist, 1852, in Wellesley, Massachusetts. Arthur Gillman was the architect. Bottom right: Armsmear, attributed to architect Octavius Jordan, the Hartford, Connecticut, villa of firearms manufacturer Samuel Colt. The 1856 house had an attached 1862 Moorish-style conservatory inspired by London's 1851 Crystal Palace. The public / private grounds, with extensive greenhouses, were landscaped by Cleveland & Copeland, colleagues of Frederick Law Olmsted.

VILLA
1829–1869

For this reason, the condition of the family home—in this country where every man may have a home—should be raised, till it shall symbolize the best character and pursuits, and the dearest affections and enjoyments of social life.

—Andrew Jackson Downing, *The Architecture of Country Houses,* 1850

LIVING LIKE AMERICAN GENTRY

When America emerged as an independent country, Thomas Jefferson and others were distressed at the ramshackle appearance of the general public's impermanent wood farmhouses and city shanties. But Democratic values of self-sufficiency and independence meant that a better way of life could not simply be imposed on the citizenry. Instead, in the decades before and during the Civil War, America evolved through technological progress, guided by social and aesthetic ideals expressed in sermons, novels, and newspapers. Preachers, moralists, and writers like Horace Bushnell, Harriet Beecher Stowe, and Lydia Sigourney defined how to live a productive and genteel American life. Architects Andrew Jackson (A. J.) Downing, Alexander Jackson Davis, and Calvert Vaux published designs for model homes and gardens appropriate to the new American way of life.[1]

A. J. Downing was the hero of America's genteel middle class. In addition to his national celebrity as a landscape designer and horticulturalist, his two landmark books, *Cottage Residences* of 1842 and *The Architecture of Country Houses* of 1850, defined the idea of "home" in America as a building set in a garden and filled with the sort of appropriate and tasteful things that properly expressed American values—refined middle-class values. As industrialization advanced, Americans had not failed to notice that with cities came certain negatives: dirt, poverty, crime. The rich had always owned both country houses and city houses, but by the 1840s, middle-class folks who could afford to looked for greener pastures (literally) beyond the borders of the city. The new houses they built outside cities—villas for professionals and cottages for workers—were unpretentious and economical.

Downing stressed in no uncertain terms the importance of furniture and decoration in creating an atmosphere that reflected the character of a house's inhabitants. He decried the confusion of *fashion* with *taste,* and he set out what was appropriate for a city house versus a country house. In country houses, away from urban corruption, Downing wrote that "we should look for the happiest social and moral development of our people."[2] The villa had a required number of public rooms—at the very least, a dining room and a parlor. A library was a nice feature, showing intellectual development and literary culture, but a well-stocked bookcase in the parlor would do in a pinch. These rooms were supposed to be ample and airy but not too large. They needed carpeting, draperies, well-painted woodwork, and appropriate wallpapers, as well as lace or muslin curtains and suitable ornaments and lighting. The genteel home had a formula, and every dry-goods merchant and every housewife followed it. In a democracy, the rewards for hard work were material comfort and financial independence, not aristocratic grandeur.

The Downing villa became the psychological model against which the White House was judged from 1830 through the end of the Civil War. Although not without dissension, Americans in 1800 had accepted the White House's grandeur as appropriate and necessary for the house of the nation's leader.

A half century later, the president's house was oddly inappropriate, a dwelling that did not reflect the new democratic values promoted by war hero and sixth president Andrew Jackson. By itself, the 2,844 square-foot East Room was larger than most middle-class *houses* in the United States and far larger than any room in the most ambitious villa published by Downing. In an era when the log cabin became an American icon, the architectural grandeur and interior splendor of the White House appeared undemocratic and morally suspect.[3] If the White House could not be transformed architecturally into a villa, its interiors, through decoration, and its gardens, through planting, could at least make the president's house livable in contemporary terms, moving it from country manor to villa.

As the city of Washington slowly urbanized, the White House was no longer really a country house but, by virtue of its extensive grounds, something of a suburban estate. Its architecture made it too aristocratic, and the number and size of its rooms made it difficult to keep clean and beautiful. Nonetheless, first ladies of the villa years struggled to wrestle Hoban's leviathan into submission and make the White House an appropriate American home.

"City of Washington From beyond the Navy Yard" during Andrew Jackson's presidency. Aquatint by William James Bennett after George Cooke, published 1832. In just 30 years since completion and rebuilding, the White House had rapidly evolved from being a country estate to a house in a prospering American city. To a visitor arriving by foot, ship, or horse, the president's residence and the Capitol were immediately visible symbols of democracy's balance of power.

VILLA DWELLERS

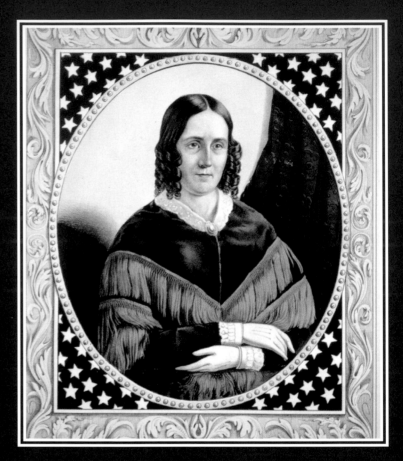

ANDREW JACKSON, bronze, Clark Mills, 1853.

Praised as the champion of the average man but himself a Tennessee plantation owner, War of 1812 hero Andrew Jackson brought to the White House in 1829 a wealthy populist's taste. He was the first president not to be intimidated by the East Room's huge scale and finally completed it. Jackson also built the first White House conservatory, near the east entrance, and finished the north portico, begun by John Quincy Adams.

In 1853 this equestrian statue was placed in Lafayette Park, belonging to the White House, by conservative democrats to complement the d'Angers statue of Thomas Jefferson.

SARAH CHILDRESS POLK, lithograph by Nathaniel Currier, after an 1846 daguerrotype by John Plumbe, Jr.

Mrs. Polk was the first woman to take charge of the decoration of the White House, at the moment when American women were becoming homemakers and the villa was the model for the ideal American house. Like other housewives in the 1840s, she relied on ready-made goods from new dry-goods emporia in major East Coast cities. She presided over a social White House and served the first annual president's Thanksgiving dinner. Competent and politically astute, Mrs. Polk advised her husband James, who oversaw the Mexican-American war that lead to the creation of New Mexico and California.

1829–37

1845–49

MILLARD FILLMORE, photograph by Mathew B. Brady, c. 1855–65.

ABIGAIL POWERS FILLMORE, engraving, c. 1850.

President Fillmore brought the authority of the presidency to the improvement of Washington and hired Andrew Jackson Downing, America's first native-born landscape architect. Downing's 1851 plan in the American picturesque style guided the development of the president's 82-acre park for the next 50 years.

A former schoolteacher and established bibliophile at a time when education for the public was new to America, Mrs. Fillmore created the first library at the White House in the second-floor oval room. She shared with her husband the period's enthusiasm for gardening. She had already studied horticulture and cultivated a greenhouse and flower garden at her Buffalo, New York, home before she arrived at the White House in 1850.

1850–53

AN AMERICAN VILLA

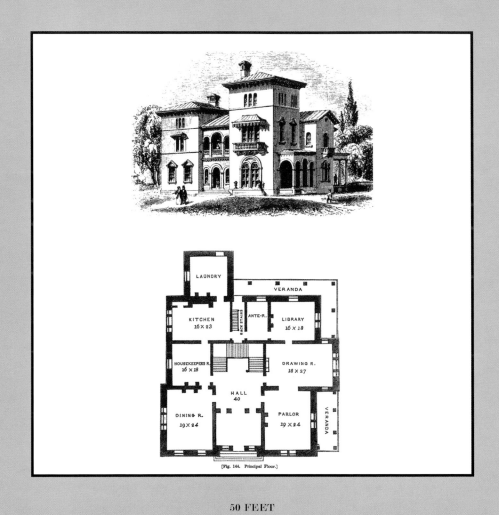

50 FEET

EDWARD KING HOUSE, 1845

Entrance façade and first-floor plan, Edward King villa, Newport, Rhode Island, 1845. Its architect was Richard Upjohn, an Englishman who learned his craft, as did America's first architects, through apprenticeship. The house was in the Italianate style, popularized by Upjohn. Andrew Jackson Downing defined villas as houses large enough to require servants, but not so large as to be castles or palaces, unsuitable for a democracy. He praised the King villa for its varied window styles that denoted the "different uses in various apartments."

THE PRESIDENT'S HOUSE
AS A VILLA

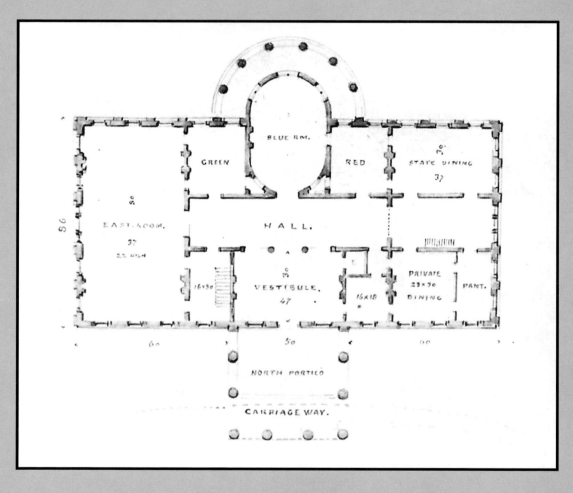

50 FEET

WHITE HOUSE, 1834

First-floor plan during the Jackson administration, drawn by Alexander Jackson Davis, 1834. At this time, the first family residence was still by far the largest house in the nation. The American villa offered a variety of spaces to meet family needs. In the almost 10,000-square-foot house for China trade merchant Edward King the drawing room was for company, the parlor was for everyday family living, and the library was a scholarly masculine retreat. The White House's 29,500 square feet rendered it too big and uncomfortable for a villa, but first ladies transformed its huge public spaces to impart some semblance of domestic coziness. The Red Room and Blue Room served as parlor and drawing room, while the president's cabinet room on the second floor stood in for a library until Abigail Fillmore created one in the 1850s.

Roseland Cottage, Woodstock, Connecticut, 1846, by English-born architect Joseph C. Wells. Built for Henry C. Bowen, a founder of the Republican Party, this villa, with a garden house and parterre garden, demonstrates the picturesque architecture and restrained scale A. J. Downing considered ideal for the American house. Republican presidents Grant, Hayes, and Harrison were guests here.

HOUSE

In the mid-19th century, as the nation grew and prospered, the rural country house evolved into the semirural villa designed in romantic styles, including variations on the Gothic, Italianate, and Romanesque. The 1845 Italianate Edward King villa in Rhode Island and the 1846 Gothic-inspired Henry C. Bowen Cottage in Connecticut represented two common romantic styles endlessly adapted for American homes before the war.

Some American houses maintained the aesthetic conservatism of the White House. The white-painted and columned Greek Revival villa, with details that echoed the north and south porticoes added to the White House in the late 1820s, had faded from popularity in the North by the

1850s. In the antebellum South, it continued to be a potent symbol, as exemplified by the 1857 house Stanton Hall in Mississippi.

Yet as restraint gave way to invention beginning in the 1840s, the White House appeared increasingly anachronistic. Its two iconic features—its architectural style and its color—both fell out of favor during the villa decades. Andrew Jackson Downing, among others, decried both the use of white paint and the building of Greek temples in America. Some Americans came to consider the color white unnatural when used extensively on a building's exterior; furthermore, for some, the Greco-Roman architecture of classicism seemed un-Christian and hence inimical to American values. However, the White House had by this time become a

Stanton Hall, residence of cotton broker Frederick Stanton, Natchez, Mississippi, 1857. Greek Revival villas like this one were built in the South up to the Civil War.

Trees, shrubs, and vines were planted to make the president's residence appear more midcentury classical villa than public Georgian palace. This is the earliest known image of the White House, taken 1846 during the Polk administration by the capital-city photographer John Plumbe Jr..

sacred building, forever associated with the founding fathers. Its architecture and its color were not open to debate and seemed to represent American values of simplicity and stability, particularly as partisan politics fueled raucous, mud-slinging campaigns.

If nothing could be done to alter the White House architecture, the house's lack of modern conveniences was a problem that could be solved. From the 1830s through the 1850s, the White House underwent changes that allowed it to extend beyond the country-house model and take on some of the new standards of comfort found in the American villa. These standards were applied in housing developments that, even before the Civil War, began appearing outside the nation's growing and increasingly industrialized cities. In 1833, Andrew Jackson installed running water. Previously, water had been drawn from a well and manually distributed throughout the White House in buckets. The new system was extended to the second floor in 1835; no effort seems to have been made to hide the requisite pipes. Martin Van Buren called for the establishment of central heating in 1837. The project was completed three years later, with extensive ductwork in the major reception rooms and several of the family quarters' seven bedrooms. In 1853 Franklin Pierce replaced this relatively inefficient heating system, which still needed to be supplemented with fireplaces, with a system that employed hot water and minimized the use of coal to ensure better-quality air.

James K. Polk had introduced gas lighting to the White House five years earlier. Gas pipes were laid beneath Pennsylvania Avenue, allowing for illumination within the house, as well as for streetlights. The number of rooms serviced by the innovation was increased incrementally over time.

During his presidency, from 1865 to 1869, Andrew Johnson considered building a new executive mansion, though he seems to have been motivated more by health and security considerations than by an assessment of the house's architectural value. The White House had long been considered unhealthful because of its frequently mildewed basement and its proximity to swampland thought to emanate toxic vapors. Additionally, following the assassination of Abraham Lincoln, as well as an unsuccessful attempt on Johnson's life, it was felt that a more secluded residence outside Washington would be easier to protect.

In the summer of 1866, the Senate began to investigate alternate sites in the Washington area. At the request of the secretary of war, Edwin M. Stanton, General Nathaniel Michler issued a report, including a drawing for a new residence and park to be built on the grounds of the Moncure Robinson estate northeast of the city. The drawing did not survive, and the proposed design remains unknown. Johnson, focused on his own impeachment, did not pursue the plan; his successor, Ulysses S. Grant, had no interest in the idea.

GARDEN

The antebellum presidents worked to domesticate not only the interior of the White House, but its north and south grounds. Their work culminated when Millard Fillmore hired A. J. Downing in 1850 to prepare a comprehensive plan for the capital mall and the White House 82-acre park. Downing's 1841 book *A Treatise on the Theory and Practice of Landscape Gardening*, dedicated to John Quincy Adams, had established him as America's leading landscape architect, with a vision that all American houses, large and small, benefitted from a private garden. He conceived the president's house as a suburban villa overlooking a landscaped park. The country house had been an object set into a landscape, a place from which nature was observed at a distance. The grounds of the contemporary villa were instead to be enjoyed through porches, verandas, and greenhouses overlooking grounds with pathways and vistas.

Andrew Jackson was the first president of the villa era. He arrived at the White House in 1829 and continued to employ the gardener John Ousley. Together they carried out extensive improvements to accommodate the increasing complexity of presidential life. They introduced new carriage drives and walkways; they replaced Monroe's curving north wall with a white parapet wall and moved the gate piers farther apart to create formal entrances at the ends of a semicircular drive. They ornamented the garden with benches, fences, and rose trellises. Jackson instructed the City of Washington gardener, Irish-born Jemmy Maher, to replace Jefferson's fast-growing but short-lived poplars along Pennsylvania Avenue with elms. This species, now long associated with the White House, was also introduced to the newly graded lawns of the president's house.

As seen in an English engraving of 1831, with the house reversed, a wooden fence separated the south flower garden from a kitchen garden planted west of the south portico and overseen by a newly hired second gardener, William Whelan. Outfitted with the most modern equipment the White House staff continued the laborious planting and care of the flower garden. From the prominent New York nurseries of William Prince & Sons and Bloodgood & Company, a wide variety of seeds and plants were ordered. Grass areas, boxwood edging, and meandering garden paths

PRESIDENT ANDREW JACKSON, *1836 portrait by Ralph E. W. Earl. The seventh president stands on the south portico, which had been completed in 1824. The gilded chair on the left from the 1817 Monroe suite by Frenchman Pierre-Antoine Bellangé has its original upholstery. In the garden, the victory arch built for Thomas Jefferson marks the end of Pennsylvania Avenue. The original Capitol building is in the distance. War hero Jackson owned an elegant Tennessee plantation and understood the scale of the White House interiors and its 82-acre park.*

South facade, English engraving, 1831, image reversed. The president's house had a private flower garden fenced from the public's pleasure grounds. The west colonnade is not shown.

smoothed with rollers lent a new refinement to the president's retreat. Flower beds bloomed with daisies, foxglove, altheas, and dragonhead.

For a nation steeped in horticulture and believing in the importance of plant study to the advancement of education and science, greenhouses provided wondrous additions to the American garden.[4] Since ancient times, the cultivation of exotic tropical plants in cold climates had been a hobby of agrarian societies. The Mount Claire estate in Baltimore had a greenhouse by 1768, and Dr. David Hosack's 1803 Elgin Botanic Garden in New York City featured a 62-foot conservatory. Washington himself had built a brick orangery for plants at Mount Vernon. In 1806, Philadelphia nurseryman, seedsman, and florist Bernard M'Mahon published *American Gardener's Calendar,* widely distributed in several editions. Based on *Gardener's Magazine,* founded by Scottish designer John Claudius Loudon, it provided detailed guidance for building greenhouses, hothouses, and cold frames. M'Mahon's patron, Thomas Jefferson, had made plans to build a freestanding greenhouse at Monticello but settled for an attached glazed loggia begun in 1806.[5]

Jackson initiated the tradition of the presidential glasshouse. Within the fenced area of his private flower garden, Jackson built an orangery using the shell of Benjamin Latrobe's Treasury vault, abandoned after the War of 1812. The supporting stone wall of this structure blocked Pennsylvania Avenue from view. A tall central section for fruit trees in tubs had south-facing windows overlooking the garden. The structure is thought to have been built for a treasured sago palm brought to the capital

from Mount Vernon after Washington's greenhouse burned in 1835.

In a much-criticized move, Jackson ordered a new national treasury to be constructed east of the original building that had burned in 1833. The building, when completed, would block the view of the White House from the Capitol. Jackson had rejected his advisors' suggestion that the treasury be built in the open park space beyond the north gates or in the fields south of the president's garden. His decision at once distanced the president's house symbolically from an intrusive Congress and assured that the public grounds at the White House were preserved.

Martin Van Buren continued to elaborate Jackson's garden, introducing decorative iron benches and urns. Although he was an advocate of gardening, Van Buren's progress in the garden was curtailed by a self-aggrandizing campaign waged by Pennsylvania congressman Charles Ogle. At a time of national economic depression, Ogle's ranting before Congress in 1840 expressed once again the anxiety that the president's residence was inherently antidemocratic. Ogle feared that the continued expenditures on the interior and exterior of the White House were making it a "royal establishment." From the public coffers, he complained, the president was paying for a man to do no more than weed and "pick up fallen leaves." He singled out for criticism the private flower garden, which he accurately described as a locked sanctuary for the president.[6]

The years from the end of Van Buren's presidency in 1841 until the arrival of Millard Fillmore in 1850 were a middle period in the evolution of the White House landscape into a private park. The earliest known

Beaverwyck, the Albany, New York, property of American art patron and Dutch descendant William P. Van Rensselaer. The Classical Revival villa, remodeled by architect Richard Upjohn, had a greenhouse and grounds praised by Andrew Jackson Downing. Wood engraving, c. 1840.

The renowned garden at Hyde Park, along the Hudson River in New York was laid out by André Parmentier and the estate's owner, Dr. David Hosack, an influential horticulturist and friend of early presidents. It influenced A. J. Downing and picturesque gardening in America. Wood engraving, c. 1840.

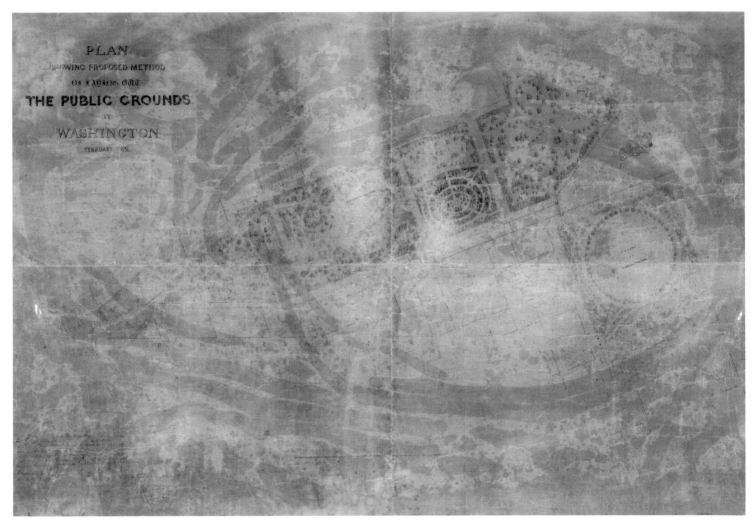

An 1867 drawing after the now-lost 1851 plan for the capital-city parks and White House garden by Andrew Jackson Downing, who died in 1852 before his vision could be realized; drawn by the federal government officer in charge of public buildings, engineer Nathaniel Michler. The president's house was to have a fenced garden on the south side, leading to a circular, public parade. Before the city park movement developed later in the century, American estates, like Armsmear (1856) in Hartford, Connecticut, had grounds open to the public.

photograph of the White House, circa 1846, shows that Maher and Ousley kept the grounds well maintained with lawn rollers and a watering machine for the hot summer months. The established vegetable garden southwest of the house continued to supply the increasing demands of the White House kitchen, and beyond the south stone wall, sheep grazed. The grounds close to the house had become an American domestic garden, not the formal park imagined by L'Enfant half a century before.

From the late 1840s into the 1850s, the federal government took steps to landscape Washington, D.C. A Congress divided by the North–South debates of the antebellum period concurred that an improved capital city would enhance Washington's degraded reputation for being unfinished and serving as an active center of slave trade. At a time when public gardens were believed to be both pleasurable and educational, influential politicians and businessmen, both Democratic and Republican, agreed in principle on the development of the Mall and its related garden areas.[7]

Influenced by the determinist landscape theories of Loudon, A. J. Downing guided America toward natural landscape design responsive to existing natural conditions and the social needs of an increasingly urban society. He embraced a deep nationalism and shared the period's conviction that gardens enhanced the physical and moral stature of society. As scholar Therese O'Malley has written, Downing extended this belief by theorizing that "since one's environment formed the person, a person's house and garden design should express who the person is."[8] With Downing was born the democratic ideal of the modern American house as a reflection of individual taste. Until the first decades of the 20th century, this ideal was reflected in the design of the gardens and, for that matter, the interiors of the White House, which changed with first families' likes and dislikes.

A. J. Downing's residential villa designs called for simplified landscapes near houses, transitioning—through views framed by trees—to untouched wilderness beyond. He stressed the importance of site and of balancing the groomed and the natural. Through plantings arranged in curves that followed natural shapes, nature's irregularity could be preserved and the imposing, artificial order of the aristocrat's garden avoided.

Downing illustrated his theories with engravings of modern American residences that exemplified his vision for a prosperous democratic society. Beaverwyck, the New York estate of William P. Van Rensselaer, was a Classical Revival house remodeled circa 1840 by a popularizer of the Italianate style, architect Richard Upjohn. The house had an adjoining conservatory set on a lawn overlooking "hill and dale." Its grounds, wrote Downing, "are . . . six or seven miles of winding gravelled paths and walks . . . their boundaries now leading over level meadows, and now winding through woody dells . . . and give the stranger or guest, an opportunity of seeing the near and distant views to the best advantage."[9]

Along the Hudson was Hyde Park, the estate of W. Langdon, Esq., developed by its previous owner, Dr. David Hosack, a founder of the New York Horticultural Society; Hosack brought John Adams, Thomas Jefferson, and the Marquis de Lafayette to the society as honorary members. Hyde Park's picturesque grounds were, as Downing wrote, "one of the finest specimens of the modern style of Landscape Gardening in America." They overlooked the Hudson for 60 miles and had been laid out to preserve "their natural state" with walks and drives down to the river. There were "costly hot houses," a Greek Revival garden temple, and "numerous pavilions and seats commanding extensive prospects."[10] Estates like Beaverwyck and Hyde Park influenced Downing's landscape designs, including his capital city plans for President Fillmore.

Millard Fillmore and his wife, Abigail, belonged to the generation of rural Americans who attended the nation's early schools; he had been a surveyor before becoming a lawyer, and she, a schoolteacher and book collector, had studied botany and created a renowned flower garden and greenhouse at their Buffalo, New York, house.

The educated Fillmores were well prepared to appreciate the implications of the capital city plan Downing presented in February 1851, with eight pages of commentary accompanying a colored drawing on linen.[11] In a March 1851 letter to the president, Downing wrote that the objective of his plan, for six interconnected landscapes exemplifying garden types, was threefold: "to form a national Park, which would be an ornament to the Capital of the United States"; "to give an example of the natural style of Landscape Gardening which may have an influence on the general taste of the Country"; and "to form a collection of all the trees that will grow in the climate of Washington, and, by having these trees plainly labeled with their popular and scientific names, to form a public museum of living trees and shrubs where every person visiting Washington would become familiar with the habits and growth of all hardy trees."

Downing called for the integration of public and private spaces of equal scope. His plan of a varied rolling terrain and treelined streets would provide a "healthful intercourse" and "relief" from L'Enfant's enduring classicism. Washington's public grounds, which included the President's Park, as the original planners of the model capital had hoped, would become a "Public School of Instruction in every thing that relates to the tasteful arrangement of parks and grounds."[12]

The White House's split personality as a residence and government office was paralleled by Downing's public–private vision for its grounds. South of the president's house, Jefferson's stone wall was to be demolished and an open lawn planted with trees to screen the house. Downing planned to connect the White House garden to a public "parade" where spectators and tourists could gather. Beyond the parade, a grove of American trees

For the Gothic villa of furniture and paper merchant Smith Ely, Staten Island, New York, Alexander Jackson Davis, a colleague of A. J. Downing, designed a conservatory on a colonnade A similar plan was followed when a glasshouse was built in 1857 on the White House west terrace. Watercolor, 1850, by Alex. J. Davis.

would surround the unfinished Washington monument. On the north side, the grounds of Lafayette Park, dedicated in 1824 to America's French hero the Marquis de Lafayette, were to be formalized to receive an equestrian statue of Andrew Jackson. Congressional Democrats commissioned this monument as a counterpoint to the statue of Jefferson placed in the north garden by James Knox Polk. Lockable gates, defined entrances and exits, and planting screens made Downing's plan the first programmatic approach to presidential security, then under threat owing to the sectarian hostilities that led to the Civil War.

To frame the east entrance and make coherent the off-axis position of the White House in relation to Pennsylvania Avenue, Downing called for a marble arch to replace Jefferson's brick-and-stone entrance. Even though the arch itself was Roman in style, Downing associated the classicism of its design with Greek culture and "the agitation of politics and a life passed chiefly in public." Straight lines and linearity were "often interesting as expressive of power."[13]

With specifications for "increasing the beauty and seclusion of the President's grounds" to follow from the architect, Downing's plan was approved in April 1851. President Fillmore instructed that improvements should begin south of the White House and on the congressional grounds. Fillmore fired the elderly Ousley and hired young Scotsman John Watt to assure changes were made efficiently. Work proceeded apace in the authorized areas. To curtail the stench from the White House sewage dumped into the south park, and to clean the fetid Tiber River that flowed through a canal along today's Constitution Avenue, terracing and planting were undertaken in the fields leading down to the Potomac marshes. In Lafayette Park, trees planted to Charles Bulfinch's plan for James Monroe were thinned, and ground was prepared to receive the Jackson statue, installed in 1853.

Downing's plans proved more complex than anticipated. After his sudden death at the age of 36 from a steamboat explosion in April 1852, city officials were unable to continue without his ongoing guidance and detailed drawings. However, the theoretical and political implications of Downing's plan influenced the design of the White House grounds for 50 years. He reaffirmed L'Enfant's triangulation of the Capitol, the monument to George Washington, and the White House, and he defined the

The second White House glasshouse, ordered by President Pierce, was a modest wood-and-glass building on the west terrace. It was completed in 1857 for President Buchanan, who had admired the 1851 Crystal Palace while living in London. A glass passage connected the president's conservatory to the first-floor hall. Stereoscope, 1860s.

No. 108.—The White House, Washington.

"Miss Lane's Conservatory," an 1858 woodcut of the new White House glasshouse. The care of greenhouses and the decoration of residential interiors were acceptable pastimes for women in the antebellum period. At the center of the presidential greenhouse was George Washington's sago palm brought from the Mount Vernon greenhouse after it burned in 1835.

president's grounds as being both private and public by surrounding the entire park with open fencing. From the White House south garden down to the public parade and parks above the Potomac, he called for the planting of American trees to provide further security and privacy for the president's house. Downing's concept of national trees echoed the early botanical nationalism of John Quincy Adams and foreshadowed the White House tradition of associating trees with the presidents who planted them.

From the administration of Franklin Pierce until the arrival of Ulysses S. Grant, the grounds of the White House within the walls remained largely unchanged. Ongoing maintenance and the replacement of Jackson's original board enclosure of the flower garden with a white picket fence continued the gentrification of the White House garden.

When construction began in 1855 on the southern extension to the 1842 Treasury east of the White House, dirt from the new foundation was contoured into the south lawn. This grading created what became known as the Jefferson mounds southeast and west of the south facade. This change was consistent with the natural landscape style then influencing the development of the White House grounds and further defined the gardens along the south facade as the president's own.[14]

The Treasury extension required the destruction of Jefferson's arch, the president's enclosed flower garden, and Andrew Jackson's orangery, which was replaced by parterres. The White House may have sacrificed its fenced garden to the Treasury, but it did not forfeit the executive privilege of a private retreat. To this end, the greenhouse tradition of the White House continued in the fall of 1857 when a new wood-and-glass conservatory was designed by Edward Clark, now thought to have participated in the design of the 1857 national Botanical Garden greenhouse.[15] By the beginning of the administration of James Buchanan, John Watt had already moved plants into the newly completed wood-and-glass structure built 12 feet from the president's house on top of the west terrace.

Safe, private, and exotic, the president's greenhouse became an extension of the White House interiors. Just as the reception rooms were decorated with printed, woven, painted, and carved flowers and foliage by this period, so were the White House glasshouses filled with living avatars of the same species, each of them redolent with meaning. The president's glasshouse served as a haven from public life and kept the costly executive horticultural collection safe from congressional scrutiny. The conservatory was appropriately modest compared to the fashionable glasshouses of

By midcentury, the attached conservatory was a fashionable room in the prosperous American home. The president's own conservatory served both as a private sanctuary and public receiving room for invited guests. The besieged Southern Plains Indians visited the president on March 27, 1863. Visible from the south glass wall were the Potomac River and the unfinished monument to George Washington. Carte de visite, photograph by Mathew B. Brady.

English aristocrats, but its rare plants rivaled those avidly collected by the wealthiest Americans.

In the 19th century, botany, the domain of intrepid explorers and scientists, was introduced not only to the male population at large, but to women and children as a safe and educational discipline. Women were encouraged to participate in the planning and planting of gardens. Through the study of plants in illustrated books, poetry, and parlor games, women developed a language of flowers to communicate sentiments otherwise inexpressible.[16] Downing singled out greenhouses as particularly suited to women because they afforded "many hours of pleasant and healthy exercise and recreation."[17]

The 27-year-old Harriet Rebecca Lane was President Buchanan's niece and hostess. She championed the cause of the American Indian and the creation of a national art gallery. She and her uncle opened the White House conservatory to guests on reception days. In March, 1858, the popular journal, *Leslie's Weekly*, published a front page report on "Miss Lane's Conservatory" that conjures up the exoticism rare specimens held for 19th century homemakers. "As you enter the conservatory itself, it seems almost like penetrating into the luxurious fragrance of some South American island, so warm and odorous is the

atmosphere, and so full of tropical bloom and verdure is every nook and corner. Here you may see a group of orange trees covered with golden fruit, and close by is a lemon tree, whose pale green balls are gradually ripening in the flood of sunshine that pours through the glazed walls. Rows upon rows of prickly cactus plants of every size and shape--aloes, with their huge, solid-looking leaves, rare and graceful forms--and camellia japonicas, covered with exquisite blossoms of white and rose-color, meet the eye at every turn."[18] This imported tropical paradise, in the middle of a mid-Atlantic city, was a privileged world reflecting America's increasing sophistication. From carefully tended pots came fresh flowers for table bouquets and recently cultivated vegetables for presidential meals, prestigious luxuries new to American homes.

Significantly, *Leslie's* illustrated its story with a woodcut of two ladies admiring the White House's horticultural collection. The greenhouse, under the influence of Miss Lane, who possessed "womanly taste in her pursuits and inclinations," became a feminine domain. In the closing decades of the 19th century, first ladies and their children, seated in the glasshouse, appeared in stereoscopic prints and official photographs. These presented to the public a domestic world sheltered and safe at a time of

Before the south garden was largely closed to the public after the Civil War, visitors were invited to hear what Thomas Jefferson called "the president's own," the Marine Band, play from Abraham Lincoln's bandstand. By the 1880s, the band's director John Philip Sousa made such pavilions ubiquitous in new city parks; photograph, 1860s.

Pierre-Jean David d'Anger's statue of Thomas Jefferson was at the center of the antebellum north garden where the public strolled and gathered to hear President Lincoln speak from the second floor; photograph, c. 1865.

war and political strife. When Abraham Lincoln received a delegation of Southern Plains Indians, photographer Mathew Brady posed the president's guests with Lincoln's secretary, John G. Nicolay, in the conservatory. The social order was preserved as the Indians sat at the feet of Nicolay and White House ladies. The harmony of the photograph was fleeting. All four Indians in the front row were dead from natural causes or slaughter 18 months later.[19]

After her arrival at the White House in 1861, Mary Todd Lincoln and the gardener John Watt developed a close friendship. Together they lavished care on the glasshouse while leaving the grounds south and north of the house a simple open park. Here the public strolled along the drives and around the statue of Jefferson. During the Civil War, the fields south of the White House wall were a stockyard and a slaughterhouse.

President Lincoln guarded what privacy he had by remaining out of public view, walking in the south garden early in the morning and visiting with his family in the greenhouse. His keen sense of the White House

as the nation's meeting place extended to his use of its grounds as a public forum. He gave speeches to an anxious public that gathered outside the Executive Mansion and invited guests to hear the Marine Band play from a tented pavilion on the south lawn. On the morning of May 10, 1865, the president appeared at the window above the north portico, a favored secular pulpit. Here he welcomed citizens who swarmed across the White House grounds to celebrate the end of the Civil War.

Industrialism replaced the agrarian methods of the 18th century with improvements in farm cultivation and greenhouse construction. Expanded spaces framed in steel instead of wood could be heated and made leak-free. When the president's greenhouse burned in 1868, the leading American greenhouse manufacturer, New York's Lord & Burnham, submitted folio-size renderings for a new sprawling glass-and-steel house in the prevailing Gothic Revival style. Their design was not carried out but guided what became an extensive collection of glasshouses over the next quarter century.[20]

FAMILY GROUP, *painted by Frederick R. Spencer in 1840, shows a prosperous villa parlor, with neutral walls and vivid colors in the curtains, carpet, and upholstery. Such interiors would have been models for Sarah Polk as she decorated the White House.*

INTERIORS

Before the Civil War the White House interiors, like its gardens, followed the model of the villa. At the close of John Quincy Adams' administration, the public interiors had taken on a decidedly French accent. With the election of Andrew Jackson in 1828, the vaguely imperial tone of American politics was swept aside by the powerful presence of "Old Hickory." Although he was a wealthy plantation owner, Jackson was neither a scholar nor a diplomat, as all of his predecessors had been. He was the first president who presented himself as a "man of the people," and he opened up the White House in a way that emphasized its public charac-

ter. In his official portrait by Ralph E. W. Earl, however, Jackson was not too much of a populist to use an ornate gilded chair as an appropriate prop. The red upholstery shown on the chair undoubtedly was based on the textiles used in the Monroes' oval drawing room. [see page 75]

President Jackson's years in the White House formed a bridge between George Washington's vision of an English country house and the new American ideal of the villa that emerged in the 1830s. Congress provided Jackson funds to complete the East Room, which Hoban had initially envisioned rather imperially as the "Great Audience Chamber." With its

Jackson East Room in the 1830s, with new black marble mantelpieces, center tables, and pier tables made by Anthony Quervelle of Philadelphia in 1829. By 1829, ready-made luxury goods were available through retail merchants in every major American city, making elegance accessible to anyone who could afford it.

Franklin Pierce's cabinet room in 1856, little changed from Andrew Jackson's era. Jackson's French marble clock is on the mantelpiece, and his classical furniture is all still in place. Only the carpet and the curtains were in the new rococo style of the 1850s.

22-foot-high ceiling framed by the massive anthemia of Hoban's plaster frieze added in the 1814 restoration, the East Room had, up to this point, served as an occasional half-finished large banqueting room. Philadelphia merchants L. Veron & Company oversaw the East Room's decoration. This was off-the-rack shopping such as any prosperous American might have done—only on a far larger scale—and it established the custom of American presidential families using commercial retailers for the White House. There was as yet no such thing as a professional decorator in America, and what we think of as interior decoration was normally handled by upholsterers or, increasingly, furnishings retailers.

Four black "Egyptian" marble mantelpieces with slender columns were installed in place of the original wooden ones found in the East Room. Such mantels became ubiquitous in well-to-do homes in the 1820s, and Jackson later used the same sort of mantelpiece at his own Hermitage plantation.[21] Massive rectangular sheets of mirror in gilt Grecian-style frames topped each fireplace and filled in the walls between the windows at either end of the 80-foot-long room, making it seem even bigger and airier. Three large plaster medallions in the classical style were applied to the ceiling, and from them hung three enormous crystal chandeliers with 18 whale-oil lamps, coordinating with sconces on the walls and oil lamps on the tables. With the advent of new kinds of artificial lighting, candles had become secondary, used only for minor task lighting (and, of course, by the poor). Such modern lighting, made possible by a booming whaling industry, was far brighter and easier to control than candles and must have increased the light level dramatically in the room. Although the White House had incorporated glass chandeliers in its state rooms earlier, they were still uncommon in private houses before the 1820s. The chandeliers Jackson used in the East Room were on a scale suitable only to public spaces, but they parallel the rise in popularity of crystal chandeliers in American parlors from that time onward.

Then, as now, taste in colors shifted in America according to what could be produced locally and, for those who could afford it, what could be imported. Textile dying was constantly affected by advances in dye technology. The naturally derived colors of the 18th century were more muted, and the introduction of chemistry to dying produced brighter colors by the end of the century. These brilliant, saturated colors were part of the neoclassical taste in Europe and were taken up in the United States, both in wallpapers and in textiles.

The East Room was ablaze with new colors. The walls were covered with lemon yellow paper bordered with what seems to have been blue velvet. The window curtains combined bright blue and yellow in an updated variation of Grecian drapery, with gilt cornices featuring large eagles. Wall-to-wall looped Brussels carpeting coordinated with the overall color scheme.[22] The mahogany furniture from 1818 was upholstered in blue satin damask.

Jackson's ability to cope with the East Room may have stemmed from seeing it not as a domestic space, but rather as akin to something new in American building, the luxury hotel. Boston's Tremont House, built in 1828–30, had similar spaces decorated with corresponding elegance. Perhaps the East Room got finished because it finally had an appropriate American model.[23]

The American villa offered a variety of spaces to meet a family's needs. The parlor was for formal social interaction, and the library was

Polk chairs, Meeks & Company, New York, 1847, and sofa, United States, 1830s. Sarah Polk used gothic-style chairs and a late-Classical-style sofa for the president's cabinet room, which filled the role of a library in the White House until Abigail Fillmore created a library in the 1850s. Lincoln cabinet room; drawing by C. K. Stellwagen, 1864.

designated for more casual, intellectual pursuits. In many villas the library became a de facto family room, while the parlor, which received the best and most costly decoration, was less often used. In a large villa such as Edward King's Newport house (see page 70 for plan), a drawing room—using a British term that was perceived as upper-class—in addition to a parlor offered an extra level of formality reserved largely for parties.

The White House offered more and larger rooms than any villa, but it had fewer family amenities on the state floor. The Red Room was the closest thing to an everyday parlor and had been used as such since Dolley Madison's day. The Blue Room served as a more formal drawing room, something not uncommon in larger villas, and the Green Room functioned largely as a reception room for the East Room, which served as a ballroom—an unheard-of feature in even the wealthiest American homes before the Civil War. As had been true since Abigail Adams, family life in the White House retreated to the upper floor, where the informal comforts of a villa were available.

Whatever eclectic style villas' exteriors might have adopted, such as the picturesque Italianate design of the King villa, their insides were more or less uniformly decorated, varying somewhat according to geography and economics. It was expected that genteel homes would have wall-to-wall carpeting, modern lighting fixtures, ample draperies with lace undercurtains, and appropriate paint or wallpapers, each in keeping with the style and function of the room. Advances in lighting technology made rooms brighter, and new chemical dyes made household furnishings more colorful. These conventions, at least, were available to the first ladies who tackled the forbidding spaces of the White House.

As was true in many other older homes in America, the White House developed layers of decoration. Although it constantly needed renewal, there was never enough money to redo the White House entirely, and decorative schemes from previous occupants always had to be worked around. The Van Burens, Harrisons, and Tylers did little to the interiors Andrew Jackson left behind in 1837, but with the Polks the White House's worn-out interiors were recast and took on a luxurious, colorful, patterned elegance.

Modern French parlor in Fountain Elms, Utica, New York, c. 1855. This museum installation in a wealthy lawyer's Italianate villa has the sort of vivid midcentury color scheme for curtains and upholstery that inspired style-conscious first ladies from Sarah Polk to Mary Lincoln.

President Polk and his wife, Sarah, brought a sober, conservative, and devoutly middle-class attitude to the White House. The couple had no experience with large-scale interiors, but at the White House they learned to be good American consumers, bent on decorating their home in the appropriate way and filling it with the right sort of things.[24] W. W. Corcoran, Washington banker and art collector, became the de facto agent for Mrs. Polk, traveling back and forth from New York to find appropriate wallpapers, carpets, and fabrics for the White House. Sarah Polk would have embraced A. J. Downing's notion that the home should be a genteel, beautiful, and cultured place, and she likely approached the daunting scale of the rooms with the outlook of a housewife furnishing a garden villa, not that of an empress outfitting a palace.

For the first time, style became associated with gender. The American villa parlor was French and feminine, while libraries were Gothic or Elizabethan, seen as masculine in character. Dining rooms were expected to be Renaissance, but bedrooms were always a mixture of styles, because they represented personal, rather than public, taste. It was hard to fit the White House into this gendered model. Although it had lots of parlors, and two dining rooms, the president's residence was not laid out like a villa. Nonetheless, the general "modern French" Rococo Revival tone of the Polk first-floor decorations was appropriate for the time because it was an elegant, feminine style.

Gas illumination changed the way homeowners saw colors. When the Polks introduced this new technology to the White House, the brighter and cleaner light went hand in hand with decorating changes that identified

Grace Hill, an 1857 villa in Brooklyn, New York, by architect A. J. Davis. The house was built for railroad pioneer and real-estate magnate Edwin Litchfield and named for his wife. Top: Villa libraries provided an informal, masculine living space akin to the one that schoolteacher Abigail Fillmore created in the upstairs oval room in the White House. Bottom: The parlor was decorated in the "modern French" style, comparable to the Red and Green rooms as they were decorated under Presidents Polk and Buchanan.

Drawing room, Grace Hill, 1857. With its suite of gilded French furniture in the modern rococo style, this grandly formal room paralleled the decor chosen by White House hostess Harriet Lane for her uncle James Buchanan's Blue Room in 1859.

for the first time the main state rooms by their vivid primary colors. More intense than their 18th-century counterparts because of the development of chemical dyes, blues, reds, and greens made up standard parlor color schemes in the midcentury American home. The White House was exceptional for having all three hues.

Although no images of the original Polk schemes survive, fragmentary descriptions align with prevailing taste for genteel houses. The best parlor next to the state dining room officially became the Red Room, with the Stuart portrait of Washington prominently displayed. It featured crimson velvet curtains and red and green plush upholstery. The Green Room followed suit with green curtains and upholstery. The new carpeting for the Green Room and the adjacent East Room had a ruby red ground with a design of eagles and stars. The Blue Room had blue-and-white damask curtains, and the Monroe Bellangé suite was reupholstered to match. This space remained softly lit because Mrs. Polk insisted that the original candle chandelier not be altered.

These three state parlors were not unlike comparable parlor–drawing room combinations that appeared in the grander villas of this period. The Italianate villa Grace Hill, designed in 1857 by Alexander Jackson Davis for the railroad pioneer Edwin C. Litchfield in Brooklyn, New York, had a grand drawing room full of gilt French rococo-style furniture, comparable to the Blue Room, and an adjacent parlor that, while luxurious, was intended for daily use. It was this sort of modern high-style villa interior that Sarah Polk would have wished to emulate as she redecorated the White House.

The White House state dining room had curtains of purple and gold figured material and purple velvet upholstery.[25] The existing blue and yellow color scheme of the East Room was changed by the installation of red silk damask curtains and upholstery. Damask was by no means universal in American homes, but it was the iconic elegant textile for the American parlor. Complementing the intensity of the colors, the woodwork throughout was painted white and the walls papered in neutral tones.

Prince of Wales bedroom, barely changed since the early 1860s, with its gold crown and bed curtains still in place. Filled with store-bought luxury goods, Mary Lincoln's state bedroom was a middle-class fantasy of royal elegance. Photograph, c. 1875.

The ceilings were given ornate cast-plaster moldings and scrollwork that made them look French.

Abigail Fillmore made the first crucial alteration to the second floor of the White House. The center oval room, a sitting room since Abigail Adams' time, was transformed into a library, a role it played until Teddy Roosevelt changed it again. A love of books and learning was seen as an essential part of the genteel life for prosperous middle-class America. In the 18th century, books had been for the rich, and private libraries were few and far between. The fact that Washington, Adams, and Jefferson all had personal libraries is proof of their status and success. Although nominally a mascu-line room, and decorated as such, the White House library, like others across America, became a family sitting room in which the values of liter-acy and education were shared. Edwin Litchfield's 1857 library at Grace Hill was just such a room, filled with culture and comfort.

President Pierce and his wife, Jane, continued to modernize the White House. Working with Thomas U. Walter, architect of the Capitol, they introduced new bathrooms and heating. Americans expected their homes to be comfortable and convenient, and advances in plumbing and central heating in American villas far outstripped progress in Europe, where large numbers of servants still took care of daily inconveniences.

For decorative changes, the Pierces continued the French mode. Outdated classical mantelpieces were replaced in the East Room and the Red, Green, and Blue rooms by white rococo-style marble mantels whose arched grates, designed for burning coal, appeared all over the country at this time. The broad, flat whitewashed ceilings of the state rooms, with their classical plasterwork, were modernized with painted decoration in bright rose, blue, green, and gold. The large-scale geometric patterns were intended to look (what else?) French. Massive gilt overmantel mirrors, ubiquitous in villa parlors, were supplied by L. R. Menger of New York for all of the main first-floor rooms as well as the upstairs library. [see page 127] New wallpapers were largely white, with patterns that picked up the dominant color of each room. Coordinating fitted carpets were made for all the rooms, with special Axminster weaves for the Blue Room and the second-floor library.

James Buchanan was the first president to receive a member of the British royal family, Edward, Prince of Wales, at the White House. The pending visit in 1860 called for updating the White House interiors. While the Pierce-era "frescoes" were simply repainted in the same patterns, Harriet Lane, the president's niece and official homemaker, introduced different textiles for the drapery and upholstery. Morocco, a fine leather from goatskin, was probably used for the upstairs library and cabinet room, and chintzes most likely in bedrooms. Brocatelles, satins, and silk reps, typical parlor fabrics, each with a distinct texture and sheen, were probably mixed in the state rooms to give variety to the monochromatic color schemes. Both the fabrics and new carpets in patterns based on the ceiling designs would have been in brilliant chemically enhanced colors. Every room became a complex visual display, very different from even the most opulent rooms of the earlier classical styles of the years from Jefferson to Jackson. One rather unkind reporter described the state rooms as being "a perfect *cholera morbus* of drapery and furniture." Even though Miss Lane's taste reflected the preferences of well-to-do housewives everywhere, not everyone admired it equally.

Harriet Lane purchased a Gothic gasolier for the library upstairs, which was in keeping with the room's masculine character. The gilded brass gasoliers in the state rooms at this period were all in the prevailing Rococo Revival style, with elaborate floral and foliate motifs. The Monroes' French ormolu objects survived the style shift and remained in the state parlors. Although technically out of fashion, they were elaborate enough and French enough to be glamorously appealing to the new midcentury decorator. [see pages 15 and 128]

Mary Lincoln tried hard to make the White House into a home, even as the country went to war. She was well trained as a homemaker, and decorating the White House was not so different from outfitting her villa in Springfield, Illinois, just exponentially grander. She traveled to A. T. Stewart's New York department store—considered the first department store in America—and to William Carryl's Philadelphia retail furnishing warerooms. She purchased stock French wallpapers, lace curtains, furniture, window cornices, and new carpets for several rooms, including the heavily used East Room. She spent a whopping $7,500 (over $171,000 in 2007 dollars) in Carryl's store alone.[26] The state parlors and East Room got hundreds of feet of gilded molding and special-order papers from stock lines of French goods "of the richest style." The East Room paper was described as "in Parisian style of heavy velvet cloth paper, of crimson, garnet and gold." The carpeting in this room was pale green with a design of roses and received a good deal of publicity. In patronizing Stewart's department store, Mary Lincoln established a tradition that continued, both in the White House and in the American home, through the middle of the next century.

Upstairs, the decoration was expectedly simpler. Lincoln's office/cabinet room was papered in dark green with gold stars and had a dark green and tan fitted carpet. This decor was suitable for the room's masculine function.[27] [see page 87] In vivid contrast, the one state room on the second floor, the best guest room, received a lavish makeover. Named the Prince of Wales Room after its most distinguished occupant, this space represented a middle-class American housewife's fantasy of regal splendor.

Decorated in a Renaissance–rococo mixture typical for bedrooms, the room had lavender wallpaper with a foliate design in gold, which created a background for purple satin bed curtains trimmed with gold fringe. These descended from a half-round gilded "crown" with the state shield over the bed and were underhung with lace draperies. The window curtains were of gold satin with purple fringe and trimmings, while the brilliant chemical colors of the floral carpet must have harmonized with the whole.

When Andrew Johnson became president following Lincoln's assassination in April 1865, the White House's interiors were badly worn and had been vandalized by souvenir hunters who had regularly stolen pieces of carpeting, upholstery, and curtain trimming. Ultimately the Johnsons' daughter, Martha Patterson, took on the role of decorator. All of the state parlors were repapered in the neo-Grec style, with Pompeian-red banding and black and gold borders. Mrs. Patterson's major triumph was the repainting of the East Room ceiling in an opulent baroque manner still meant to be French. Ultimately, Martha Patterson spent $135,000 refurbishing the interiors by 1869.[28] If the upstairs rooms continued to be decorated and lived in according to the less ambitious standards of America's villa dwellers, the state floor had begun to tip irrevocably toward a style that was richer and more elaborate than anything imagined by Washington for his dream house.

Johnson East Room with newly painted ceiling, looking northwest, 1867. Although the painted ceiling, new carpeting, and silk draperies represented the latest in modern style for Andrew Johnson's daughter, Martha Patterson, she retained the 1818 Monroe chairs made by William King of Washington, D.C.

FURNISHINGS

Just as there was a formula for decorating villa interiors, standard "ingredients" were expected to fill those interiors. Increasingly, furniture forms evolved to suit the nuances of genteel function and style for the various villa rooms. As the century progressed, the things that went into the rooms, like the rooms themselves, became increasingly French.

During Andrew Jackson's tenure, the last phase of classicism in America made its mark on the objects in the president's house, most dramatically with the finishing of the East Room in 1829. At the same time, the two new porticoes were completed, transforming the conservative English country house of 1800 into a modern Greek Revival villa, examples of which sprouted up all over the United States between 1825 and 1845. Jackson, like many prosperous Americans in the 1820s, was no longer intimidated by large, high-ceilinged rooms and went to a single source for everything, using Philadelphia furnisher Louis Veron. Although Congress in 1826 had rebelled against the wholesale importation of foreign goods

for the president's house, the French influence on American style continued to gain momentum.[29] The East Room ended up being furnished like a vast Greek Revival double parlor.

The tradition of custom-ordered furnishings began to fade early in the 19th century, even for the wealthiest Americans. Regardless of economic status, Americans started to furnish their homes with ready-made goods, and both craftsmen and upholsterers (the forerunners of the modern decorator) geared up to keep a handy supply of elegant goods for whoever walked in the door with cash to spend. Veron probably sought out several local furniture suppliers, including Anthony Gabriel Quervelle, a French-born furniture maker of high-quality goods. Quervelle supplied three circular mahogany center tables inset with the same gold-veined black Egyptian marble that was used for the mantelpieces in the room, one for each of the new crystal chandeliers. On a larger scale, this is just what many American homeowners were then doing time in the same style. [see pages 16 and 86]

The four Quervelle pier tables also represent a form that became ubiquitous in elegant Greek Revival houses throughout the United States. Intended to go between two windows beneath a pier mirror, pier tables were a standard part of the Greek Revival home, although most houses had only one or, at most, two. As a group, the Quervelle tables exemplified the iconic elements of genteel parlor furniture consolidated during the first quarter of the 19th century in America: rich, dark wood, usually mahogany, and marble tops, decorated with carving and / or gilding, depending on local fashion and budget. By the 1890s, all of these tables had been removed from the East Room. One of the center tables had found its way into the oval sitting room on the second floor. The surviving pier tables, given white marble tops in the 1850s, were being used as serving tables in the Family Dining Room on the main floor by the 1880s.

The black marble mantel clock acquired for the oval room from Veron's shop in 1833 represents the continuing desirability of French accessories in the American parlor. So influential that it was imitated for middle-class customers by Aaron Crane in Newark, New Jersey,[30] Jackson's French clock quickly became associated with him and ended up on the mantelpiece in the president's office under Jackson's portrait at least by Franklin Pierce's term in office.[31] When Frances Benjamin Johnston photographed the clock in the late 19th century, she commented that it, as well as a pair of bronzed allegorical figures of Industry and Agriculture, "stood in President Lincoln's office," and it was still there in the 1890s during McKinley's presidency.[32]

Jackson used funds from a major sale of outmoded White House furnishings to purchase a large, rather dated—but *French*—silver service in 1833, from the estate of Russian diplomat Baron de Tuyll. Most of the 130 pieces he acquired were made between 1809 and 1819 by Martin-Guillaume Biennais, a Parisian silversmith who had worked for Napoleon. With all of the fine silver being produced in American shops at this time, Jackson's purchase was strangely at odds with both American consumption patterns and his other choices for the White House.[33]

The monumental pair of ormolu torchères, apparently given to President Jackson for the White House in the 1830s by General Robert Patterson of Philadelphia, was said to have come from the New Jersey estate of Napoleon's brother Joseph Bonaparte.[34] Even grander in scale than the Monroe ormolu, these massive tripod candelabra exemplified the "modern French" style that began rising to dominance in the American parlor at about this time. Certain silver shops, especially Baltimore's Samuel Kirk and Philadelphia's Bailey & Kitchen, began to produce silver in this hybrid classical–rococo style by the late 1830s, but they were in the vanguard.[35]

Martin Van Buren, beset with criticism that he and his wife lived regally, added no significant high-style furniture to the White House, instead contenting himself with sprucing up the tired and shabby furnishings already in place. He did fit out what was by then called the Green Room with a group of entirely padded and upholstered furniture popularized by the French and known as *confortables*. Inexpensively made of packing crates and leftover fabrics, a divan, or armless sofa, with large cushions, was an early use of coiled steel springs to make upholstered furniture more comfortable. Such furniture was recommended by A. J. Downing in *The Architecture of Country Houses.*[36]

After James Polk took office, Sarah Polk was the initial president's wife to take on the role of "first homemaker" of the nation, at just the moment when it had become a woman's job to make the home comfortable, beautiful, and cultured. It is hard to imagine the Empress Eugénie or Queen Victoria shopping for furniture at a department store, but this was how Sarah Polk made the White House a villa, just as thousands of her peers did across the country.

Familiar with shopping in large eastern retail establishments, Mrs. Polk had William W. Corcoran's help in refurnishing the main floor of the White House. Mrs. Polk's choices reflected the latest upper-middle-class taste of the time. For the Red Room, she purchased a rosewood parlor suite in the modern French style from the New York firm of John & Joseph W. Meeks.[37] Known today as the Rococo Revival style, its curvaceous forms were based loosely on Louis XV forms of the mid-18th century, and it was called (somewhat randomly) "French antique," "Louis Quinze," or even "Louis Quatorze." [see page 128]

Downing wrote that modern rococo was already the most highly esteemed style in the country, being largely feminine and suitable for female-dominated spaces, such as the drawing room.[38] Walnut—typically, American black walnut—was the standard wood for less expensive furniture and for pieces used in rooms other than parlors. During the summer and when there was no company, loose slipcovers protected the glossy finish of villa furniture. Although made of the most fashionable wood, the White House suite was the simplest sort of Rococo Revival. Meeks and other firms offered much fancier (and more expensive) furniture. It represented a standard parlor suite (matching armchairs, side chairs, sofa, center table), which was still a new idea in America, where previously only sets of matching chairs had been the norm. A now-lost side chair that was in the Red Room featured an elaborately carved tall back and was known as a "fancy" or "reception" chair. These were typical additions to parlor suites, and Downing illustrated similar pieces as "Elizabethan" drawing-room chairs.[39] The grand piano seen in the room somewhat later was purchased by Abigail Fillmore and was the standard choice for well-to-do American villas.

Top left: Marble clock, France, 1833, purchased by Andrew Jackson. Despite a "buy American" attitude among politicians in the 1830s, French-made goods still attracted affluent American consumers. This trend continued throughout the century. Top right: Patent clock, Aaron Crane, Newark, New Jersey, 1830s. So popular were stylish French clocks that an American clockmaker patented a painted-wood imitation for the burgeoning American middle-class market. Center left: Silver, Martin-Guillaume Biennais, Paris, from the de Tuyll service, purchased by Andrew Jackson, 1833. Although the French Empire style was familiar to well-to-do Americans by 1833, President Jackson's purchase of a huge French silver service for the White House must have enraged American silversmiths. Bottom left: Sofa, United States, 1830s. This is likely the sofa that was in the Lincoln cabinet room from the 1830s until 1869. Here, it is still in use in the office stairway during the Harrison administration, c. 1890. Bottom right: Ormolu torchère, France, given to Andrew Jackson, c. 1830. Such objects were in the tradition of the Monroes' ormolu and were far grander than things most Americans owned. This opulence signaled the taste for modern French design that flourished among America's elite in the coming decades.

Two sets of chairs ordered by the Polks are important evidence of the villa style applied to specific settings. The notion of a villa's rooms having a masculine or feminine character, popularized by Downing, meant that different styles of furnishing were called for. Rococo suited feminine parlors and drawing rooms, and manly, intellectual styles, such as Gothic and Renaissance, were right for libraries and dining rooms. This approach differed radically from the norms of preceding periods.

Although the White House had no library until the Fillmores arrived, the president's office and cabinet room served similar masculine functions. The Meeks firm in New York supplied the White House with two dozen side chairs for President Polk's cabinet room in 1846 and 1847, in a striking but simple style merging classical and Gothic Revival. If not for the trefoil piercings in the crest and the lancet openings of the back, the chairs would be purely Grecian. They were still in use in 1864 during Lincoln's presidency; they appear in a remarkable drawing of Lincoln's office by C. K. Stellwagen. Along with furniture dating back to Jefferson's years, the large scroll-arm sofa in this drawing is a Grecian form from the 1830s and may have survived into the 1890s, when a similar sofa appeared at the foot of the office staircase. Such lingering of outmoded but useful objects was typical of every American home.

The 42 rosewood chairs ordered for Polk's State Dining Room from New York furniture maker Charles Baudouine show an early form of the Rococo Revival, blended with restrained Greek Revival details. Baudouine was among an increasingly influential group of French-born furniture makers in New York encouraging the shift toward French modes in the American villa in the 1840s.[40] [see page 129]

Genteel dining had become part of upper-class life in 18th-century America. As the nation prospered and the villa ideal matured, the dining room became the second key arena for the display of genteel behavior. With more refined dining came all the accoutrements once associated with aristocracy but now part of middle-class aspiration. The Polks' French porcelain was a mixture of modernism and restraint. By this time, the American hunger for fine French porcelain had eroded England's dominance in the American market. A. T. Stewart's New York department store supplied the White House porcelain from the French factory of Edouard Honoré. In typical American style, the dinner service was restrained, limited to gilt trimmings on ornately molded white bodies. The dessert service was much more highly decorated, with an apple-green border and lush floral decoration. Aside from the custom presidential decoration, it was like the porcelain every well-off housewife aspired to. Because dessert services were used more gently, costly hand decoration was more commonplace. Here, as with the Meeks and Baudouine chairs, a lingering classical influence reigned in the design.

Abigail Fillmore converted the oval sitting room upstairs to a "start here" villa requisite—a library—adding built-in mahogany bookcases and walnut furniture that was appropriately masculine and informal for a private sitting room, as Downing would have recommended. The costly grand piano she ordered was probably the one used in the Red Room until Mrs. Hayes replaced it with an upright.[41]

The porcelain that the Pierces introduced to the White House in 1853 had a similar sense of classical propriety pushed just slightly over the edge into rococo extravagance. The only out-of-the-ordinary objects were the centerpieces or fruit stands, which towered over the Monroes' ormolu fruit stands of 1817. As was the practice in the day, the Pierce service was purchased blank from foreign manufacturers and custom decorated, by the New York retailer Haughwout & Dailey.

For the State Dining Room the Pierces bought four walnut console tables, thought to have been made by Anthony and Henry Jenkins in Baltimore. They accompanied two now-lost sideboards and a new dining table. Customized with a carved shield with stars and stripes—to coordinate with the huge mirrors ordered from L. R. Menger in 1853—the tables show an unusual mixture of classicized rococo and what tastemakers like Downing called "Elizabethan." While no villa dining rooms would have needed so much furniture at this time, these handsome consoles were no finer than any villa dining room might have boasted. [see page 129]

For her uncle James Buchanan, Harriet Lane brought the Blue Room into the villa era with a large suite of gilt furniture that finally displaced the Bellangé seating furniture in 1859. Produced by the high bourgeois firm of Gottlieb Vollmer in Philadelphia, the set was clearly envisioned as an updating of the "gold modern French" idiom established by the Bellangé suite. The rather clumsy mixture of Louis XV and Renaissance forms might have been intended to make the furniture sturdy enough to withstand the onslaught the Blue Room inevitably suffered. The circular settee, a new form, was intended to be placed under the chandelier at the center of the room. Inspired by a French salon piece called an ottoman by Downing in 1850, it was the latest thing for such formal spaces.[42] [see pages 15 and 126]

For the Green Room, Vollmer also supplied in 1859 a much more graceful ebony-and-gilt "Louis"-style suite, still in use during the Grant administration. This furniture was more likely ebonized, or lacquered black, than made of solid ebony. [see page 127]

The idea of "accessorizing" a room came into its own for middle-class homeowners during the villa era. Accessories for the Buchanans were purchased from Bailey & Company in Philadelphia. Like Tiffany & Company, its counterpart in New York, Bailey was a retailer of fancy goods, including both American-made silver and imported luxury wares.

Top left: Dessert plate, Edouard Honoré, Paris, c. 1847, from the Polk service. The Polks' porcelain followed the trend, established by the 1830s, of upscale Americans, favoring French porcelain. By 1850, Sèvres and Limoges, porcelain-making centers in France, were virtually brand names that indicated refinement and elegance to American consumers. Top right: Fruit stand, decorated by Haughwout & Dailey, New York, 1853, from the Pierce service. The Pierce monumental centerpieces—colorful, ornate, and obviously costly—would have been the pride of any mid-Victorian housewife. Bottom left: Porcelain service, Haviland & Company, Limoges, France, decorated by E. V. Haughwout & Company, New York, and purchased by Mary Lincoln, c. 1860. Bottom right: Clock, Japy Frères, Paris, 1859, for James Buchanan's second-floor oval library. Such figural clocks, imported from France and sold in jewelry stores, were status symbols in the America villa.

A figural clock, made by Japy Frères in France, was purchased for the second-floor oval library in 1859.[43] This kind of Romantic figural clock was the high-bourgeois offspring of the aristocratic Monroe clocks from 1817. The seated figure, which would have been seen as literary because of his pose and his costume, was perfect for a library.[44]

Mary Lincoln fully understood the symbolic importance of the White House as the nation's home. To make sure it embodied American domestic ideals of comfort, beauty, and gentility, she shopped at upscale dry-goods stores in New York and Philadelphia.[45] Her Haviland porcelain, custom decorated at Haughwout's New York shop, had a very modern deep purple border, with an overscaled rope-and-bead design in gold around the rim that was still classical. Only in its distinctive color and the use of the eagle crest was Mary Lincoln's china noticeably different from what other ladies used on their tables.

Left: Gothic Revival side chair, probably Meeks & Company, New York, c. 1845. This chair is nearly identical to the chairs purchased by Sarah Polk for her husband's cabinet room in 1847. Such gothic/classical chairs were used in the more masculine spaces of American 1840s–1850s villas. Right: Abigail Fillmore's grand piano and a fancy chair with a high carved back, probably purchased by Sarah Polk in the late 1840s, are shown in the Red Room in loose summer slipcovers that would have been typical during the villa era. Photograph from the Grant administration, c. 1869.

The dominant French accent in American furniture of the antebellum era was adapted for the bedroom, where a mixture of Rococo Revival and Renaissance designs was typical. The most important acquisitions Mary Lincoln made were two rosewood bedroom suites, one in 1861 and one in 1864. Oddly enough, based on surviving pieces and photographs, neither seems to have been a true suite, because the pieces did not match and were not even by the same manufacturer.

The mix-and-match 1861 furniture from William and George Carryl of Philadelphia was for the "Prince of Wales" guest bedroom. It appears to have been assembled from available stock and was probably selected with some eye to budget. A standard bedroom set at this time would have been a bed, one or two side chairs, a wardrobe, a nightstand, and a chest of drawers with a mirror. Because of the scale of the room, Mary Lincoln added part of a parlor set to the standard array, including two armchairs and four side chairs, as well as a parlor table. The surviving chairs and the parlor table from the guest room were manufactured by John Henry Belter of New York, and these items were apparently sold wholesale to retailers in other cities. The chairs were much plainer than the table and the bed and would have been appropriate for the informality of a bedroom. The table was too fancy for an average bedroom—fancier than either the Red or Green Room parlor tables—but it was suited to the special nature of this VIP guest room. It did not match the bed, a mixture of Renaissance-style

architectonic forms with rococo and Gothic carving. The mixture of real and imitation rosewood on the bed suggests the Cincinnati firm of Mitchell & Rammelsberg, which wholesaled furniture all over the country and is known to have produced furniture using exactly this mixture of real and imitation rosewood.[46] Certainly, Mary Lincoln assumed she was getting all rosewood on the bedstead.[47] [see pages 91, 176–177]

A chest and mirror associated with Mary Lincoln's guest-room furniture coordinates with but is again different from the wardrobe, which seems to have been part of the original grouping and was always used with the rest of the set. By contrast, the distinctive dressing chest and mirror, probably purchased by Martha Patterson for her father Andrew Johnson in 1865, has lost all traces of the Rococo Revival. It is a restrained, sophisticated rosewood piece in the newly emerging Neo-Grec taste—the latest "modern French" style that swept into America's homes after the Civil War ended and the Gilded Age began.[48]

The homemakers who lived in the White House during the nation's villa years tried their best, and within their budgets, to adapt A. J. Downing's notions of the genteel American home to the outsize and old-fashioned rooms of George Washington's dream house. The families who witnessed the Gilded Age from within its venerable walls, however, cast off Downing's ideals and embraced a more ambitious vision for the home of the president.

Upper left: Walnut console, Anthony and Henry Jenkins, Baltimore, c. 1853, for the Pierce administration. Because of the vast size of the State Dining Room, Mrs. Pierce would have felt justified in ordering custom-made furniture to provide adequate serving space for large dinners. Upper right: Gilded armchair and stool ordered by Harriet Lane in 1859 from Gottlieb Vollmer & Co. of Philadelphia, for her uncle James Buchanan's Blue Room. Its awkward heaviness was probably intentional, making it better able to withstand the heavy use from large public receptions. Lower left: Dressing chest, in the latest "neo-Grec" style from France. United States, c. 1865, purchased by Martha Patterson for her father, Andrew Johnson. In the Lincoln Bedroom, Reagan administration, 1983. Lower right: Buchanan's Gottlieb Vollmer & Co. gilt furniture suite in Martha Patterson's 1865 Blue Room.

AMERICAN MANSIONS

Top left: Elm Park, in Norwalk, Connecticut, 1868, by architect Detlef Lienau for railroad and banking magnate LeGrand Lockwood. At over 20,000 square feet, it was one of the first private mansions to approach the scale of the White House. Herter Brothers and Leon Marcotte, who provided decorations for the Grant and Theodore Roosevelt White Houses, furnished the residence. Top right: Linden Towers, Menlo Park, California, 1878, by architects August Laver, Jacob Lenzen, and William Curlett. This white post–Civil War mansion was built for mining millionaire James C. Flood. Bottom left: William K. Vanderbilt house, New York City, 1882, by architect Richard Morris Hunt. The English aristocracy's houses and way of living had inspired the design of the White House; almost a century later, William K. Vanderbilt also turned to England for social authority and married off his elegant daughter, Consuelo, to the impoverished Duke of Marlborough, heir to Blenheim Palace. Bottom right: Addison G. Foster, grain merchant and Republican U.S. senator, built his house in St. Paul, Minnesota, in 1883, with Clarence H. Johnston as architect.

MANSION
1869–1889

Its study is as important, in some respects, as the study of politics; for the private home is at the foundation of the public state, subtle and unimagined influences moulding the men who mould the state.

—Harriet Spofford, *Art Decoration Applied to Furniture*, 1878

KEEPING UP WITH THE JONESES

By the time America had emerged from its bloody internecine war, Andrew Jackson Downing's romantic dream from 1850 of a villa-filled America must have seemed part of a quaint, distant past. Along with the loss of prewar innocence, the United States was no longer an agrarian commercial backwater. The industries built to fuel and supply the war, connected by a network of railroads and canals, had created a new class of people with ambition and money—money on a scale never before imagined in America. This new wealth allowed Americans to reinvent themselves and to reset the boundaries of what was domestically possible and acceptable. This was the Gilded Age, a term coined by Mark Twain in his novel of that title, published in 1873. Twain meant the term to be derogatory, in contrast to the Golden Age of Washington and the founding fathers.

The post–Civil War American with lots of money was not inclined to settle for a comfortable eight-room villa that had hitherto been considered appropriate in a democracy. Downing's own admonishment against building "great establishments" in a republic had fallen on deaf ears.[1] Inspired by the French glamour of Emperor Napoleon III and his beautiful wife, Eugénie, newly rich America embarked on an era of mansion making with the fervor of religious converts. Middle-class women continued to live out the Downing-era model of wifely domesticity, but the wives of freshly minted moguls and magnates stormed the fancy-goods stores and upholsterers in America's booming cities. Ordinary people (albeit rich ones) were building bigger, more elaborate, and more richly decorated houses than any seen before in America. For the first time in the nation's history, rooms the size of the East Room, now baldly referred to as "ballrooms," were expected in the best homes. Elegance and luxury were the keywords of the day, and Downing's warnings about confusing fashion and taste were lost in the rush.

The 1868 LeGrand Lockwood house in Connecticut was among the first American houses to approach the White House in scale, although its picturesque outline evoked Downing's modest plans. The 1878 James C. Flood house in California used the general form of the 1840s Italianate villa; but the mining magnate owner dressed it in an outrageous skin so the house in the end seemed to cry out, "My owner is really rich!" Both mansions paid lip service to the villa ideal but were conspicuous in their opulence and aristocratic pretensions.

The houses the new rich built were villas magnified to new, previously unimagined proportions. They boasted vast spaces with high ceilings for specialized purposes no villa had ever required: music rooms, reception halls, morning rooms. Moreover, the decor and furnishings took on increasing complexity and richness as these American consumers spent their boundless new wealth. The chateau-style 1882 William K. Vanderbilt house, on Fifth Avenue in New York City, with its two-story "dining hall" and breakfast and billiard rooms, was just such an inflated, elaborated villa-turned-mansion. With castles such as this, the president's residence no longer stood in splendid isolation among America's homes; the mansions of the Gilded Age were gaining fast on George Washington's dream house.

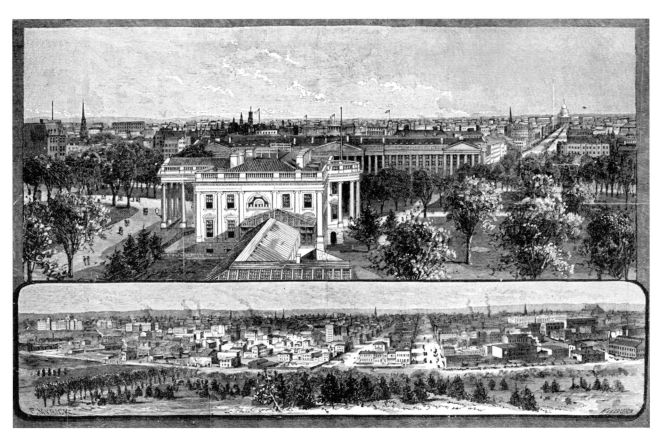

In the last quarter of the 19th century, the White House became a city mansion with private-house luxuries, including greenhouses and decorated interiors furnished with purchases from department stores. American engraving, 1884.

MANSION FURNISHERS

JULIA DENT GRANT, by photographers Levin C. Handy and Mathew B. Brady, c. 1876.

GENERAL ULYSSES S. GRANT, on June 11 or 12, 1864, the time of the great cavalry battle at Trevilian Station, at his headquarters in Cold Harbor, Virginia.

Mrs. Ulysses S. Grant had lived in a log cabin and in a comfortable villa, but when she moved into the White House in 1869 she began to transform it from an overscaled villa to a showy mansion worthy of the Gilded Age. Mrs. Grant established the tradition of sending floral arrangements from the White House conservatory to diplomats and created a special room for orchids, a favorite flower of post–Civil War society.

The Civil War hero became the 18th president of the United States. He had a patriotic affection for the White House and oversaw extensive landscape improvements that defined the president's garden within the White House's 82-acre park.

1869–77

RUTHERFORD B. HAYES AND LUCY WEBB HAYES, c. 1870–80.

CHESTER ALAN ARTHUR, c. 1880.

President Hayes, the 19th president, was a wealthy lawyer from Ohio and a Civil War veteran. He and his wife were abolitionists and advocated the rights of women and blacks. By creating the Ellipse and introducing the tradition of the annual Easter egg hunt, for which the public was permitted into the president's garden, Hayes further defined the White House's park as both private and public. He began the tradition of planting commemorative presidential trees on the south lawn, and Mrs. Hayes created the first White House rose garden, inside a greenhouse along the west colonnade.

Chester Arthur was a lawyer and the collector of the port of New York before becoming the 21st president. His conservative Republican colleagues were chagrined when Arthur brought civil service reform to the federal government.

A fashion-conscious New Yorker, the widowed president introduced to the White House its first avant-garde interiors. Beginning in 1882, the Aesthetic Movement decorator Louis Comfort Tiffany transformed the state rooms into spaces that rivaled the finest "artistic" interiors in the mansions of America's industrial rich.

1877–81

1881–85

AN AMERICAN MANSION

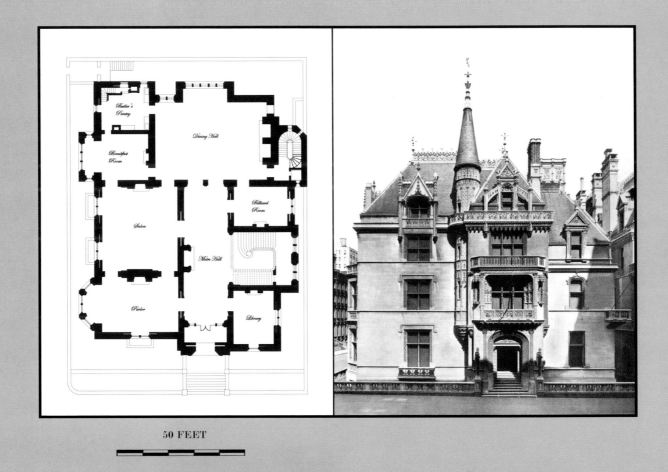

50 FEET

WILLIAM K. VANDERBILT HOUSE, 1882

First-floor plan and entrance, William K. Vanderbilt house, New York, 1882, Richard Morris Hunt, architect. The 31,000 square foot, four story, Fifth Avenue chateau of the New York Central Railroad heir had rooms that were just as large as those in the White House, but they were more opulently furnished and decorated.

THE PRESIDENT'S HOUSE AS AN EXECUTIVE MANSION

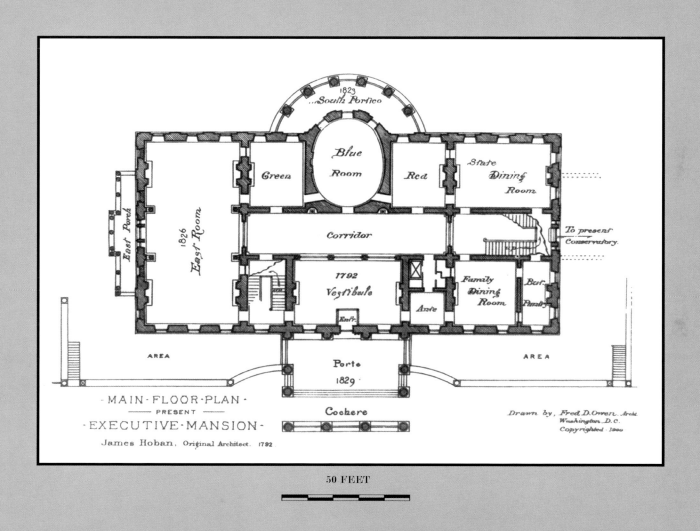

WHITE HOUSE, 1880s

First-floor plan drawn by Frederick D. Owen in 1900, as the White House appeared in the 1880s; dates of architectural additions are noted in the plan. Postwar first ladies elaborated and enriched the high-ceilinged spaces of the White House until it had the colorful, layered opulence of a true Gilded Age mansion. Ulysses S. Grant kept up with American millionaires by creating a billiard room on the first floor.

The White House south facade, 1884, with Chester A. Arthur greeting guests from the portico. The residence, in a private garden, was now too small for the needs of an increasingly powerful presidency.

HOUSE

The mansions of post–Civil War America reflected a society stratified by wealth and ostentation. America had matured with the war, and charming villas and Gothic cottages were unsuited to the bigger-than-life personalities and fortunes of the new industrialism.

The real-life hero Ulysses S. Grant was such a figure, and, like his military predecessors George Washington and Andrew Jackson, he transformed what it meant to live like a president. The Georgian-style White House that had been decorated and landscaped as a genteel American villa by antebellum administrations became the mansion of the nation's leader. Taciturn, dowdy Ulysses S. Grant—who, frankly, could not have cared less for the high life—became forever associated with the new lavish style of the Gilded Age and its shadow, the political corruption that accompanied America's rise to imperial pretensions.

A building boom among the very rich followed the war. In 1878 Comstock mine millionaire James C. Flood built his mansion Linden Towers outside San Francisco. Three stories of white-painted towers, gables, and cupolas sat in a landscaped park. Like many Americans with lavish amounts of time and money, Flood ordered up rooms solely dedicated to pleasurable pastimes, including smoking and music. Changes to the White House were almost exclusively decorative, but Grant did expand the first-floor conservatory and moved billiards from the basement to a newly built room in a prime public location between the stair hall of the main floor and the 1857 Buchanan greenhouse on the west terrace, just off the State Dining Room. Incorporating large windows to the north and south, it was entered through French doors in the stair hall and required blocking up the windows at the western end of the dining room. [see page 129]

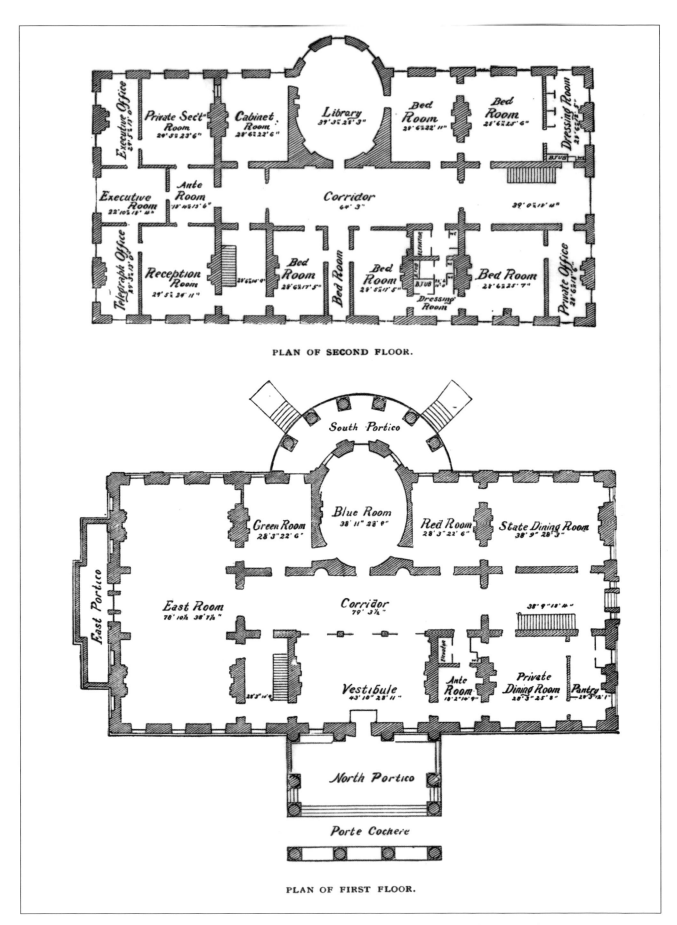

PLAN OF SECOND FLOOR.

PLAN OF FIRST FLOOR.

First- and second-floor plans, c. 1890, showing the dimensions of the major White House rooms as they were until 1903.

Roses, one of the rare flowers cultivated in American colonial gardens, were carved over the north entrance to greet the first White House guests in 1800. Colored glass panels in the north entrance doors, created during Louis Comfort Tiffany's executive mansion redecoration for Chester Arthur, prepared visitors for the decorator's extravagant entrance hall screen. Tiffany and painter John La Farge pioneered the American art glass movement and the fashion for panels in residential hallways, private chapels, and dining rooms; c. 1889.

The new east entrance by architect Alfred B. Mullett, 1868, for President Andrew Johnson. It had the first fountain of the mansion-era White House garden.

In 1881, Chester A. Arthur, who became president following the assassination of James Garfield, revisited the idea of rebuilding the White House to accommodate the growing public needs of the presidency. In contrast with Andrew Johnson's proposal, Arthur sought to maintain the White House in its Washington location. Unable to garner the requisite support of the Army Corps of Engineers, which was responsible for public buildings, Arthur proposed a large wing to the south of the existing house to serve exclusively as private living quarters for the president and his family. Although a bill appropriating $300,000 for the wing was passed by the Senate, the House of Representatives rejected the legislation. Arthur's alterations of the house were limited to interior decoration and the installation of a hydraulic elevator.

In 1884 the journalist E. V. Smalley noted in *Century*, "The Executive Mansion, in these modern days of wealth, luxury, and display, appears a small and modest dwelling for the chief magistrate of fifty millions of people."[2] Smalley specifically pointed out the house's relatively few bedrooms (seven) and the constraints imposed by having both bedrooms and the presidential offices on the second floor. "If a President has a

moderately numerous household," Smalley wrote, "as General Grant, Mr. Hayes, and Mr. Garfield had, he can hardly spare guests more than the big state bedroom. A President may wish to invite an ambassador and his family, or a party of distinguished travelers from abroad, to spend a few days at the White House, but he cannot do so without finding lodgings elsewhere for members of his own household. It has been said over and over again, in the press, that Congress should either provide offices for the President, or should build for him a new dwelling, and devote the Mansion exclusively to business purposes; but Congress is in no hurry to do either."[3]

Smiley's critique reflected the sensibility of a nation on the brink of becoming a world power. In a country where a self-appointed aristocracy composed of buccaneer capitalists now built houses with luxuries rivaling those of European palaces, the White House was no long an exemplar of commodious and grand accommodation. Practically and symbolically, the 18th-century model of the country house, even dressed up as a mansion, no longer functioned as residence and workplace. It would take a new century and a president with a grandiose vision to bring the White House into the imperial era.

The White House gardeners kept up with the fashion to collect exotic specimens, planting aloes in the north flower parterre and arranging palms from the conservatory along the north portico. Bright displays of recently cultivated annuals replaced long-established perennials in American gardens. Photograph, 1880s.

GARDEN

Concerned for the safety of the president and inspired by travels to Europe, government officials initiated plans in 1864 to replace the White House with a new residence in a suburban park, designed to rival estates in France, Germany, and Italy. What had been palatial for George Washington, who had also wanted an American palace to revival Europe's finest, was now outmoded and run down. The Army Corps of Engineers considered building a "princely mansion" for the president on 200 acres in what is today Rock Creek Park.[4] Proposals were presented, but the government's will for change dissipated after the failed impeachment of Andrew Johnson and the arrival of General Ulysses S. Grant in 1869. The modest 82-acre lot of the White House would have to suffice for a residence that now competed with new American mansions sited on

hundreds of acres. If the president and his family wanted a rural experience, they could leave their city house and join other urban dwellers on a drive to the Maryland countryside.

The late 19th-century residential garden reflected a society emboldened by postwar prosperity. Across America, fountains, expressing a new formalism, returned to gardens. In the gardenesque style, flower beds in intricate mosaic patterns and specimen plants were ostentatiously displayed on open lawns to highlight the architecture of newly built mansions. Homeowners of midcentury villas pruned their wooded, picturesque gardens to open up vistas and decorated new flower gardens with fashionable iron furniture. When mining millionaire James C. Flood built his 1878 estate Linden Towers outside San Francisco, he hired

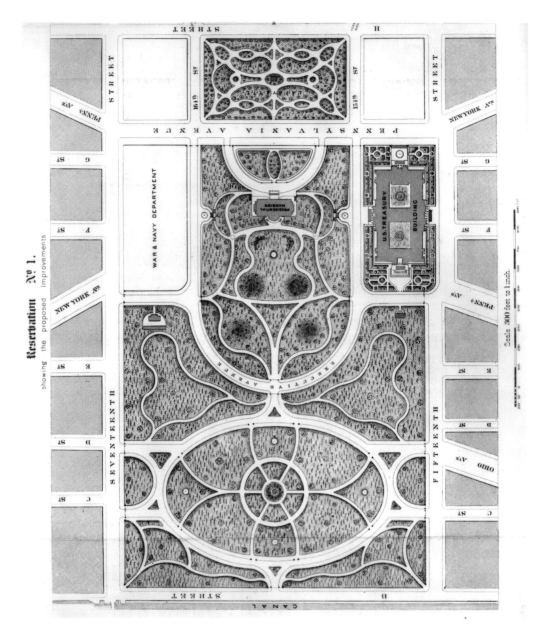

This 1868 plan was proposed by government architect Alfred B. Mullett. Like others drawn up after the Civil War,
it returned to A. J. Downing's 1851 conception of the president's south park as both private garden and public parade.

German émigré Rudolph Ulrich to landscape its grounds. The finished garden close to the house included a broad, arching drive, a multitiered fountain, specimen plants, and floral carpet beds. These became features of the White House garden under Presidents Grant and Hayes.

Grant embraced the history of the White House and the capital city. In 1872 he modernized the city's sanitation systems and filled the stinking Tiber Canal at the edge of the president's park. At the White House itself, the president transformed the neglected grounds. Planning initiated in the 1850s and continued by architect Alfred Bult Mullett under Andrew Johnson guided the improvements. In his 1868 text to a schematic plan, Mullett supported a return, in form and spirit, to the plan of the "lamented Downing." A desire for the public good guided his

recommendation that land south of the White House garden and west of the Capitol be improved with pathways to form "an ample park for the recreation and amusement of [Washington's] citizens, and one that from its location is available to the poorest as well as the richest."[5]

Mullett's plan was one among several similar ones of the 1870s used by the Grant administration to landscape the garden after it was extended southward. By the 1880s, the White House garden and park were a synthesis of these plans. A drawing first stamped 1878, and used through 1898 to note improvements, shows the White House grounds as they appeared in the last quarter of the 19th century. In this period, the president's house came to have a garden of its own, defined by perimeter fences. While this garden had expansive views traditionally associated with

Government proposal for the president's park and garden, 1877, one of several plans that were Victorian gardenesque elaborations of A. J. Downing's 1851 vision for the nation's capital city.

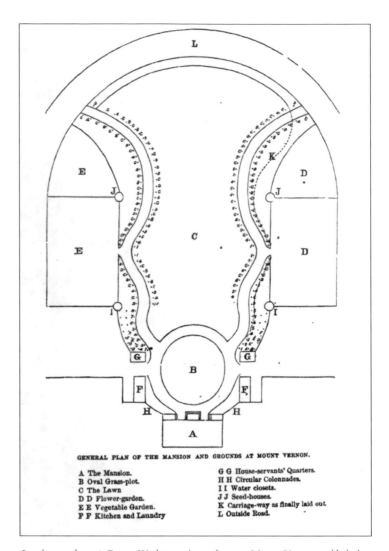

GENERAL PLAN OF THE MANSION AND GROUNDS AT MOUNT VERNON.

A The Mansion.
B Oval Grass-plot.
C The Lawn
D D Flower-garden.
E E Vegetable Garden.
F F Kitchen and Laundry

G G House-servants' Quarters.
H H Circular Colonnades.
I I Water closets.
J J Seed-houses.
K Carriage-way as finally laid out.
L Outside Road.

Landscape plan of George Washington's residence at Mount Vernon, published in 1859. The White House south carriage path, laid out in the Grant administration, resembled the entrance drive to this revered colonial plantation.

aristocratic parks, the extended north and south grounds, though still legally part of the 82-acre president's park, were finally set aside for public enjoyment. Decades of democracy, embodying the idea that every American family should have a home and garden of its own, had finally resolved that the White House, as a house, not a palace, could do with a remarkably modest 18-acre garden.

Grant hired his Civil War colleague General Orville E. Babcock to oversee landscape improvements. The general was head of the Office in Charge of the Public Buildings and Grounds at the Army Corps of Engineers, created by Andrew Johnson in 1867 to oversee White House building projects. Babcock demolished the remains of Jefferson's crumbling stone wall. South of where it had been, as suggested by Mullett, Babcock built a semicircular drive that joined the east avenue along the Treasury and the west avenue fronting the State, War, and Navy Building, begun in 1871 to Mullett's design. An iron fence, in the Greek Revival

style of the north fence, outlined the new road along the south boundary of the enlarged president's garden. This fence unified the public appearance of the White House and left the park open to public view. A curving drive immediately in front of the south portico joined the semicircular road and created an eye-shaped lawn as originally envisioned by Downing. A carriageway in the form of a guitar crossed the lawn. Echoing the design of the entry drive at America's first national house monument, Mount Vernon, this pathway through the south lawn paid homage to George Washington, America's first general and president.[6]

Grant expanded on the conspicuous formalism introduced to the White House grounds by Mullett with his 1868 east entrance pool and double stairway. The statue of Jefferson, a symbol of Enlightenment restraint, was moved from the north lawn to the Capitol Building. In its place, a circular basin was built and surrounded by a pinwheel carpet bed of brightly colored annuals tightly planted. This 1873 parterre was designed by John Stewart, a

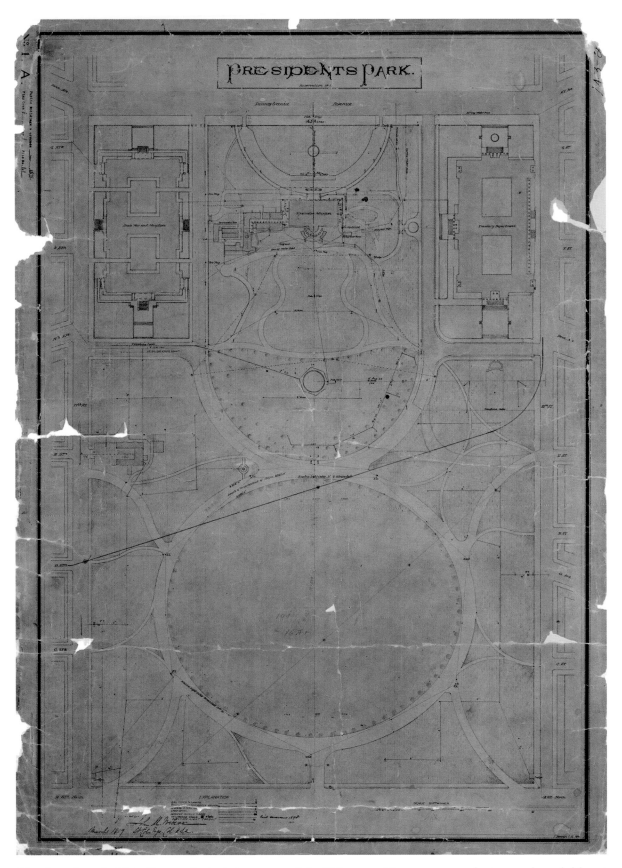

This plan reflects the White House garden in the last quarter of the 19th century. The now ornamented private garden and elaborate conservatory filled with prized specimens reflected the tastes of America's wealthy bourgeoisie. The document is dated 1878, with changes dated 1889, and was signed by John Stewart, the government surveyor who signed the plan for President Grant's elaborate 1873 north facade parterre.

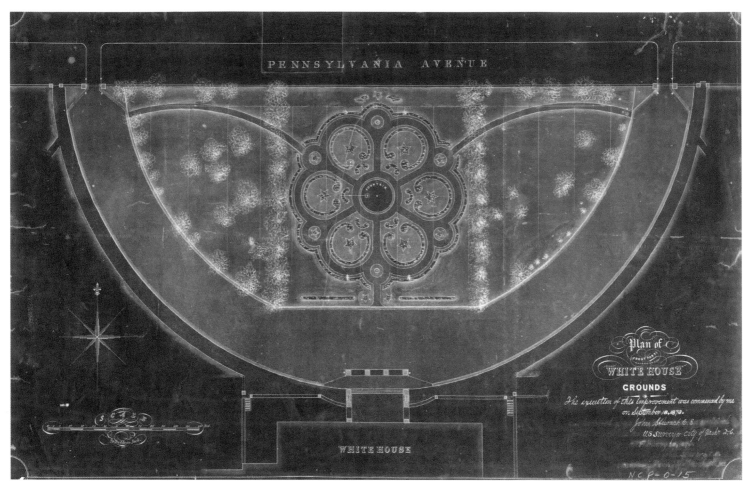

Plan of the north lawn flower parterre, planted in 1873 for Ulysses S. Grant, signed John Stewart for the Army Corps of Engineers, which oversaw the development of the president's grounds. The pinwheel design with patriotic stars celebrated the general—president who had preserved the union.

surveyor with the Army Corps of Engineers. A third pool was built on the south lawn and animated with sprays from an imported French fountain jet. Between the south facade and an openwork metal fence along the arching drive were flower beds. Grant restored parterres southeast of the house and returned life to the garden by hosting outdoor receptions.

Accompanied by his family on the south portico, whose balustrade overflowed with flowering vines, President Grant surveyed the realm as if it were his own. As the public symbol of America's hard-won peace, he had earned the new luxury of the renovated mansion. The president from his porch rocker and the public from their place along the new fence could mutually admire what a united nation had preserved. No longer the problematic palace of an emerging democracy, the White House, with its fountains and flower pinwheels, was a dream house now within reach of any prosperous American.

The State, War, and Navy Building changed the White House garden forever. When its construction required the destruction of the president's vegetable garden, the colonial tradition of combined pleasure and service gardens ended. The looming Second Empire edifice and the neoclassic

Treasury left the White House a mansion within the semipublic confines of a fenced park, visible from all sides and from the floors of the east and west government buildings. The south garden was no longer a private sanctuary but a greensward within a city that grew to a half million in the 19th century. As the century closed, the White House became surrounded by roads and fences that guided travel to and from the president's residence. Its grounds offered little privacy, but the interior, artificial paradise of the presidential greenhouse remained a privileged retreat.

With the changes carried out by Babcock and his government office, a professionally conceived presidential garden moved closer to realization. Rutherford B. Hayes, a former state congressman and governor of Ohio, was married to Lucy Webb Hayes, an abolitionist, devout Methodist, and teetotaler. Together they continued the Grant administration's improvements, assisted by a new gardener they hired from Cincinnati, Henry Pfister. With a staff of nine men and one woman, he simplified the White House parterres and moved the French spray to the north pool. At the center of the south pool, Pfister placed an Italianate, tiered fountain that had been installed on the south lawn in Andrew Jackson's administration.

Linden Towers, in Menlo Park, California, begun in 1878 for mining millionaire James C. Flood. The 140-acre garden, visited by President Grant in 1879, had bedded parterres along a curving drive. Its tiered iron fountain was on axis with the mansion, whose ornate, carved wood exterior was painted white to suggest stone. Photograph, c. 1890.

Though its historic architecture remained unchanged, Gilded Age formality came to the executive mansion in 1871 when General Babcock built a 75-foot-diameter pool on the south lawn for President Grant. At its center was a terra-cotta fountain purchased by Andrew Johnson. A similar pool was built on the north lawn in 1873, on axis with the north portico. Photograph, c. 1875.

The Philadelphia Centennial Exposition of 1876 fostered a renewed enthusiasm for America's past after the bitter divide of the Civil War. The president and his friends participated in the Colonial Revival movement, decorating their houses with furnishings and art evoking the lost world of the first colonists. They collected romantic landscapes of a pristine American West, untouched by Indian massacres and railroads, painted by German artist Albert Bierstadt. In March 1878, the president invited the revered painter to the White House. During this visit, Bierstadt captured the view south from the Red Room, where Hayes, in March 1877, became the first president to take the oath of office in the White House. Bierstadt now saw George Washington's view to the Potomac across the recently created "Jefferson" mounds.

Hayes extended his patriotism to the President's Park by initiating the tradition of planting trees in the White House grounds, to commemorate American presidents. From colonial times, trees had been an invaluable commodity, and their abundance across the continent represented America's vast economic potential. By joining the political with the natural in the presidential grove of elms, oaks, and beech, Hayes created an enduring symbol of democracy's emergence from the American wilderness.

Security, as well personal taste, continued to influence the design of the White House garden. Before entering office, Hayes had received assassination threats. He ended the tradition of concerts on the south lawn and moved Lincoln's bandstand, still at the White House when he arrived in 1877, to the grounds of the Corcoran Museum of American Art (now the Renwick Gallery), designed by James Renwick Jr. in 1871. Public access to the president's garden within the White House fence was restricted, but at the instigation of the president, the tradition of the annual Easter egg roll on the south lawn was introduced in 1879.

With the rapid urbanization of America after the Civil War, the public parks movement expanded. Open areas in small and large cities were preserved and landscaped as amenities for all classes. Reflecting the national trend, begun in 1860 with Central Park in New York City, President Hayes expanded the public enjoyment of of the greater park south of the White House. Downing's conception of a parade inspired the creation of a 17-acre oval ringed by a 50-foot-wide roadway shaded with American elms. To either side, picturesque "woodlands," as imagined by Downing, were planted. The park was named the "central ellipse" before becoming the Ellipse. The completed area provided a verdant transition from the White House to the recently completed Washington Monument.

Mrs. Hayes and Henry Pfister created the first White House rose garden inside a one-story greenhouse built in 1878 on the site of today's west-wing garden. Since 1800, carved stone roses above the north entrance door had welcomed visitors to the White House. Roses, a prized feature of colonial gardens, were among the few flowers planted at Mount Vernon.[7]

VIEW FROM THE WHITE HOUSE RED ROOM TO SOUTH PORTICO AND GARDEN, *painted by German landscape artist Albert Bierstadt while visiting Rutherford B. Hayes in 1878. The open park of trees had a naturalized slope formed with dirt excavated from the site of the 1855 Treasury Building extension.*

Private conservatories were elegantly finished rooms attached to houses, while greenhouses were independent service buildings. At Elm Park, the 1868 LeGrand Lockwood mansion in Norwalk, Connecticut, the conservatory, with a half dome etched with fleurs-de-lis, was off the first-floor library. In the mansion's 28-acre garden on Long Island Sound a grapery and potting house, a forcing house and hot house were each equal in scale to the simply finished glasshouses that made up the president's conservatory. Photograph, 1961.

The more than 125-foot White House conservatory was merely serviceable compared to this greenhouse at Lyndhurst, the Hudson River estate of railroad tycoon Jay Gould. The 376-foot steel-and-glass structure, in a park ornamented with patterned floral beds, was built in 1880 by Lord & Burnham. The Tarrytown, New York, firm had drawn up gothic-style plans to rebuild the president's greenhouse after it burned in 1867. Because of budget concerns, a more modest building, similar in overall design, was built. c. 1890.

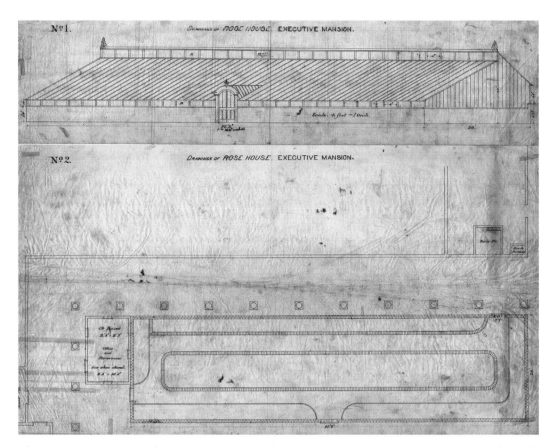

Plan of the rose house designed for First Lady Lucy Webb Hayes in 1880. This simple structure, 26 feet deep and 97 feet long, was built of brick, glass, and pine, and housed the first rose garden at the White House.

The south facade parterre and conservatory complex, in the 1880s, with Lucy Hayes's rose house parallel to the first-floor greenhouse on the west terrace. The profusion of available horticultural specimens in the 19th century led to ostentatious displays in greenhouses and intricate flower beds.

Entrance from the south park to the president's conservatory, late 1880s. Romantic rockery grottos, mossy and damp year-round, were made possible by new technologies that kept greenhouses insulated in the winter.

White House conservatory, 1880s. First ladies cultivated fresh flowers for bouquets that were status symbols in American mansions.

The collecting and planting of roses in American gardens expanded after Frenchman Jean-Baptiste Guillot introduced the first long-blooming hybrid tea rose in 1869.

The opening of the Crystal Palace at the 1851 Great Exhibition in London was a watershed moment in the history of the glasshouse. Industrial design had finally caught up with, if not exceeded, the invention of nature. In London the sprawling palace dazzled American visitors with what President Hayes called its "colossal" scale.[8] Like other Americans, firearms pioneer Samuel Colt returned from London with notes he later used to design the Moorish style conservatory he added to his 1857 Connecticut villa, Armsmear. At the White House itself, President and Mrs. Hayes improved the Grant greenhouses. Collectively known as "the conservatory," they were impressive in scale but modest in design, with shelves and narrow alleys. Lucy and Rutherford Hayes domesticated the interiors by widening walkways and adding decorative iron benches, plant stands, and basins. The greenhouse became a world of private garden rooms.

By the 1880s, the presidential greenhouses were a spectacle. From the south drive, an arched classical doorway opened to a grotto vestibule with a fountain in a rockery base.[9] On the second floor, orchids, lilies, hydrangeas, and chrysanthemums planted under towering tree ferns and palms were safe from the bitter winter cold. Strolling through the blossom-scented interiors, the president and his guests admired the view of the Potomac. The natural beauty of the unspoiled panorama contrasted with the artificiality of the hothouse interiors.

As the century came to a close, the 82-acre President's Park was clearly defined. The president no longer lived like a landed aristocrat but as a rich, bourgeois businessman. His city mansion had a garden, ornamented with fountains and beds of bright annuals. To the north and south were public parks. Like city dwellers throughout America who stared through the gates of private houses along new boulevards, Washingtonians admired the privileged life of the White House residents through black iron fences and gates that defined the presidential estate.

Greenhouse collections reflected the globalization of American and European economic power in the 19th century. Intrepid plant collectors working in the jungles and deserts of colonized countries exported rare cycads, fan palms, orchids, bromeliads, fruits, and vegetables to western conservatories, including the president's own. Photograph, c. 1875.

Grant East Room. Left: Looking northwest, c. 1871, before alterations. During her husband's first term, when her budget was smaller, the socially ambitious Julia Grant had to make do with the colorful villa-style interiors left by her predecessor, Martha Patterson. Right: As seen after the 1873 renovations, c. 1874. With Julia Grant's elaborate new gold-and-white decoration, the room was now more splendid than it had ever been, equal to the ballrooms of the nation's grandest mansions.

INTERIORS

When General Ulysses and Mrs. Grant moved into the White House in 1869, America was poised on the leading edge of the Gilded Age, and A. J. Downing's vision of a nation of genteel, cultured villa dwellers was being abandoned in a stampede for wealth, splendor, and self-reinvention. The previous era's futile project of making the White House, with its huge rooms and public functions, fit into the villa-as-dream-house model was now unnecessary.

William K. Vanderbilt's chateau-style house, built on New York's Fifth Avenue in 1882, offered rooms that were just as large as those in the White House, and far more opulent. The Vanderbilt residence was, however, still laid out quite like a villa, with a variety of rooms on the main floor to cater to the family's needs. A library and billiard room offered masculine privacy and comfort, while a parlor and a drawing room—here called a *salon*, then an even more upper-class term—provided the ladies of the house with formal and less formal social spaces. Although the original main-floor rooms at the White House still didn't offer the kind of functional variety found in this mansion, they at least had—thanks to James Hoban—a high-ceilinged grandeur that made them worthy canvases for first ladies' decorative ambitions.

The decoration of Alexander T. Stewart's New York City house of is a good example of an early Gilded Age mansion interior. Stewart invented the concept of the luxury department store (Mary Lincoln had shopped at his establishment and had been entertained by the Stewarts) and was for a time in General Grant's cabinet. His city mansion's drawing room was perhaps the first room in America that made the Johnson East Room of 1869 look timid. Next to the opulence of Stewart's master bedroom, Mary Lincoln's Prince of Wales bedroom looked homey.[10] With this sort of house as its model, the White House, for the first time, fit in.

General Grant was not much interested in aesthetics and let his wife handle issues of shopping and decoration. His one major influence on the White House decoration was the addition of a billiard room to the state floor in 1869. Billiard rooms were a standard appurtenance in mansions of the day, even as the public playing of billiards in pool halls was decried as a symbol of moral decay. Grant, not wanting the billiard room inconveniently in the basement, placed his new room to the west of the State Dining Room. Though no photographs or drawings exist, construction notes suggest that the billiard room, with exposed wood framing, was paneled in varnished woods. The billiard room also

Drawing room in Alexander T. Stewart's house, New York, with a mansion interior, 1864–69. The opulent architecture, rich woods, and shimmering textiles made this cosmopolitan drawing room of a department-store founder outshine the state rooms of the White House.

accommodated the gendered etiquette of Victorian dinners, after which men retired to a masculine place to smoke and talk politics, while the ladies retired to the genteel, feminine parlor to gossip. The addition of such a personal room to the state floor suggests how much less intimidating the house was at the dawn of the Gilded Age than it had been at the start of the century.[11]

While leaving the Red and Green rooms essentially as inherited from Johnson, Julia Grant gussied up the Blue Room with blue satin curtains and upholstery, floral carpeting, and an enormous crystal gasolier.[12] Despite the increasing elaboration of the decorations, the dominant theme of the mansion years was still French, although the curves and naturalistic motifs of the rococo shifted toward to a new, more Renaissance-inspired angularity.

The old double-flight grand staircase was replaced for Mrs. Grant with a massive stairway having a single main flight. Upstairs, Mrs. Grant turned the newly gained floor area of the west hall into a sitting room for the first time, adding family space for daily use. The even larger East Hall had long been used as a lobby for the presidential offices, which took up nearly one-third of the second floor. Although she couldn't alter the office situation, Mrs. Grant redecorated the cabinet room in an appropriately masculine

style. But her most ambitious mansion upgrade came in her husband's second term, with the dramatic redecoration of the East Room in 1873–74.

Elaborating on James Hoban's 1817 gold-and-white anthemion frieze, the vast East Room was subdivided into three large sections with a pair of beams across the ceiling, supported by four enormous freestanding Corinthian columns. Complex new mantelpieces and overmantels, which were massive and architectonic to fill the cavernous space, complemented the architecture. Three new gasoliers, even bigger and fancier than Jackson's massive fixtures, filled the room with glittering light. The Monroe-era furniture was finally carted away, replaced by overstuffed furniture with upholstery in two contrasting colors of shimmering silk velvet that coordinated with the draperies. The East Room now looked less like a hotel parlor and more like a ballroom, an increasingly popular feature of urban mansions in America. It was as spectacular as any space in any American house of its day and made a fitting background for the marriage of the Grants' daughter, Nellie, to an aristocratic Englishman in May 1874.

Like many American homemakers, Julia Grant rarely got to do complete makeovers, and neither Lucy Hayes nor Lucretia Garfield had much chance to interpret the new mansion mode while at the White House. The Green

Grant Blue Room, southeast view, 1870–75. Julia Grant updated the Blue Room with new textiles and a splendid gasolier.
Because they were still fancy enough to be impressive, and for reasons of economy, Mrs. Grant left the Buchanan-era furniture
by Vollmer and the ornaments from earlier presidents in place.

Room remained little changed during the Grant era and beyond and was stylistically still more haut-bourgeois villa than mansion. The Red Room, which Mrs. Grant saw as the family's "best parlor," similarly kept its prewar identity. Even the addition of new furniture from New York's fashionable Herter Brothers in 1875 did not change the overall scheme.

The widowed Chester Arthur was one of the few men to have a significant impact on the White House decor in this period. His years in the White House coincided with a watershed moment in American interiors. By 1870, Downing's villa model for interior decoration, even upgraded to mansion pretensions, was no longer adequate for America's elite. The emergence of professional interior decorators from the furnishing trades and the concept of the artistic interior went hand-in-

hand. Newly rich (and newly richer) Americans, tired of standard furniture forms and formulaic interior treatments in place since the late 1830s, looked for ways to differentiate themselves from the mass of prosperous middle-class homeowners.

Continuing to emulate European aristocratic standards of luxury, elite Americans embraced the British concept of the artistic interior, promoted by such aesthetic theorists as Charles Lock Eastlake (1836–1906) and William Morris (1834–1896). Ironically, both men decried aristocratic pretensions and targeted the middle class much as Downing had, but their passion for the handmade and the artistic took hold among the very rich. Opulent interiors filled with costly objects became the ideal path to social differentiation in the later Gilded Age. Starting in the

Grant Green Room, looking northeast, 1875–80. Mrs. Grant left the room mostly alone, choosing to spend her redecorating budget elsewhere. The Buchanan 1859 ebony suite by Gottlieb Vollmer & Company of Philadelphia is still in place, as is the wall treatment done for President Johnson.

Grant Green Room, looking northwest, 1875–80. Although somewhat out of date, the elegant villa interiors left by the Johnson administration would have been the most elaborate rooms the Grant family had ever known.

1870s, in the hands of the new decorator–furnishers such as Herter Brothers, rooms became more than just an assemblage of coordinated objects in more or less the same style; they became unique settings in which to showcase art. These self-consciously exotic and expensive interiors set their owners apart from, and above, everyone else. This kind of elitism had never existed before in America and resulted directly from post–Civil War wealth.

The hugely expensive two-volume book *Artistic Houses*, published in New York in 1883 and 1884, became the Gilded Age's response to Downing's *The Architecture of Country Houses.* The houses shown in the 203 lush monochrome photographs represented America's elite in all its splendor. As a New Yorker, Arthur had seen these modern city mansions and brought to the White House one of the first professional decorators in the country, New York–based Louis Comfort Tiffany. Tiffany's own interpretation of the artistic interior was evident in his first major domestic commission, the 1879 interiors of the Fifth Avenue mansion of George and Juliet Kemp, which were later published in *Artistic Houses.*[13] [see page132] The Kemp rooms were not just opulent—they were new, unlike any interiors seen before in America, and emphatically not French. Their magical color and mixture of Asian and Middle Eastern must have enthralled the new president. Louis Tiffany's work at the White House in 1882 made the state rooms a showcase for all that was luxurious, artistic,

and modern. For the first time in White House history, entire interiors were custom-made, not purchased from a department store.

Tiffany did not change the Green Room, which had been decorated for the conservative (and small-town) Garfields. They had invited Herter Brothers but chose the low bidder, local Washington furnishers W. B. Moses & Sons. The result was an interior just like the drawing room of any upper-middle-class house in the country. Moses had applied an embossed paper and brought in new ready-made Aesthetic Reform-style furniture, covered to match the draperies. An Anglo-Japanese étagère with a black finish filled one corner of the room, distracting visitors from the 1850s gasolier and overmantel mirror. Moses also redecorated the Family Dining Room, and it, too, ended up being an archetypal industrialist's dining room: dark, masculine, with busy paper and carpeting. [see page 137]

Tiffany's most dazzling change was the replacement of Thomas U. Walter's institutional 1850s iron-and-glass screen in the ground-floor entrance hall with a colored glass wall. Beyond its aesthetic brilliance, the Tiffany screen created a lush private passageway out of the blank cross hall.[14] An ideal in the Gilded Age mansion was privacy—something always hard to achieve in the White House—and the Tiffany screen made the house feel more like a mansion and less like a city hotel.

In the East Room, Tiffany had to work with the amber silk plush drapery and upholstery that had been installed by Moses & Sons for

Grant Red Room, looking northwest, 1874. Having known severe economic hardship herself, Julia Grant economized at first by leaving President Polk's 1847 Meeks & Company rosewood suite in place, along with the decoration carried out for President Johnson.

Mrs. Hayes in 1881. But he updated the flat surfaces with intricate arrangements of ivory-, bronze-, and copper-colored papers, applied between the ceiling beams added by Mrs. Grant. This sophisticated treatment gave the finished interior a vaguely Moorish style. Its subtle hues were far from the intense aniline reds, greens, and purples of the previous generation. Because of its scale, this interior was included in *Artistic Houses* in 1883–84, adjacent to images of Tiffany's own apartment.[15]

For the dining room at the other end of the state floor, Tiffany's contributions included a new color scheme of "glowing yellows" with painted stenciling in silver and huge circular sconces of hammered silvered metal.

In the state parlors, Tiffany again mixed his distinctive style with existing furnishings. In the Blue Room, he reupholstered the Buchanan chairs and settees in pale blue silk canvas. He shaded the walls from dark blue at the bottom to pale robin's egg at the cornice. To the ceiling and walls he applied lacy snowflakes picked out in ivory and silver. The coordinated window curtains were dark blue velvet in the lower section and light blue satin in the upper. Four custom-made gas sconces, each three feet in

Grant Red Room, looking northeast, 1874. Like other first ladies, Mrs. Grant used the Red Room as her "best parlor." The monumental portrait she hung there left no doubt as to her social ambitions for her family.

The western windows of the State Dining Room were blocked up to accommodate President Grant's new billiard room, which was built in between the house and the conservatories. The Monroe ormolu plateau from 1817, the Polk dining chairs of 1847, and the Pierce console tables of 1853 are still being used.

Enlarged James Monroe plateau, Jean-François Denière et François Matelin, Paris, 1817. The original Paris plateau was not fancy enough for Julia Grant's mansion; she enlarged and expanded it to fit her idea of what a mansion centerpiece should be. She continued to use the Charles Baudouine dining chairs acquired by Sarah Polk. In the Grant State Dining Room, 1871.

Center table, Anthony Quervelle, Philadelphia, 1829, for James Monroe. Although they quickly become inconvenient in the East Room, for which they were purchased, the Quervelle center tables continued to be useful elsewhere. Seen in the oval library, late 1860s.

Faux-bamboo suite, unknown maker, probably New York, c. 1877. Although possibly purchased by Julia Grant, this was used by Lucy and Rutherford Hayes for their master bedroom. Not since Mary Lincoln had the White House had such a stylish new bedroom suite.

diameter, "composed of fantastic shapes of colored glass interspersed with little mirrors, [produced] a scintillating effect"[16] impossible to see in photographs.[17] [see pages 15 and 134]

In the Red Room, Tiffany retained the still-stylish Herter Brothers furniture from Julia Grant. He used the same effect he had in the Blue Room, painting the walls a modern "purplish Pompeian red" and the wainscot a darker red. The walls grew paler toward the cornice, with a frieze of abstracted stars and stripes. Bronze and copper stars covered the ceiling, glittering in the light of the 1850s gasolier. The woodwork was painted dark red rubbed to a high shine. A massive cherrywood mantelpiece and overmantel mirror filled the western wall, inlaid with red leather and glass jewels and faced with red tiles Despite the positive press they received, all of these remarkable interiors, but for the East Room, were swept away by the time Theodore Roosevelt became president in 1901.

FURNISHINGS

Julia Grant and Mary Lincoln both knew how to run a household, but unlike her predecessor, Mrs. Grant had actually lived in a log cabin in Missouri. Following her husband's rising star, Mrs. Grant had the opportunity to study elegant homes and changing fashions in Philadelphia, Washington, and New York, where, despite the war, demand for imported and American-made luxury goods skyrocketed during the

1860s. The genteel villa taste Julia Grant had struggled to maintain since her marriage in 1848 had been pushed aside by the newly rich in favor of a style that was more aggressively luxurious.

Mansion-taste eclecticism in the Gilded Age followed parallel tracks: historical revival styles, adhering to patterns established during the villa years; and modern styles, which came out of the Aesthetic Reform movement begun in the 1860s in England. In the final decade of the century, mansion style tipped decidedly in favor of historicizing. By the time she settled in at the White House, Mrs. Grant had a clear idea of the latest styles in household goods, as well as where to buy them. With high aspirations for herself and her husband, she began in 1869 to transform the White House from an oversize Greek Revival villa with a French accent into a modern mansion.

The White House began to shift from villa to mansion when William Cogswell's mammoth 1867 portrait of the Grant family replaced Gilbert Stuart's portrait of Washington in the first family's best parlor, the Red Room.[18] The picture shows Julia at its center, refined, genteel, sublimely middle-class, surrounded by her life's work—her children and her husband. Grant is portrayed as a general, but his position is secondary and supportive.[19] Only in the more public Green Room did an equally huge equestrian portrait of the general allow him center stage. The scale of the pictures suggests the scale of Mrs. Grant's domestic agenda.

Top: Entrance hall, c, 1893. James Hoban's original marble columns from the 1814 rebuilding create a frame for Louis C. Tiffany's 1882 aesthetic fantasy in colored glass. Tiffany reused the framework of Thomas U. Walter's 1853 iron-and-glass screen, installed to minimize drafts in the vast hallway. Bottom: Arthur East Room, still with its c. 1880 Garfield decoration.

Parlor, George Kemp House, New York, as decorated by Louis C. Tiffany in 1879. Tiffany's Arabian Parlor for this drug manufacturer's residence exemplified the artistic interiors used by Gilded Age millionaires to distinguish their homes from those of the merely affluent.

Among her many enhancements to the White House collections, Julia Grant enlarged the Monroe ormolu plateau with brass wire arches and a massive new central candelabrum-cum-epergne. Apparently, 14 feet of glittering ormolu wasn't enough for her ambitions. It appeared in *Frank Leslie's Illustrated Newspaper* on April 1, 1871, in its updated form. Julia Grant's Haviland Limoges porcelain dinner and dessert service, its enameled floral botanicals circled with a simple scalloped rim and yellow-buff enamel band, would have been at home in America as far back as the 1830s. Purchased from Boteler & Brother in Washington, it was more conservative than the Polk service of 1846 and the Pierce service of 1853. Only the standing compotes make note of the Neo-Grec style that had supplanted the Rococo Revival in American homes by this time.[20]

The furniture Mrs. Grant ordered for the cabinet room in 1869 exemplifies the hard-edged modern style of the early Gilded Age. Produced by Pottier & Stymus in New York, it was carved in walnut, suitable for the all-male work space. Both the sofa and the custom-made cabinet table were heavily scaled, architectural in form, loosely Greco-Roman in detail.[21] The chairs were also in the angular Neo-Grec mode, while the president's own chair was simply office furniture—a chair that swiveled and rocked. The top-heavy Grant sofa relates closely to a much richer set of four sofas, designed at the same time by Herter Brothers in the late 1860s for what was the most opulent country mansion of its day, Elm Park, the LeGrand Lockwood house in Norwalk, Connecticut. Both the Lockwood and presidential sofas were meant for use that was not quite domestic in nature and thus look different from parlor sofas.[22] [see pages 138 and 179]

By the time Mark Twain had published *The Gilded Age* in 1873, the firm of Gustave and Christian Herter had surfaced in New York as the first furniture makers and upholsterers in America to offer full-service interior decoration. Their interiors and furniture appeared in the most opulent houses from New York to Boston to Chicago to San Francisco. For the Red Room, Julia Grant ordered a large group of furniture from the Herter Brothers firm

Top: Julia Grant couldn't afford to edecorate the Red Room entirely during her husband's two terms in office, but she did purchase a large assortment of ultramodern furniture by New York's Herter Brothers in 1874. It was stylish enough that Louis Comfort Tiffany kept most of it in place for his redecoration of the room for President Arthur in the early 1880s. This view is the earliest phase of Tiffany's decoration scheme. Bottom: In the second phase of Louis Comfort Tiffany's redecoration of the Red Room for Chester Arthur, he replaced the Chinese vases by the new mantelpiece with a pair of large figural French urns. To the Herter Brothers furniture purchased by Julia Grant in 1874, Tiffany apparently added cabinets of his own design, seen on either side of the doorway in this c. 1883 picture.

Arthur Blue Room, looking west, 1886. The Monroe 1817 pier table by Pierre-Antoine Bellangé of Paris remained in place. Louis Tiffany himself typically used old objects in his artistic interiors, both for budgetary reasons and because he enjoyed the aesthetic variety that old things brought to a room.

in 1875. It represented both the edgier eclecticism of the period and the disintegration of the standard parlor suite of the Polk era. The suite included a variety of rosewood settees, armchairs, and side chairs in the "Japanese" style closely related to chairs Herter had made just a year earlier for the parlor in the James Goodwin mansion in Hartford, Connecticut.[23]

The incised gilt lines and flattened linearity on all the furniture show the influence of the Aesthetic Reform movement, which had recently come from England. French style hadn't lost cachet, but it just wasn't enough to satisfy the eclectic tastes of America's mansion builders. A pair of gilded armchairs from the suite, seen in images of Chester Arthur's Red Room circa 1882, had no prior parallel in domestic furniture forms, having been designed as objets d'art rather than merely as useful furniture. The idea of "art furniture" emerged as America's wealthy sought greater and greater opulence, being less concerned with practicality than with status and show.

THE GREEN ROOM.

THE RED ROOM.

Arthur Green and Red rooms, c. 1885. Mansion interiors were lush and visually complex. This rare photo lithograph gives some idea of the colors and patterns of the luminous Louis C. Tiffany interiors.

Though similar in overall style, the richly carved and ornamented center table from the Herter suite stayed in the Red Room the shortest time. It was the only Herter piece removed from the room by Louis Comfort Tiffany in 1882, when it was banished to the second-floor oval library. [see pages 175 and 192]

The Gorham Manufacturing Company of Providence, Rhode Island, emerged after the Civil War as the largest manufacturer of sterling silver in the world, second in celebrity only to Tiffany & Company in New York.[24] Julia Grant chose a symbol of America's finest manufacturing for the state dining room from Gorham's display at the Centennial Exposition in Philadelphia in 1876. The silver "Hiawatha" centerpiece, just under four feet long, evoked *The Song of Hiawatha*, a popular American epic poem by Henry Wadsworth Longfellow. This was not an object for a villa—it

was a mansion tour de force and was Julia Grant's ultimate response to the aging foreign grandeur of the Monroe ormolu plateau.[25] The centerpiece survived the purge of Victorian furnishings from the White House in 1903 but was so alien to 20th-century eyes that it was publicized in 1940 as having been given to Mrs. Grant by the Iroquois Indians "who made it."[26]

Gilded Age eclecticism continued after the Grants left the White House in 1877. The Hayes family broke with the White House tradition of ready-made furniture and added two pieces of custom furniture to the redecorated Family Dining Room, where their state china was displayed when not in use.[27] A massive sideboard and matching table, designed by Cincinnati craftsman Henry L. Fry, were commissioned in 1880. The mahogany sideboard was laden with symbolism, from flora representing

Louis Comfort Tiffany updated President Arthur's East Room with a new ceiling in the early 1880s, while retaining the store-bought furniture in the Aesthetic style purchased by Lucretia Garfield.

Left: Arthur Family Dining Room, 1880s. The custom-made 1880 sideboard by Henry Fry of Cincinnati, one of the few pieces of custom furniture acquired during the frugal Garfield presidency, holds pieces from the Hayes porcelain service. Right: Arthur Green Room, 1880–85. The room remained unchanged after the Garfields, retaining standard mansion interior schemes and finishes created by a local Washington, D.C., decorating firm.

Ohio—the president's home state—to a richly sculpted American eagle guarding a stars-and-stripes shield.[28] The Anthony Quervelle pier tables from Andrew Jackson's East Room, with white marble tops added in the 1850s, were also in this room, finding a new life as serving tables.

Upstairs was a faux-bamboo bedroom suite used by President and Mrs. Hayes. The forms recalled the Renaissance mode of the 1860s, but the imitation of bamboo was inspired by the large Japanese and Chinese displays at the Philadelphia Exposition. Similarly, a chair made of steer horns appeared by the Hayes years in the informal upstairs sitting hall next to the main staircase. These exotic novelties, a by-product of the Texas cattle trade, were typical conversation pieces in late 19th-century houses.

Lucy Hayes bought four monumental gilded brass candelabra from Tiffany & Company for $500 in 1880. Their historicizing style was probably seen as French or Italian and looked to past models for their details. They were just the sort of conventionally splendid objects that stores like Tiffany sold routinely to mansion owners all over the country. In startling contrast to these was the Limoges porcelain dinner and dessert service, ordered by Mrs. Hayes and completed in 1880, which was radical and modern. America's porcelain industry, centered in Trenton, New Jersey, was beginning to make strides in luxury goods by 1880, but the Haviland name still dominated the tables of America's mansions.

This was also the moment when china painting was becoming popular among amateurs (women) and professionals (men) in America. Lucy Hayes chose Theodore Davis, an illustrator specializing in the American West, to design both the enameled patterns and the shapes. It was the first—and, truthfully, the last—avant-garde design ever to grace the White House table. Some of the forms were standard functional pieces such as dinner, salad, and soup plates, some with fluted edges, and others decagonal with slightly scalloped rims. Specialization was encouraged by manufacturers to promote sales of large sets of silver, ceramics, and glass. Variety became a necessity for tablewares. The more inventive forms in the Hayes service, rectangular and square dishes with folded corners, were inspired, loosely, by Japanese design, as part of the Aesthetic Reform movement. Davis used his familiarity with American flora and fauna to create the designs, but he laid them out in distinctly foreign ways, imitating the asymmetry and stylized naturalism of Japanese prints and paintings. The snowshoe on the ice cream plates referred both to ongoing American interest in Arctic exploration and to the special status of ice cream as a luxury dessert.

Caroline Harrison was the first president's wife to look seriously at things acquired by her predecessors. Her choice of conservative French porcelain suggests her awareness of the historical patterns that had accumulated in the cupboards and closets of the White House. Paul Putzki, a professional

Sofa, Pottier & Stymus, New York, purchased by Julia Grant, 1869, for the cabinet room. The strange high-backed sofa was more like ones used in semipublic spaces than those intended for parlors.

china painter and teacher, designed the Harrison service for production by Tressemanes & Vogt in Limoges in 1891. The conservative design, with ears of corn and wheat in gold on a dark blue brim, evoked the Indiana heartland from which the Harrisons had come and seemed to hark back to White House china from the 1830s or 1840s.

The silver ordered for the White House in the 1880s reflected ready-made mansion taste of the period. Electroplated pepper casters, footed olive dishes, and compotes were part of Tiffany & Company's new line of nonsterling wares. Tiffany produced electroplate, first in Providence, Rhode Island, and then in Newark, New Jersey, in order to capture the vast middle-class market for silver.[29] The plated pieces reflect the ubiquitous foliate and floral repoussé style of the 1880s, based on the dense, overall patterning seen as "oriental" in this period.[30]

A silver-plated electrotype of the Milton Shield was proudly shown in the White House. Photographer and journalist Frances Benjamin Johnston, during her documentation of the president's house in the 1890s, took special care to include the shield, produced by the English silver plating firm Elkington & Company of Birmingham. It was a replica of the original made for Elkington's display at the 1867 Paris Exposition Universelle by French sculptor Léonard Morel-Ladeuil (1820–1888). The complex low-relief scenes that fill the shield are taken from John Milton's epic poem *Paradise Lost.* The original shield won a gold medal in 1867 and was purchased for the South Kensington Museum (now the Victoria and Albert Museum in London). Electrotype copies of the shield were purchased by

wealthy Americans for years afterward, and the White House version was displayed in the upstairs oval library. Like the Hiawatha centerpiece, it was an object meant to be studied at leisure and to give status to its owner.[31]

Louis Comfort Tiffany's love of color and texture was evident in the objects he chose for his interiors in the Arthur White House. In the State Dining Room, he kept (or was forced to keep) most of the existing revival-style furniture and mirrors spanning several decades but replaced the curvaceous Polk-era dining chairs with rectilinear walnut side chairs. The monumental Chinese vases he originally positioned by the fireplace in the Red Room featured the dense, overall pink, green, and gold enamel decoration that had appealed to American taste since the 1830s.[32] He replaced these vases with large French-style painted urns, equally rich and dense in both color and pattern.

It seems that Arthur did acquire some custom-made furniture as part of the second phase of Tiffany's Red Room. Two cabinets that flanked the door into the main hall appear to have been part of a group of furniture including a center table and a curtained cabinet. These pieces closely match the Louis Tiffany mantelpiece, with its glass and leather decorations, and are completely unlike any commercial furniture of their day. Still in the room long after the Tiffany decoration had been replaced, they were specially photographed by Frances Benjamin Johnston. Although no record exists of Tiffany's designing furniture for the Red Room, he did have his own furniture-making business in New York and might well have produced these remarkable pieces of furniture, swept away in the purge of 1903.[33]

Top: Center table, Herter Brothers, New York, 1875, for the Grant Red Room. Louis C. Tiffany removed this table when he redecorated the Red Room in 1882, probably because it was bulkier and more old-fashioned than the rest of the Herter pieces. Bottom left: Side chair, Herter Brothers, New York, c. 1874. "Japanese" style chairs of this form, but in rosewood, were purchased by Julia Grant for the Red Room. Bottom right: Faux-bamboo chair from the master bedroom, 1870s. Possibly purchased by Julia Grant, this piece was used by President and Mrs. Hayes.

Center table and cabinet, possibly by Louis C. Tiffany, 1882–83, for the Arthur Red Room. Custom-made artistic furniture lent prestige to status-conscious Gilded Age mansion builders. Although no records survive to prove it, photographs document several pieces of furniture created to match Tiffany's mantelpiece in the Red Room. Pictured in the Harrison Red Room, c. 1890.

Vollmer's ebony Louis XV suite, which had been in the Green Room since Buchanan's time, was replaced by the Garfields with standard upper-middle-class Aesthetic-style furniture, available at any fine furniture wareroom. This included a center table and a sofa, as well as side chairs with fretwork frames. In another image of the Green Room dominated by the portrait of Lucy Hayes, Louis Tiffany's big Chinese vases from the Red Room have appeared, along with an American Empire-style center table. This table was brand-new—a bit of Colonial Revivalism—since Empire was seen as colonial in the Gilded Age mind. That the table remained in the Green Room after the Roosevelts "restored" the space in 1902 is testimony to its colonial attributes.[34]

The East Room received at least two large suites of stylish but department-store-quality Aesthetic-style furniture during the late Hayes and early Garfield years, all, like the Green Room furniture, probably from W. B. Moses in Washington. It was dark, angular, and vaguely Oriental, densely covered with shallow carving and incising. All of it would have appeared cutting-edge to visitors to the White House in the 1880s but would have dated quickly, and consequently it was disposed of in 1903 by President Roosevelt.

Until the mansion era, the upstairs and downstairs rooms at the White House had always been approached aesthetically in the same way, albeit with different levels of funding. By the end of the mansion era, however, the state floor rooms were tipping from mansion to palace in style and splendor, while the private quarters stopped changing as dramatically. They began to take on that look of pragmatic eclecticism—reusing old things and making do with new wallpaper and paint—that typifies any household with a limited budget lived in over long periods. The oval library looked just like the library in any wealthy house of its day. President Harrison adopted the Lincoln guest-room furniture from 1861, and Mrs. Harrison made do with assorted secondhand upper-middle-class goods that had been around since the 1870s and earlier. Mrs. McKinley used the same Neo-Grec wardrobe in her bedroom in 1897 but switched to newly fashionable (and hygienic) brass beds. Mrs. McKinley's other modernizing included a Windsor-style rocking chair and heavily carved center table, both in the new colonial mode, as well as a little side table with carved legs by the fireplace that was surely from the 1820s and thus would have been seen as a colonial relic.

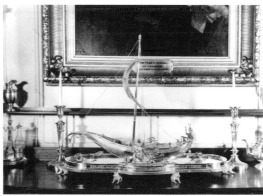
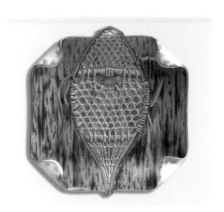

Top left: Dessert plate, Haviland & Company, Limoges, France, 1869, from the Grant service. Mrs. Grant appreciated the beauty and status of imported French porcelain. The hand-painted flowers, different on each piece, demonstrated both her good taste and her deep pockets. Top center: Hiawatha centerpiece, Gorham Manufacturing Company, Providence, Rhode Island, 1875, for the Grant State Dining Room. Julia Grant chose this remarkable sterling centerpiece because it was American-made and was a mansion object in its scale and elaborate design. Only the wealthiest Americans would have had silver of this size. Pictured in the Franklin Roosevelt family dining room in 1940. Top right: Ice cream plate, Theodore R. Davis for Haviland & Company, Limoges, France, 1879, from the Hayes service. Middle left: Game plate, Theodore R. Davis for Haviland & Company, Limoges, France, 1879, from the Hayes service. Middle center: Soup plate, Theodore R. Davis for Haviland & Company, Limoges, France, 1879, from the Hayes service. Although many Americans had Limoges porcelain, the Hayes service was unique in the nation both in form and in decoration. Middle right: Dinner plate, designed by Caroline Harrison and Paul Putzki, Tressemanes & Vogt, Limoges, France, 1891, from the Harrison service. Mrs. Harrison's interest in historical White House china probably influenced the conservative design of her state service. Bottom left: Ormolu candelabrum, Tiffany & Company, New York, for Lucy Hayes, 1880. Mansions had to be filled with ostentatious objects, and Mrs. Hayes would have had that expectation in mind when she purchased this. Bottom right: Silver-electroplated wares, Tiffany & Company, Newark, New Jersey, for James Garfield, 1882.

AMERICAN PALACES

Top left: Ogden Mills house, Staatsburg, New York, 1897, designed for the heir to a Pacific Coast mining, railroad, and banking fortune, by architects McKim, Mead & White. Top right: Frederick W. Vanderbilt house, Hyde Park, New York, 1899, by architects McKim, Mead & White for the Yale University benefactor and New York Central Railroad director. This Classical Revival mansion was built on the historic 1830s estate grounds of Dr. David Hosack, horticulturist and friend of early presidents. Bottom left: Lynnewood Hall, residence of Peter A. B. Widener, Elkins Park, Pennsylvania, 1900, by Horace Trumbauer, architect. Bottom right: Whitemarsh Hall, house of financier Edward T. Stotesbury, Wyndmoor, Pennsylvania, 1916–20, by Horace Trumbauer, architect. The Georgian Revival house was set in a parterre garden designed by French landscape architect Jacques Greber. The McMillan Commission conceived a similar landscape plan for the White House in 1901–02.

PALACE
1889–1921

There is something very palpable, and not in the least subtle, about the impression of wealth afforded by the greater contemporary residence. It has as little modesty about it, and makes as loud a proclamation of its own merit as any other characteristic American achievement.

—Harry W. Desmond and Herbert Croly, *Stately Homes in America,* 1903

KEEPING UP WITH THE VANDERBILTS

By 1900, America had developed an aristocracy of its own, one based on recently acquired industrial wealth rather than land ownership. The country had long forsaken the democratic belief that Americans should not live in palaces. The eclectic mansion of the 1870s, designed by builder architects familiar with European houses through books and journals, seemed provincial to wealthy Americans who now traveled abroad and experienced firsthand the castles and palaces of Europe's waning aristocracy. What house owners retained from the mansion era were Victorian notions of domestic comfort and convenience, even as Victorian notions of form, color, texture, and line were being rejected in favor of increasingly academic concepts of continental taste.

With architects professionally trained in American schools and French academies, American plutocrats embraced European period architecture and interior design. If Americans were going to be players on the international stage, they needed houses that conformed to aesthetic ideals associated with power. Along the avenues of America's major cities and in fashionable watering holes like Newport, Rhode Island, and Lenox, Massachusetts, luxurious, palatial houses sprang up. Carved and gilded chateaus and manors had formal French-style gardens with alleys of pleached lindens framing open lawns that were American imaginings of the French *tapis vert.* Inside, spaces as large as the White House's East Room were parqueted and paneled with ornate woodwork from baseboard to cornice, fitted out with the most costly draperies, chandeliers, carpets, and marble from around the world. Stylistically these fixtures were interpretations of French and English aristocratic interiors from every period up through Napoleon's empire.

America's relationship to European traditions was ambiguous. After all, only a century before, a revolution had been waged to forge a country with traditions of its own; and this revolution had been followed by the inferno of the Civil War, waged to protect what had been pioneered in the first half of the 19th century. This ambiguity was manifest in the design of American houses. As some of the rich became enchanted with the pleasures of Paris and London, others embraced ideas of the Colonial style, often more linked to Georgian England than to colonial America. Colonial became synonymous with good taste, and the "General Grant style," renamed Victorian, came to denote bad taste.

Continental and colonial traditions were seamlessly combined when Theodore Roosevelt undertook the first major renovation of the White House after his election in 1901. "Theodore the First," as Edith Wharton called the new president, brought to the White House his generation's expectation of how the rich—and, by association, the president of an international empire—should live.[1] Even though his Long Island country house, Sagamore Hill, was no more than a large villa, Roosevelt knew that the president's house had to be something more; it could not be overshadowed by private palaces built outside the nation's industrial and banking centers. To bring the White House up to par with American estates, Roosevelt turned to the New York architects McKim, Mead & White.

When Charles Follen McKim began his work for the president, his firm's reverence for the White House was already evident in their 1890s designs for the New York palaces of Ogden Mills in Staatsburg and Frederick Vanderbilt in Hyde Park. When asked in 1902 by architect Charles Moore if "among the great houses that have been built during recent years in the general style of the White House—many of them larger and much more costly—is there any one that in part of architecture, surpasses the White House?," McKim replied modestly, "No, there is not one in the same class of it."[2] George Washington had created a radiant white house that brought the authority of a Georgian country residence to the capital of a new republic. A century later, Charles McKim returned to Washington's colonial vision but amplified it with the European, aristocratic taste of the contemporary American plutocrat.

In 1902, President Roosevelt formally established the name of the president's residence as the White House. Hoban's looming edifice was not simply a government building. It was the home of a world leader. Roosevelt fulfilled L'Enfant's dream of a President's Palace, but democracy prevailed. The White House was now just one among many in a nation of palaces.

Caroline Harrison's dream house was a vast Colonial Revival palace with wings leading from the 1800 south facade to a new conservatory. Drawing by architect Frederick D. Owen, c. 1890.

PALACE BUILDERS

CAROLINE LAVINIA SCOTT HARRISON, c. July 1889

Mrs. Harrison was the daughter of an Ohio Presbyterian minister and supported the Daughters of the American Revolution, an influential group before women's suffrage. She had grand aspirations for an extensive White House renovation to coincide with the 1889 centennial celebration of George Washington's inauguration, but settled for electric lighting and the replacement of Chester Arthur's Tiffany decor with fashionable continental interiors. Mrs. Harrison began the tradition of collecting presidential china after she discovered some discarded dishes in a White House closet.

1889–93

THEODORE ROOSEVELT in his new office, c. 1905.

Responsible for the first complete renovation of the White House as a Beaux-Arts palace, the gregarious and imperial president Theodore Roosevelt sought to make the White House into a setting grand enough to represent America's global influence. With architect Charles McKim, he finally moved the executive offices in 1902 out of the second floor. The White House became a combination home-office with a three-part division that still exists today: state rooms, second-floor residence, and west-wing offices.

1901–09

EDITH CAROW ROOSEVELT at her writing table in the oval sitting room, c. 1905–09.

President Roosevelt's second wife, who had been his childhood friend, oversaw the radical modernization of the family quarters in the White House. She resisted the rising tide of anti-Victorian taste by rescuing old furnishings used in past presidencies, including the Lincoln Bed. Her creation of a portrait gallery of first ladies in the renovated ground-floor entrance hall reflected a new regard for women in American history.

In a nod to both America's colonial heritage and the formalism of the renovated White House, Mrs. Roosevelt planted Charles F. McKim's new south parterres as formal flower beds based on the garden at Mount Vernon.

ELLEN AXSON WILSON, standing by a window with contemporary landscape paintings, c. 1912.

The first Mrs. Wilson, from Rome, Georgia, disliked the gloom of the formal White House and moved its interiors in a more modest and comfortable Colonial Revival direction. A gifted painter and gardener, the intellectual Mrs. Wilson planted the 1913 rose garden at the White House following the fashionable Italianate style of American country estates.

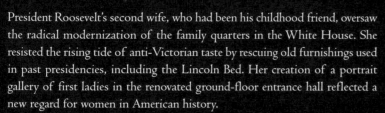

1901–09

1913–14

AN AMERICAN PALACE

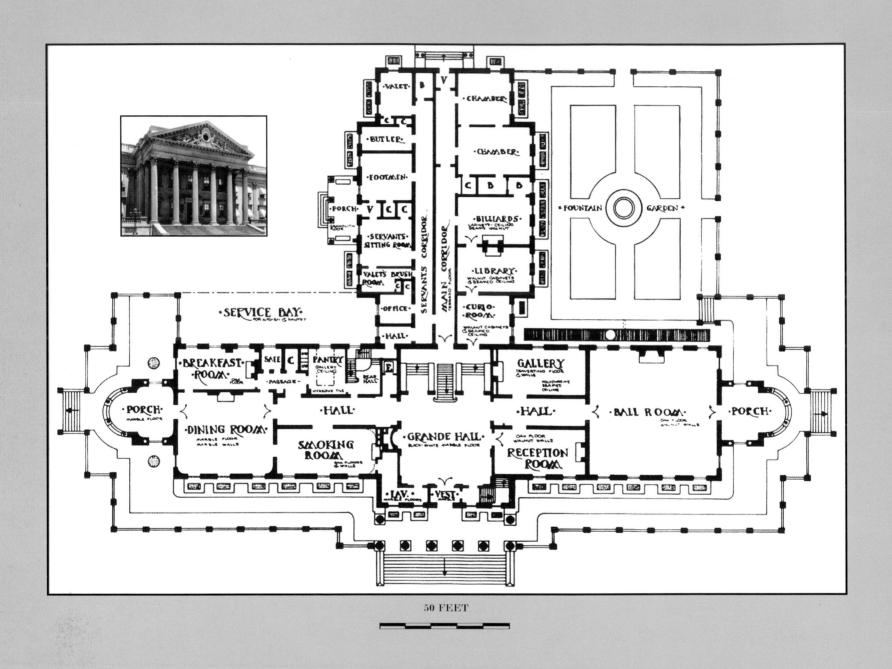

50 FEET

LYNNEWOOD HALL, 1900

Entrance (inset) and first-floor plan, Lynnewood Hall, 1900, Elkins Park, Pennsylvania. Architect Horace Trumbauer used Beaux-Arts conventions to organize the 110 rooms of this over 40,000 square-foot house, built in a 36-acre residential park and garden for Peter A.B. Widener, a trolley car investor, founder of U.S. Steel and the American Tobacco Company. The Georgian Revival house reflected the national respect for the White House.

THE WHITE HOUSE AS AN
AMERICAN PALACE

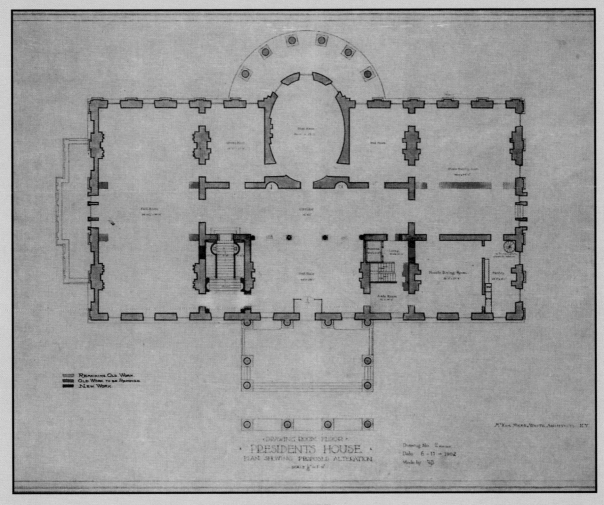

WHITE HOUSE, 1902

First-floor plan, reflecting proposed changes for the Roosevelt administration, 1902. By 1900 the 29,500 square-foot White House had become outmoded in comparison to contemporary American estates like Lynnewood Hall. Theodore Roosevelt made the house more palatial by rearranging rooms and adding a west wing for the executive office.

Marble House, Newport, Rhode Island, inspired by the White House and the Petit Trianon, designed by Richard Morris Hunt, 1892, for New York Central railroad heir, William K. Vanderbilt. Architecture critics Harry W. Desmond and Herbert Croly wrote in 1903 that the palace "invites comparison with some of our earlier post-revolutionary classic buildings, and it can hardly be said that the modern building gains by the comparison…The absence of charm robs it even of its impressiveness." No matter how much money they spent, the rich could not buy the reverence that Americans held for the founding fathers.

HOUSE

At the peak of the Gilded Age, rich Americans built houses along Fifth Avenue in New York, on the Philadelphia Main Line, at resorts such as Newport, Rhode Island, and Lenox, Massachusetts. Nowhere was the preference for the grand and imperial more apparent than at Marble House in Newport, designed by Richard Morris Hunt for William and Alva Vanderbilt and completed in 1892. Marble House is arguably the first American house that crossed the line from mansion to palace, in scale, in materials, and in aristocratic pretense. At the same time, the classical building, with its symmetrical composition and pale stone cladding derived from Ange-Jacques Gabriel's design for the Petit Trianon at Versailles, strongly echoed James Hoban's White House of the late 18th century.

Although Marble House arguably fulfilled the needs and requirements of the Vanderbilts for a palatial summer "cottage" by the ocean, the White House, despite its great size, was no longer functional as the residence and workplace of the president. In 1889, the Army Corps of Engineers addressed the problems stemming from the White House's now-too-small size, suggesting that an executive office building be constructed immediately to the west. First Lady Caroline Harrison, who found the presidential living quarters wholly inadequate, took the corps's proposal as an opportunity to pursue ambitious building schemes, seeking the help of engineer Frederick D. Owen, a personal friend.

Owen's proposal called for the original house to become the southern component of a sprawling quadrangular complex. To the west, a wing somewhat larger than the White House was to house presidential offices; to the east, a matching building was identified on drawings as the Historical Art Wing. On their north ends, these wings were to be attached

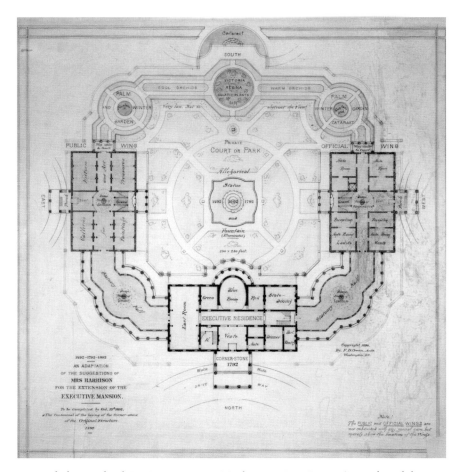

Proposed plan, Frederick D. Owen, circa 1890, showing Mrs. Harrison's presidential dream house, which never materialized.

to the White House with both rectilinear and circular forms wrapped in colonnades. To the south, low-lying conservatories and a centrally located pavilion containing a lily pond were to enclose a courtyard. It is important to note that the architectural vocabulary used in this massive dream house mimics closely the classical Hoban design. The scale of the project, however, has become imperial. Some elements of the proposal, including highly visible domes, significantly altered the building's profile, providing a jarring contrast and transforming the White House into an overblown civic structure. A bill calling for the proposal's realization failed to gain sufficient political support, and while Benjamin Harrison shared his wife's belief that it would serve as an appropriate architectural tribute to the centennial of the presidency and the Constitution, the proposal never came to fruition.

In 1897, during the administration of William McKinley, the Army Corps of Engineers, headed by Colonel Theodore A. Bingham, with Owen now on staff, produced preliminary plans for a radical expansion of the White House. The plans' development was soon stymied by the outbreak of the Spanish-American War in April 1898. Following the war's cessation four months later, Bingham and Owen began to revise the Harrison administration scheme, conducting extensive research about previous plans and renovations, so as to be able to justify the design in historical terms.

In December 1900, Bingham presented a model of a new scheme. The quadrangle-defining east and west additions had been replaced. To the west, a rectangular Ionic colonnade surrounded a circular building that was to be surmounted by a shallow dome and contain a banquet hall and guest rooms. To the east was to be a similar structure, but its colonnade adopted the curve of the building. A smaller structure, farther to the east, had a principal entrance crowned by a pediment. The wings to the east were to house presidential offices and space for the increasingly influential press. Collectively, the three planned structures more than doubled the width of the White House's principal facade. Consistent with the existent building, the wings were to incorporate smooth sandstone walls, rusticated bases, sandstone balustrades, window enframements, and pilasters. Attending the presentation was Senator James McMillan, who was highly critical of Bingham and Owen's scheme. McMillan was also head of the powerful eponymous commission given the task of creating a master plan for Washington. One of the members of the commission was Charles Follen McKim, principal of the esteemed architectural firm McKim, Mead & White.

In the spring of 1902, following McKinley's assassination and Theodore Roosevelt's swearing in as president, First Lady Edith Roosevelt invited McKim to consult regarding possible changes to the White House. With funding for the renovation of the house secured by McMillan, the Roosevelts put McKim in charge, dramatically shifting power from the Army Corps of Engineers to an established architect, giving newfound status to the architecture profession, still in its early years in terms of training, practice, and recognition in the United States. The choice of McKim also set the architecture of the White House in a decidedly different direction than in past years. Embarking on the most extensive renovation the White House had undergone up to that point, McKim brilliantly synthesized an intellectually rigorous classicism, emboldened by the success of the White City of the World's Columbian Exposition of 1893, with a deep appreciation of early American architectural forms.

With Glenn Brown, the secretary of the American Institute of Architects, serving as project architect on-site, McKim called for the demolition of the White House's Victorian conservatories. At first the Roosevelts were reluctant, but McKim successfully argued that the conservatories' removal would enhance the house's original architecture. The architectural historian Leland Roth has noted that following Buchanan's construction of the White House's first greenhouse in 1857, "subsequent presidents added to the greenhouses as they fancied flowers or grapes or cucumbers, until the aggregation was said to resemble a commercial florist's."[3] Indeed, Charles Moore contended that Colonel Bingham's "hobby was greenhouses" and that had his alterations to the White House been realized, "he would have made the President of the United States the largest grower of flowers in Washington."[4]

In an effort to remove most office functions from the house, McKim built a temporary executive office building to the east. McKim also restored the flanking colonnades designed by Jefferson and Latrobe, providing, as he put it, an adequate "saucer to the cup."[5]

McKim then focused on the house itself, reconfiguring plans on the ground and first floors to enhance the sense of procession deemed appropriate to the increasingly elaborate and protocol-based affairs of state. A new entrance for guests was added to the ground-floor level, where laundries and storage rooms were converted into modern amenities, including cloakrooms and bathrooms. The first-floor State Dining Room was extended about 20 feet into the transverse hallway to allow for more seated guests. Throughout the house, McKim realized dramatic structural changes, exchanging wooden joists for steel ones and replacing existing warped floorboards with new wood-and-stone floors resting on a foundation of Guastavino tiles. While the remodeling to a large extent celebrated the house's original classical design, removing layers of stylistically inconsistent renovations and additions, it had a destructive dimension, as well. Many architectural elements, including doors, windows, stairs, and railings, were simply discarded. The original Ionic gray marble columns installed by Hoban ended up in the Potomac River. The house became a sleek white palace, but at a cost to its colonial integrity.

Much of the immediate response to McKim's remodeling was negative. As Charles Moore noted, "It is not to be expected that the radical changes in the White House would escape criticism; but the chorus of objection amounting to vituperation was not anticipated." In time, however, opinion shifted. Moore pointed out that "people began to realize that in the restored White House they had a President's House expressive of the simplicity and dignity of the Republic, and at the same time in its appointments and elegance fit for any king on earth."

Moore posited that much of the criticism arose from the shift from public to private that McKim's design effected. Moore stated, "While the offices were in the White House, that building belonged not to the President and his family, but to the public. . . . Senators and Congressmen had access day and night, not as a courtesy but as a right. With the relegation of the offices to the office building, the President ceased to 'live over the shop.' . . . Naturally some of the Men on the Hill resented having to ring the bell instead of entering unannounced. Such a change smacked of monarchy and exclusiveness."[6] Writing in *Architectural Record* in 1903, the noted critic Montgomery Schuyler praised McKim's work, conjecturing that Hoban, "could he visit the scene of his labors, would be as delighted as surprised to see what has come of the development of his ideas."[7]

◆ ◆ ◆

DETAILS OF DINING ROOM

0 1 2 3 4 5 6 7 8 9 10
·SCALE·

ALTERATIONS TO THE WHITE HOUSE, WASHINGTON, D. C.
1903

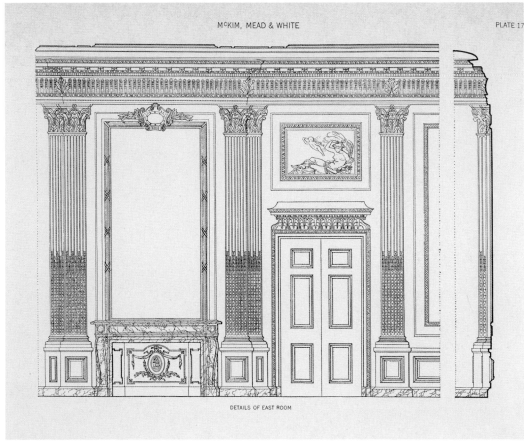

McKIM, MEAD & WHITE   PLATE 17

DETAILS OF EAST ROOM

Charles F. McKim applied Beaux-Arts proportions to American colonial design for the panelled State Dining Room (top) and the East Room (bottom) that he created for Theodore Roosevelt's presidency, 1902.

The government printed postcards to publicize the crisp elegance of the renovated president's residence, officially named by President Roosevelt the White House. The west executive office wing at the end of the west colonnade, the east public entrance, the east and west colonial gardens, and first floor terraces were featured, c. 1910.

View through the north portico after the Theodore Roosevelt renovation. Though topiary boxes now stood where exotic conservatory plants had been in the mansion era, the 1873 circular pool still had its showy French spray purchased for President Grant. It was replaced with a restrained jet like those found in European parks. Photograph, c. 1904.

By 1890, the president's private conservatory was a vast complex. Its patchwork design reflected the changing horticultural interests of post–Civil War presidents and first ladies.

GARDEN

Before its demolition by Theodore Roosevelt, the White House conservatory was the de facto president's garden for the predominantly Republican administrations at the close of the 19th century. Set in a park laced with serpentine pathways, the sprawling palace of glass, lush with prized botanical specimens, symbolized presidential power and exclusivity. Frederick D. Owen intended to extend this exclusivity by creating a private courtyard, closed from public view by a glittering conservatory between east and west wings. Had Owen's plans for First Lady Caroline Harrison been realized, the democratic intent of L'Enfant and Downing's open landscape plans would have been lost.

When Theodore Roosevelt arrived with his family at the White House in 1901, the presidential grounds were part Anglo-American park and part Victorian parterre garden, with mature shade trees and densely planted carpet beds. William Cullen Bryant's *Picturesque America* captured their domestic spirit. "The front is not imposing," wrote Bryant. "At the back, a small but beautiful park, adorned with plants and flowers, varied by artificial hillocks and spread with closely trimmed lawns, stretches off to a high road." The south portico staircase was "overgrown with ivy and other clinging parasites . . . The most prominent object seen from these president's grounds is the red Smithsonian Institution, which from here seems a very feudal castle."[8] This was not the garden of a president

determined to impress the world with America's new cosmopolitan culture and refinement. The White House, like Roosevelt himself, now had to compete with the best the Continent had to offer.

Frederick Law Olmsted Jr., along with city planner Charles Burnham, joined the McMillan Commission to oversee the landscape plan for the capital city and ensure the White House was commensurate in ambition with the building plans of Charles F. McKim. Olmsted was the son of Frederick Law Olmsted, the father of the naturalized American park and landscape architect of the Capitol grounds, laid out in 1874. The Olmsted firm in Boston was well suited for the job of providing a garden for the White House, now being restored to its imagined colonial Georgian splendor. They had designed the Beaux-Arts grounds of the 1893 Chicago World's Columbian Exposition and the 1894 French-inspired formal gardens of George Washington Vanderbilt's Biltmore estate in North Carolina.[9]

To understand the historical origins of the White House garden and park, Olmsted and his fellow commissioners cruised the Potomac, visiting colonial estates and traveled, like wealthy American families, to royal parks in Europe. From their observations, they presented to Congress and the president their vision for a renewed capital city. Like L'Enfant a century before, the commissioners, as architect and congressional liaison Glenn Brown observed in 1904, presented a triangular plan that "contemplated

Schloss Schönbrunn, Austria (top), and Château de Compiègne, France, c. 1900. The gardens of these 18th-century palaces influenced the design of the south parterres and topiary on the first-floor terraces of Theodore Roosevelt's White House.

Charles F. McKim's imagined French parterre outside the new executive office building, as drawn by illustrator Jules Guérin, 1902.

Bird's-eye view of the White House garden and capital-city improvements, after the 1901–02 plan by the McMillan Commission. For a newly rich nation with international ambitions, Charles F. McKim and his colleagues returned to Major L'Enfant's conception of the White House as a palace with an open formal park linked to the Capitol's mall. Rendering by Francis L. V. Hoppin, who apprenticed with McKim, Mead & White.

the Capitol as the East and the President's house as the West of the great Government garden, with numerous great buildings between these structures."[10] The plan was at once symbolically democratic and aesthetically imperial. The private White House garden and park, fenced and shaded, would become a broad, public *tapis vert* opening to terraces at the Washington Monument. Drawings by Jules Guérin, the architectural illustrator who had worked with McKim on the Chicago Fair, reflect the formal reserve intended for symmetrical parterres along the south facade.[11]

The imperialism of the McMillan Plan was moderated by practical suggestions from President Roosevelt and his wife, for whom the White House was home. In February 1903, Charles McKim sent Olmsted a preliminary plan accompanied by an explanatory letter. The plan honored the president's request to retain the south lawn and a driveway, redesigned as a formal arc, for cabinet members and diplomats to enter the house at the south portico. A dark line defined where Mrs. Edith Carow Roosevelt envisioned a driveway reduced in width to expand the north lawn. Instead

of the cramped flower gardens that existed along the south facade, McKim proposed symmetrical square parterres. At the far end of the west parterre, Mrs. Roosevelt intended "some sort of lattice work, such as we saw at Compiègne, to be used by her as a drying room for clothes, but so screened as to appear to be an arbor." The arbor, explained McKim, might be functional, or a "bosquet, or a mass of shrubbery, of box or linden, or other trees, as you may suggest, cut to give it formal shape, like Schoenbrun [*sic*, the royal palace in Vienna]." For the planting of the Jeffersonian first-floor terraces, now extensions of the White House garden, McKim recommended "formal trees, say Bay Trees, to be placed both upon the roofs . . . at the distance that one would expect to find them in France and Italy." Trees on the White House grounds were to be moved and replanted "formally."[12]

What McKim and Olmsted realized fell far short of the McMillan vision. Like the interiors, elements from both colonial America and aristocratic Europe were assimilated in the final planting. By June 1905, a new formalism had been introduced to the grounds, with the overall

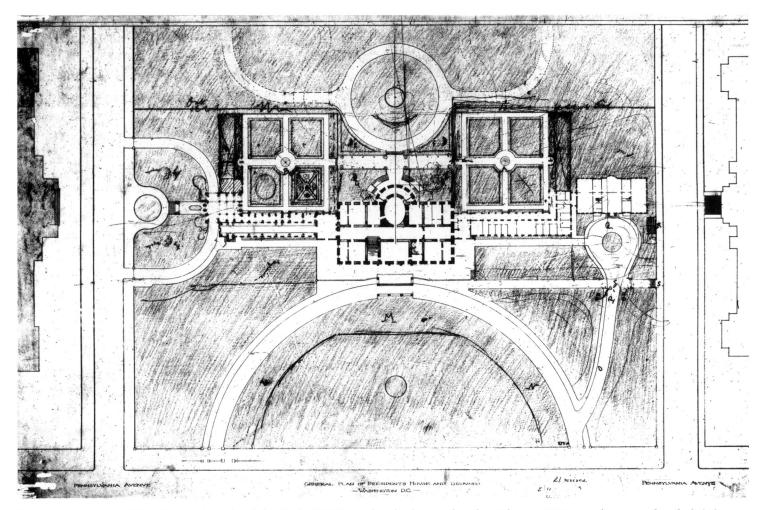

Preliminary plan for the White House garden and park, by Charles F. McKim and Frederick Law Olmsted Jr., February 1903. Formal terrace gardens flank the house.

conception of the White House as a home with a private garden preserved. The conservatory had been razed.[13] The perimeter wall remained, as did the historic guitar-shaped path McKim and Olmsted had planned to remove. The north drive was as Mrs. Roosevelt had requested, and the laundry area parallel to the new west wing was simply screened. Clipped hedges along the north facade, symmetrical parterres east and west of the south portico, and 10-foot-high Belgian topiary on the first-floor terraces were palatial in spirit.

At the end of the 19th century, women emerged as leaders in the new field of professional landscape design. In the wake of the landscape preservation movement, women organized the Garden Club of America in 1913 and founded their own schools to provide professional landscape training.[14] Edith Roosevelt began the tradition of presidential wives overseeing the design of the south portico gardens, claiming them as the president's own.

In a 1903 letter, McKim outlined a suggested planting for the newly graded terraces south of his east and west wings. "What is desired by Mrs. Roosevelt and her friend Mrs. [Edith] Wharton (who is a woman of great taste), seems to me . . . desirable—that these gardens should be extremely simple, and should present something of the character of Mount Vernon, namely divisions into parterres, surrounded with close-cut hedges. These are slightly sunken, say 18 in. to 2 ft. at the most, thus giving a better perspective, as well as additional height to the terraces upon which they abut."[15]

It is not surprising that Mount Vernon was suggested as inspiration for the White House gardens. Mrs. Roosevelt and the president had frequently visited George Washington's plantation, which had become a mecca of the Colonial Revival movement.[16] Its gardens, with boxwood-bordered flower beds, were not archaeological restorations but romantic 19th-century interpretations of America's early flower gardens.[17]

Mrs. Roosevelt and gardener Henry Pfister designed the White House colonial garden as an homage to Mount Vernon. Sweet peas, hollyhocks, lilies, and roses were planted in petal-shaped beds outlined with boxwood. Like the guitar-shaped drive of the Grant administration, Mrs. Roosevelt's parterres associated Teddy Roosevelt with the authority of the first president.

By authorizing the razing of the greenhouses, President Roosevelt moved family life back to the White House park, a change that foreshadowed the expanded use of the gardens in the post–World War II years. Mrs. Roosevelt

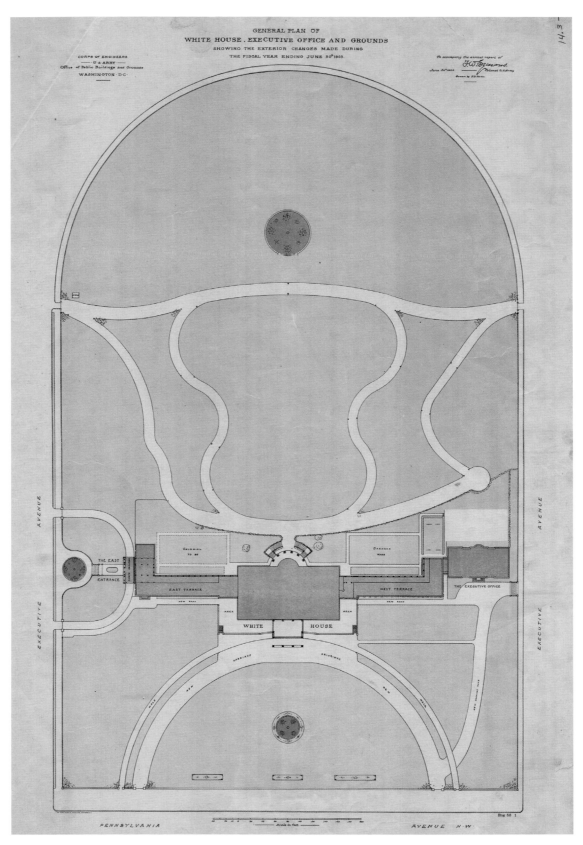

This 1903 plan by Frederick Law Olmsted Jr. reflects the president's grounds after the Roosevelt renovation. The McMillan Commission had planned to open to the public the 82 acres belonging to the White House, but in the end, the president's residence, with security and privacy needs, remained a house in a walled garden. The new symmetrical south parterres were consistent with the Beaux-Arts formality of Charles F. McKim's changes, but the curving pathway modeled on Mount Vernon's bowling green still remained.

Southwest mosaic flower bedding and conservatory before renovation, 1880s.

Edith Roosevelt's southwest colonial garden, c. 1906.

held annual spring afternoon parties at which guests were invited to stroll through the well-tended flower beds. Children played games on the south lawn and, like Lincoln's sons before them, rode a pony in the White House park. Huntsman and athlete, the president had tennis courts installed directly south of his new executive office.[18] Expressing the rise of national interest in the moral and physical benefits of outdoor life, Roosevelt wrote that sports were "admirable for developing character, besides bestowing on the participants an invaluable fund of health and strength."[19]

In form, Edith Roosevelt's colonial gardens remained unchanged through the Taft administration. The ovals in the west garden outside the president's office were replanted patriotically in red and blue. At the center were Duchesse de Brabant roses. The east garden was yellow and red.[20]

By the time Thomas Woodrow Wilson arrived in 1913 after being president of Princeton University, these boldly colored parterres were out of fashion. Landscape architects, academically trained, continued to work in formal traditions developed in American palace gardens of the 1880s and 1890s, but now they combined the formal with the painterly effects of English Arts and Crafts gardens. A concern for the integration of architecture landscape through structured plantings brought house interiors into alignment with outdoor "rooms" created with hedges around flower beds. The contemporary American country estate house, more domestic than the preceding generation's chateaus and classical in proportions, had bordered flower gardens close to the house leading to naturalized grounds.

Women of Edith Roosevelt's and Ellen Axson Wilson's generation embraced art making and horticulture as intellectual and physical necessities in an increasingly urban world. An American impressionist painter and amateur gardener, Mrs. Wilson had already designed her own loosely formal backyard gardens in Princeton when she arrived in Washington. For Mrs. Wilson, the "big garish White House," with its gilded and paneled interiors, was not a home.[21] To bring a new informality and livability to the president's house, she decided to change the south parterres. The hedge and flower gardens she planted, while intended to be as inviting as her slipcovered interiors, were still symmetrical and formal, their design influenced by American interpretations of Italian Renaissance gardens.

Planning began in earnest after Ellen Wilson's memorable 1913 summer in Cornish, New Hampshire, when she rhapsodized in weekly letters to Woodrow Wilson at the White House about the town's renowned flower gardens. The sculptor Augustus Saint-Gaudens, Charles McKim's colleague on the McMillan Commission, had founded a vibrant colony in Cornish in 1885. The community's members included the muralist of the Library of Congress, Kenyon Cox; Daniel Chester French, sculptor of the 1922 seated president for the Lincoln Memorial; and Charles Adams Platt.

Platt pioneered America's interest in Italian gardens. He discovered on his 1892 trip through over 20 villas a "harmony of arrangement between the house and the surrounding landscape." In Italy, one could be at home outdoors as well as indoors.[22] Like Charles McKim, Platt

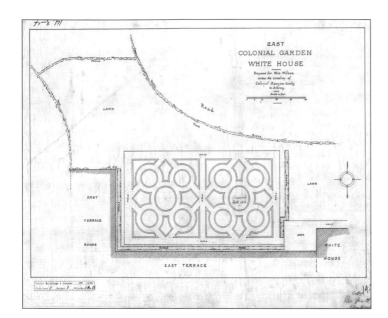 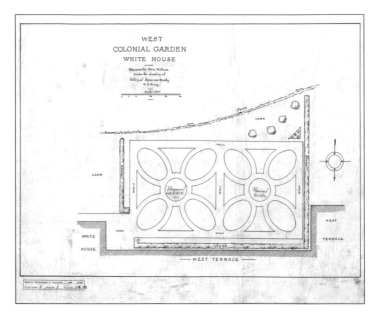

Plans for Edith Roosevelt's colonial garden along the south facade, c. 1902. The parterres were framed by McKim's new east and west wings.

The boxwood garden at Mount Vernon, Virginia, seen here c. 1910, inspired Edith Roosevelt when she created her colonial gardens at the White House.

combined his interest in formal gardens with a reverence for colonial design and the White House.[23] His interests came together at Gwinn, the 1907–14 estate Platt and landscape architect Warren H. Manning designed for industrialist William G. Mather outside Cleveland. Gwinn's resemblance to the White House itself during the Wilson years was notable. On the shore of Lake Erie, the Classical Revival house, built of concrete and stucco, was on axis with a broad open lawn, which had been a feature of American landscape design since Mount Vernon. Parallel to

the house on the south side were two defined gardens, one a wooded glen and the other a formal terrace flower garden with boxed bay trees around a shallow reflecting pool.

George Elberton Burnap, a landscape architect with the federal Office of Public Buildings and Grounds, had already planted Washington's Tidal Basin with cherry trees when Mrs. Wilson hired him in 1913 to transform the White House west garden. A White House gardener since the Cleveland administration, Charles Henlock recalled that Mrs. Wilson

Gwinn, the 1914 suburban Cleveland, Ohio, estate of mining industrialist William G. Mather, by architect Charles A. Platt and landscape architect Warren H. Manning. Its grounds combined colonial American and formal European traditions, as did the White House garden during the Woodrow Wilson years, 1913–21; photograph, 1930.

decided Burnap's initial proposal was too expensive, and he and Mrs. Wilson designed what became the first outdoor rose garden at the White House, planted in the spring of 1914 on the site of Lucy Hayes's 1878 rose conservatory.[24] In fact, the finished garden followed Burnap's final September 1913 plan. It included elements from Dingleton House, the "most beautiful and elaborate house and garden" in Cornish, wrote Mrs. Wilson to her husband in August 1913.[25] The last house in the arts colony designed by Charles Platt, the stucco villa was built in 1904 for two sisters,

Augusta and Emily Slade. Its Italianate rose garden, on axis with the house, was planned by Emily Slade and Platt.[26]

At the White House, Henlock removed Mrs. Roosevelt's west colonial parterre. He enclosed the space, traditionally open to the south park, with California boxwood hedges, clipped with Beaux-Arts refinement into a broad cone shape resembling the form of the hemlock hedge at Dingleton. When Mrs. Wilson requested a "President's Walk" to connect the house to the new Oval Office, Burnap proposed a walkway along the 132-foot-long

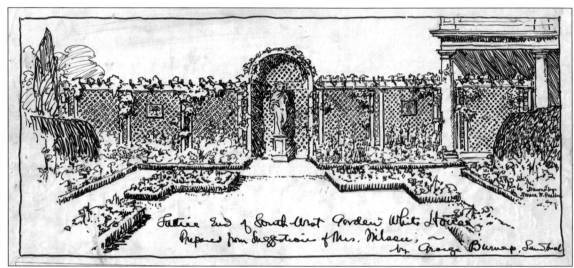

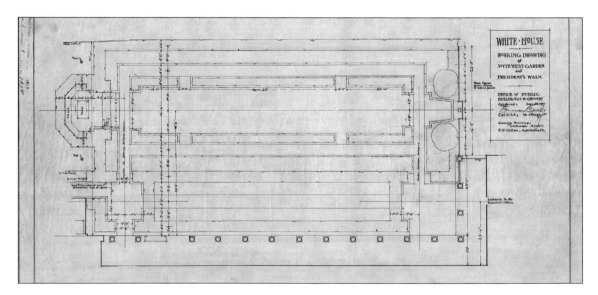

Top: 1907 rose garden and statue of Pan at the estate Dingleton House in Cornish, New Hampshire, by Augusta Slade and Charles Adams Platt. This private Italianate garden influenced the design of Ellen Wilson's 1913 west garden at the White House, photograph, c. 1920. Middle: George E. Burnap's 1913 sketch for the painting gallery as suggested by Ellen Wilson for her rose garden room. Art displayed out of doors was considered a civic improvement. Bottom: George E. Burnap's September 1913 plan for Mrs. Wilson's west garden.

Top: Ellen A. Wilson Rose Garden with statue of Pan; domestic practicality often trumped design at the White House; the lattice screened the laundry yard outside the president's offices. Bottom: The hedge and curved bench in First Lady Ellen Wilson's west rose garden. The president's walk along the colonnade to the west wing office had topiary arches. Photographs, c. 1917.

Looking west over the Wilson southeast garden. Its design combined the naturalism of Arts and Crafts gardens with the formality of estate parterres; c. 1920.

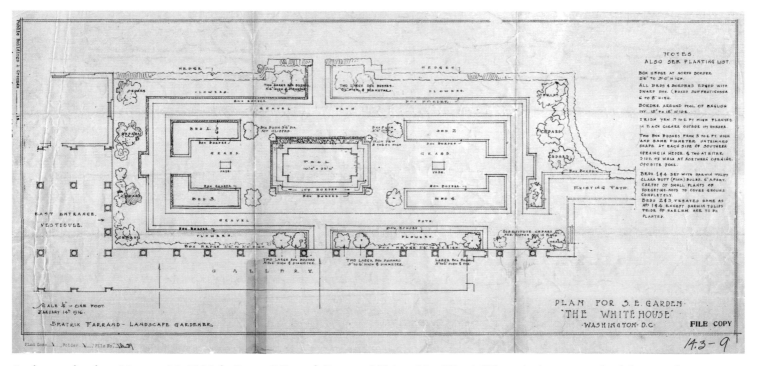

Southeast garden plan of January 14, 1916, by Beatrix J. Farrand. Begun in 1913 for Mrs. Ellen A. Wilson, the design was realized three years later.

Looking east over the southeast Wilson garden. Charles F. McKim's east wing closed the garden from public view. Flower beds bordered with boxwood unified both south gardens, but the west garden was deeper because of the president's walk; c. 1916.

Beatrix J. Farrand watercolor sketch for the east garden, undated [late 1915, early 1916]. The lily pool was 10 feet by 22 feet, and was framed by iris and cypress.

President Wilson and his second wife, Edith, in the southeast garden, c. 1916.

west colonnade, ending at a classical archway. This walk became a gravel path with topiary arches at each end. A hedge below the General Jackson *Magnolia grandiflora* at the south portico stair formed a niche where a curved white bench faced west across rose beds to a statue of Pan, the god of nature, under a rose-covered wooden arch. Similarly, at Dingleton, a Pan figure stood beyond an arbor at one end of the circular rose garden. When it was completed, the White House west garden, wrote Mrs. Wilson's daughter Eleanor, "had a suggestion of Italy, a lovely illusion of vistas that make it by far the most attractive of the two [south gardens]."[27]

Behind the sculpture, Henlock, per Burnap's plan, built a decorative lattice screen to close the view from the garden to the White House laundry outside the executive wing. A sketch prepared by the landscape architect in consultation with Mrs. Wilson shows that the first lady intended to hang paintings or reliefs on the decorative fence, completing the conception of the space as a private outdoor room.

Mrs. Wilson's west garden was exemplary of the turn-of-the-century revivalist garden that emerged as American designers, through university programs and travel, studied the period gardens of England, France and Italy. In the 1880s, pioneer woman critic and proponent of a landscaped America, Mariana Griswold Van Rensselaer called for the elevation of

landscape design from the domain of the gardener-designer to a profession on a par with architecture and painting.[28] This became possible when landscape architects like George Burnap graduated from academic programs.

Andrew Jackson Downing's conception of landscape as a civilizing force was fully embraced by Burnap's generation of trained professionals. Through the American Civic Association, endorsed by President Wilson, preservationists, architects, and city officials advocated for professionally planned parks and gardens that "created a positive environment capable of influencing human thought and behavior."[29] J. Horace McFarland, the president of the association, wrote that beauty encouraged order, while "ugliness tends towards moral decadence."[30] This was the beauty of ideals studied in academic programs. Proportion and balance now guided the landscaping of not just the president's park and Mrs. Wilson's new south flower gardens, but private and public landscapes throughout America. In these carefully conceived and groomed spaces, art, in the form of statues, wall reliefs, and architectural elements, contributed to an overall effect intended to enhance day-to-day life in America.

Beatrix Jones Farrand was the niece of Edith Wharton, a friend of Mariana Van Rensselaer, and one of the first women to become a

At times of war, the White House grounds have accommodated public need. President Wilson ordered sheep to groom the south lawn when World War I brought labor shortages; c. 1918.

landscape architect n America.[31] Since 1912 Farrand had designed gardens for Princeton University and was well acquainted with the White House through her friendship with Edith and Teddy Roosevelt. Ellen Wilson approached the architect to redesign the colonial gardens. In 1913 Farrand presented a watercolor for the east garden. Her plan, later simplified, called for boxwood flower beds and classical sculpture that would have complimented the Pan statue in Burnap's west parterre.[32] Like Ellen Shipman in the East and Florence Yoch in California, Farrand combined the formalism pioneered by Charles Platt with the color and naturalism of the English Arts and Crafts garden. Her plan for the east terrace, while conforming to the geometry of the west garden, was a lyrical counterbalance to Burnap's clipped Italianate hedges and arches. Cedars at the portico stairway and at the east wing softly defined the space. At its center, water lilies floated in a reflecting pool framed by flower beds and loosely trimmed boxwood. Faux-bois garden stools and benches from Theodore Roosevelt's administration created a sense of intimacy beneath the looming south facade.[33]

Mrs. Wilson died of Bright's disease in August 1914. Her east garden was only realized two years later with the support of Woodrow Wilson's second wife, Edith Bolling Galt Wilson.[34] In the summer of 1915, the president had courted her in the White House garden by quoting poet Thomas Edward Brown's "My Garden." The verse echoes with Emersonian transcendental sentiments and suggests the spiritual renewal Ellen Wilson's south gardens provided the president:

> A Garden is a lovesome thing, God wot!
> Rose plot,
> Fringed pool.
> Fern grot—
> The veriest school
> Of Peace; and yet the fool
> Contends that God is not—
> Not God! in Gardens! when the eve is cool?
> Nay, but I have a sign:
> 'Tis very sure God walks in mine.[35]

In the Wilson years the White House landscape, like the estates of America's industrialists and bankers, combined the elegance of parterre gardens with the sylvan retreat of a surrounding park. Echoing its colonial beginnings, a pastoral touch returned to the White House grounds during World War I. Faced with national labor shortages, Wilson had sheep brought to Washington to groom the outer reaches of the president's grounds. They grazed in the south park until they grew from 18 to an unruly flock of 40, eating hedges and flowers in the president's own newly planted garden.[36]

Caroline Harrison replaced textiles, carpets, curtains, and wall treatments with vaguely neoclassical designs to make the old mansion's interiors more palatial. Here in the Red Room c. 1890, Mrs. Harrison retained Julia Grant's still-glamorous Herter Brothers seating furniture from 1874 and also kept Louis Tiffany's nearly-new cabinets and center table made for Chester Arthur.

INTERIORS

The formality of the president's garden at the turn of the century was modest compared to the heroic redecorating of the White House interiors, begun in 1888 with the arrival of Benjamin Harrison, a Civil War general and former United States senator. His wife, Caroline, the daughter of a minister and university president, took her role as White House homemaker seriously, obtaining funds for major upgrades of decrepit and dirty service areas as well an ambitious modernizing and redecorating of the upstairs that pushed the house away from mansion and toward a fashionable palace.

In 1891, Thomas Edison's company installed electric lighting at the White House. The change was as dramatic as the switch from candles to gaslight. The olives, blue-greens, oranges, and rusty reds of Chester Arthur's Aesthetic Movement interiors must have seemed muddy in the hot-white light of incandescent bulbs. Another effect of the new electric light was to make even the upper reaches of the 18-foot White House ceilings visible, and Mrs. Harrison took advantage of this change to create a historical gallery of portraits of the White House's past occupants in the state rooms.

The general trend in the Harrison era was simplification, according to 1880s notions of simple. The East Room was mostly left alone, but while channels were dug in the walls for new wiring, the other state-floor interiors

Left: Harrison Blue Room, c. 1890. A founder of the Daughters of the American Revolution with a love of White House history, Caroline Harrison left in place the Buchanan 1859 parlor set by Vollmer & Company but covered it in opulent cut velvet, a rich textile found in industrialists' houses. The Monroe 1817 pier table by Pierre-Antoine Bellangé was not only useful, but by this time inspired romantic images of Napoleonic France. Right: McKinley Blue Room, 1899. With its new colonial frieze and overmantel, this decor was the first conscious attempt to evoke the Federal origins of the White House.

were scraped to the bare plaster. Mrs. Harrison's decorator, E. S. Yergason of the Hartford furnishings firm of William H. Post & Company replaced the custom-made exoticism of Tiffany's work with a new haut-bourgeois neoclassicism. The carpeting, wallpapers, upholstery, and applied wall decorations were strictly standard fare, selected from ready-made stock aimed at well-to-do clientele. The overall classical theme of the Harrison redecoration underscores the growing influence of the Parisian École des Beaux-Arts on American architects and designers. More than just another revival of the classical taste into which the White House was born, the new Harrison interiors represented a distinct shift in favor of historically based styles over modern ones. The 1890s saw the emergence of the Art Nouveau movement in Europe, but Caroline Harrison was turning the White House irrevocably in the different direction of mainstream American taste.

In the Blue Room, Mrs. Harrison used blue damask wallpaper against varnished white woodwork picked out in gold. The ceiling got a complex pastel makeover in shades of pink, blue, gray, and white. It was the first room in the White House to make a nod to the house's neoclassical roots. Colonial Revival was still a new style in 1889, and "restoring" the house would not have crossed Mrs. Harrison's mind.[37] However, a growing awareness of the neoclassical origins of the White House architecture would have made classically derived motifs seem more appropriate than the

overheated exoticism of Louis Comfort Tiffany. The great height of the windows was reduced by elaborate neoclassical fretwork grilles backed with blue glass, above electric blue damask curtains that harmonized with the dark blue cut-velvet upholstery.[38]

The Red and Green rooms received the same grille-over-curtain treatment, the colored glass matching the scheme of the room, as did the State Dining Room, where Tiffany's flamboyant yellow scheme was toned down to a more ochre yellow, tuned to the new luster of electricity.

In the Harrison family's private quarters, the deep Aesthetic Movement colors applied a decade before gave way to a brighter palette, with wallpapers of repeating patterns of stylized foliage and scrolls applied in horizontal bands to reduce the intimidating height of the ceilings.

Ida McKinley simplified the Blue Room even more by 1899 with ivory-enameled moldings applied to the walls and pale blue wall covering and upholstery. A new frieze of loosely Adamesque swags and medallions emphasized the colonial character of the redecoration. In the family quarters Mrs. McKinley modernized even more with softer colors and less boldly contrasting patterns.

In September 1901, with Theodore Roosevelt sworn in as president, the redefinition of the presidential dream house as a palace advanced quickly. Compared to the palaces of American plutocrats, the White House was a seedy hotel. A fortysomething couple with a large family,

Harrison State Dining Room, 1893. Although Louis C. Tiffany's decorative schemes were removed because they were too "artistic" and not palatial enough, Tiffany's rectangular dining chairs and huge hammered-copper sconces, designed for Chester Arthur in 1882, remained in place, along with the c. 1853 Pierce console tables by Anthony and Henry Jenkins of Baltimore. New to the room are Caroline Harrison's wall and window treatments, as well as the window grilles with amber glass behind them.

Edith and Theodore Roosevelt both understood making do with old furniture and department-store decorating, but it now seemed that the president's house was meant to be better than that.[39] People didn't buy palaces ready-made, and the appointment of New York architects McKim, Mead & White to oversee the transformation placed the Roosevelts on a par with the industrialist palace builders of the late Gilded Age. The architects brought a mature Beaux-Arts style to the project, highly influenced by Roman and Renaissance models studied in Europe and most fully expressed in the buildings of the White City of the 1893 World's Columbian Exposition in Chicago.

Although the White House transformation of 1902–3 was referred to in its day as "repair and restoration," the changes to the first floor were drastic. The overhaul was meant to settle forever the question as to whether the White House was an appropriate place for America's president, bringing the house up to the accepted standard for the rich and powerful of the day. The White House was compared by Roosevelt to Mount Vernon as a national monument kept in trust for the people of the country. Paying lip service to the ever-more-potent Colonial Revival, Roosevelt praised the White House's "stately simplicity" as expressive of the time it was built but simultaneously created a handy loophole for the architects by saying that "so far as is compatible with living therein it should be kept as it originally was."[40]

Despite the rhetoric, the work carried out by Stanford White for his firm involved almost no effort at preservation. McKim, Mead & White are celebrated for their achievements in the Colonial Revival, but one must remember that this was the eclectic "free-style" Colonial Revival of

Table, Herter Brothers, New York, 1875, purchased by Julia Grant for the Red Room. Louis C. Tiffany might have found it outmoded, but the table was still good furniture and continued to be used by economy-minded first ladies. It is seen here in the Harrison second-floor oval library, 1893.

the late Gilded Age, not the correct, academic Colonial Revival that emerged after World War I.

The best change to the function of the house was the removal of the busy president's offices from the second floor and the creation of the west wing. This division of living from work space also made the White House more like a European palace, in which administrative, social, and private spaces were strictly separate.[41] The second-floor offices would not have been appropriate according to the original English country-house model for the White House, but the need for space had made it necessary. The second-floor space that had served as a cabinet room since Jackson's day became the president's study, the walls covered in tan burlap, with bookcases taken from the oval library. Roosevelt's office and cabinet room in the new temporary wing were decorated with burlap walls in colonial green. They looked like the double parlor of a Greek Revival town house

and echoed living rooms of upscale suburban houses being built all over the country. By 1908, new plans for an expanded west wing were being drawn up, including the Oval Office, which eventually became the symbol of the presidency.

Along with the reorganization of the offices, the entire basement of the White House was transformed into a secondary state floor by McKim, Mead & White. Rooms that had been used for storage or for servants since 1800 got a new lease on life. The basement's oval room became the Diplomatic Reception Room and it was initially furnished with all of the Buchanan gilded furniture from the Blue Room upstairs.

The most egregious alteration to Hoban's plan was to remove the main staircase and expand the State Dining Room to accommodate larger dinners. The result was a symmetrical T-shaped entrance hall, with the doors of the East Room and State Dining Room facing each

The palace-style upgrades made by Mrs. Harrison were largely restricted to the state rooms. President Harrison was content to use the Philadelphia retail store furniture purchased in 1861 by Mary Lincoln for the Prince of Wales bedroom, seen here c. 1890.

other. The hall was classical, evoking the Grand Trianon at Versailles in its horizontal sweep and paired columns. This design paralleled similar arrangements in recent American palaces that allowed stately procession from one vast room to another down a wide stone-floored hall. [see page 149]

Horace Trumbauer's massive Lynnewood Hall in Elkins Park, Pennsylvania, built for self-made public transit millionaire Peter A. B. Widener between 1898 and 1900, had just such a plan. With the doors of its ballroom and dining room facing each other down a marble corridor, Lynnewood merged the processional spaces of a large English country house with the various genteel functions that had become necessities in the late Victorian home—not just a billiard room and a library, but a smoking room and art galleries and reception rooms. Added to all of this was the latest in technology: electricity, plumbing, central heating.[42]

The new White House dining room was paneled in carved oak made to the architect's design by Herter Brothers, the New York firm that supplied Julia Grant with furniture for the Red Room. An elaborate baroque plaster ceiling was added, and the Monroe-era marble mantels from either end of

the old room were replaced with a massive new one of carved stone in the center of the longer west wall. Silver-plated chandeliers and sconces, with imported "Flemish" tapestries, created a baronial look. Rooms like this and the 1901 dining room of steel magnate Henry Phipps in New York called to mind late 17th-century state rooms in English ducal palaces.[43]

The moose heads in the State Dining Room were a personal addition of the president's but typified the use of game trophies on the walls and floors of homes in the era.[44] The mounted animal heads express the complex relationship between America and its wilderness. While great wealth came from exploiting the forests and mines of the West, the disappearance of unspoiled nature due to industrialism resulted in a national cry for preservation. The moose itself was seen as a uniquely American animal, and, odd as it may seem today, the mounted heads in the State Dining Room symbolized the president's simultaneous commitment to conquering nature for progress and to protecting it as part of our national heritage.[45]

Inspired by Napoleon's rooms at the Château de Compiègne that Charles McKim and the McMillan Commission had visited, the new Roosevelt

President Harrison's bedroom, c. 1890, used most of the furniture Mary Lincoln had purchased for the Prince of Wales bedroom in 1861, including the center table and chairs, by John Henry Belter & Company, New York, and the accompanying dressing chest, which did not match exactly but was part of the original suite.

Blue Room was radical in its rich austerity. The French emperor was much admired by Gilded Age industrialists as a man who got things done, and neither the designer nor the client saw any irony in the Blue Room's decor being in a democratic president's house.[46] A Louis XVI–style white marble mantelpiece with ormolu mounts replaced the Victorian colonial one of the 1890s. Hidden doors connected all three of the parlors and improved circulation during state events. The walls of deep blue corded silk contrasted with the white-enameled woodwork and embroidered frieze and chair rail in a Greek key design. The matching curtains were elaborately swagged over imperial valance rods.[47] A crystal chandelier and sconces replicating 18th-century models made in New York replaced Julia Grant's gasolier.[48] The blue-and-gold Empire brocade on the furniture was also from a New York firm. With polished herringbone oak parquet on the floor instead of carpeting, the room looked more like an Empire "saloon" (drawing room) than it had since the Monroes.

The Green Room had walls and curtains in deep green velvet "copied from an old piece of Genoese velvet," while the multicolored tapestry upholstery coordinated with a modern floral-bordered carpet on the new parquet floor. One of the Monroe State Dining Room marble mantels was placed here, along with new crystal electric fixtures that were modern interpretations of French style rather than reproductions. The Red Room got the other Monroe marble mantelpiece, new crystal light fixtures, and red-on-red Genoese velvet walls and curtains that complemented the red damask upholstery. While adhering to the traditional colors of the rooms, these velvet walls recalled Italian Renaissance palazzi, a major source of inspiration for McKim, Mead & White's buildings.[49] An antique oriental rug on the floor picked up the deep reds, and Martha Washington's portrait, commissioned in the late 19th century for the East Room, hung for the first time near the Stuart portrait of her husband. All the paintings in the state rooms were portraits of historical figures. Only upstairs in the private quarters did any other genre of American art appear, a tradition that lasted until the Kennedy era.

Herter Brothers hung the fabric walls for the three parlors and produced the East Room paneling, replacing Julia Grant's interior of 1873. For this room, the pre-Napoleonic interiors at the Château de Compiègne were the source of inspiration. The massive American-made crystal chandeliers

Hygienic brass beds, United States, 1890s, for the McKinley administration. Metal beds became popular in the late Gilded Age because they prevented bedbugs and were easier to clean. They were decidedly nonmansion and reflected a pragmatic approach to furnishing the family quarters. In Ida McKinley's bedroom, 1897.

Center table, United States, 1890s, in Ida McKinley's bedroom, 1897. By the end of the 19th century, factory-made colonial-style furniture both offered novelty to American homemakers and evoked nostalgia in a rapidly changing world.

Left: McKinley cabinet room, 1898, with Julia Grant's Pottier & Stymus furniture from 1869. The presidential office spaces, in use since Andrew Jackson's time, were removed from the private quarters in 1902, creating a luxurious private apartment on the second floor of the White House and forever separating public and private areas within the residence. Right: Milton Shield as displayed in the McKinley second-floor oval library in 1898.

and mantelpiece torchères, along with the red marble mantelpieces, completed the regal French look of the room.

Such French ballroom interiors were almost a requirement for American palaces. McKim, Mead & White had designed a related room for Rosecliff, the Hermann Oelrichs house in Newport, and their competitors Carrère & Hastings made certain the New York City house of their client Henry Phipps, a steel magnate, had a ballroom spacious enough to receive that city's renowned elite.

On the second floor of the White House, changes were dramatic but far less luxurious than on the state floor. In this, the Roosevelt palace differed from industrialists' palaces, where money was no object and the same level of luxury was carried throughout the house. The oval library remained the family's living room. Its Victorian mantelpiece was replaced by a prim classical one, and bookcases were moved to the adjacent presidential study. Five new bathrooms were added to the second floor, along with pale maple floors, chintz curtains, and light printed wallpapers that gave the rooms a modern colonial look. Victorian mantelpieces remained in several of the upstairs rooms, as well as objects Edith Roosevelt had not let the architects throw out.

The state floor's palatial grandeur was largely unaltered during the Taft and Wilson administrations, but Wilson's first wife, Ellen, hated the "gloomy" state rooms. Her only rebellion against the Beaux-Arts darkness

was to remove the stuffed animal heads from the State Dining Room and to have white dimity slipcovers, curtains, and even coverings for the silk walls made for summer use in the Red, Green, and Blue rooms. This rather imperial gesture to lighten up her best parlors reflects the growing influence of such early 20th-century tastemakers as Elsie de Wolfe, who advocated brighter, lighter rooms through the elimination of dark draperies and heavy wall coverings.

Mrs. Wilson also made changes upstairs that amplified the distinctly unpalatial trend begun by the Roosevelts in the private quarters. Using a fairly modest budget and stock goods from New York decorator Robert Talmadge, Mrs. Wilson replaced the dark burlap the Roosevelts had put in the upstairs hall with amber Japanese grass cloth. She introduced bright floral chintzes and pale paint and wallpaper colors in the bedrooms.[50] This was still historicizing decoration, although the colors and textures were modern.

The sitting room next to the Wilsons' delft-blue and white master bedroom combined the Lincoln bed and Belter table with oddly folksy textiles. Instead of the gold and purple silk Mary Lincoln had once thought appropriate, Mrs. Wilson ordered upholstery and curtains of handwoven fabric by rural Tennessean Elmeda McHargue Walker. The dark blue and white "double chariot wheel" design was based on early 19th-century coverlets being collected by suburban antiquers and

Theodore Roosevelt entrance hall, c. 1903. Both James Hoban's marble columns of 1814 and Louis C. Tiffany's stained-glass screen of 1882 were replaced by classical paired columns that evoked the Grand Trianon at Versailles and created a space that was impressive rather than luxurious, palatial rather than homelike.

Ballroom, John Henry Hammond house, New York, c. 1906. Grand French-style ballrooms as large as the East Room became standard features of American industrialists' palaces by 1900.

museums in this period when an authentic America was being supported.[51] The matching carpeting was loomed in strips by North Carolinian Allie Josephine Mast, and the handwoven coverlet for the Lincoln bed came from a Washington craft show held to support the Southern Industrial Educational Association, of which Mrs. Wilson was honorary president.[52] Widely publicized as the "Blue Mountain Room," it struck a decidedly antipalace note. Perhaps, by paying homage to Abraham Lincoln's homespun rural origins, the textiles made the ornate Victorian furniture palatable by overlaying it with nostalgia for preindustrial America.

In the second-floor oval room, the McKim, Mead & White finishes brightened the interior with lighter colors, and the floor was covered with a plain velvet pile carpet. Old furniture was recovered, now appreciated for its sense of an authentic America. A piano made the large living space into an informal music room. Aside from a few old portraits, the art in this room, as well as in the upstairs hallway, was largely modern work by

American impressionists. Several of the paintings were by Ellen Wilson herself, who had exhibited at both the Chicago Institute of Art and the Pennsylvania Academy in Philadelphia.[53] The conversational grouping of the furniture huddled around the fireplace reflected the typical arrangement in most American living rooms by this time. Central heating had made fireplaces functionally unnecessary by the 1880s, but they persisted as decorative and symbolic focal points in the American home. Embraced as part of the Colonial Revival, fireplaces appeared in only the living rooms of most American homes by the 1910s, and sometimes in dining rooms. Precisely because they were unnecessary, fireplaces became status symbols, and the grander a house, the more fireplaces it had.

Edith Bolling became the second Mrs. Wilson in 1916, and within a year she took the first permanent step in moving the White House away from its role as a home and toward its new status as a museum. Caroline Harrison and Edith Roosevelt had started the presidential china collections, but Mrs. Wilson formalized them as a public collection.

East Room, c. 1903. Charles McKim specified gold silk damask draperies, although President Roosevelt wanted red. Ultimately, the architect's palace taste trumped the president's villa preferences. Americans turned to French precedents to decorate ballrooms. For the White House, Marcotte & Company of New York supplied gilt benches inspired by Louis XVI furniture at the Château de Compiègne.

From the Diplomats' Cloak Room, she created the China Room in 1917, prompted initially by Mrs. Wilson's fear that the Mission-style display cases out in the corridor, used for the china collection since Edith Roosevelt's time, would get bumped by tourists. The China Room was the first place in the White House set up for the display and preservation of historic relics in a museum-like setting.[54]

FURNISHINGS

Despite the China Room's representing a first tentative step in preserving historical artifacts in the White House, the historic meaning of surviving old furnishings was generally given short shrift during the palace years. The palatial interiors of the Theodore Roosevelt White House had to be furnished with appropriately palatial objects. Only on the second floor, which no longer held offices and thus was entirely shielded from public eyes, were stylistically out-of-date artifacts offered a safe haven from the relentless tide of progress.

Just as serious interest in the historical importance of the White House was growing, President Theodore Roosevelt authorized the last major dispersal of White House furnishings. Roosevelt's wife Edith salvaged a significant number of Victorian objects for the family quarters, including Mary Lincoln's huge Victorian bedstead and the Belter table.[55] As McKim, Mead & White transformed the White House from Victorian mansion to a Franco-Georgian palace in keeping with the late Gilded Age, they shifted the nature of its furnishings in the same direction.

McKim, Mead & White turned to a celebrated Victorian cabinetmaking firm to produce new "period" furniture for the Roosevelt dream house. Leon Marcotte & Company had been operating in New York since the 1850s and had been a major player in the cult of all things French. Marcotte produced furniture for the White House in a mixture of French and English styles that typified the furniture being used in new industrialists' palaces all over the nation. The gilded banquettes and console tables made for the East Room were the most

Gold and white furniture, Marcotte & Company, New York, for Theodore Roosevelt Blue Room, c. 1903. Custom made and based on Napoleon's furniture for the Château de Compiègne, Marcotte's suite was ideal for the White House's palace years.

Theodore Roosevelt Green Room, c. 1903, with white-painted furniture by A. H. Davenport & Company, Boston. Colorful, elegant, and distinctly upper-class, these items were seen as right for the new White House because of their Anglo-French style. In the center of the room is a specimen marble table purchased for Mrs. Tyler in the early 1840s, which brought a historical note to the space. The few old objects that survived the architects' purge of the Victorian White House had to be grand or possess substantial historical association.

American-made period-style reproduction and upholstered furniture in two views of the Theodore Roosevelt Red Room, c. 1903.

The State Dining Room as reimagined by McKim, Mead and White for President and Mrs. Theodore Roosevelt, c. 1903. With its oak paneling, silvered baroque lighting fixtures, tapestries, and taxidermy heads, the transformed space evoked the palatial dining rooms of America's industrial elite, and—quite intentionally—the aristocratic interiors of English stately homes such as the Duke of Devonshire's Chatsworth. The furniture by A. H. Davenport & Co. consciously drew on a melange of newly popular Anglo-American styles—Queen Anne, William & Mary, Regency—that managed to be simultaneously Colonial Revival and English Country house.

Palatial-scale furniture by Stanford White for A. H. Davenport & Company, Boston, for the Theodore Roosevelt State Dining Room, 1903.

purely French, although far from exact reproductions. The spectacular gilded Steinway piano made for this room (a gift from the manufacturer in celebration and as an advertisement of its own golden anniversary) had carved eagles and a lushly painted case by Thomas Wilmer Dewing. It is a superb Beaux-Arts fantasy, both patriotic and imperial. Like the Marcotte banquettes, the piano is a palatial object, as different as could be from the domesticated pianoforte that Dolley Madison put in her best parlor.

Marcotte's Blue Room suite was dominated by fairly accurate reproductions of chairs made for Napoleon at the Château de Compiègne. In an age when many rich Americans admired Napoleon, one can see the appeal of the suite modeled after French originals. Certainly Marcotte, like Charles McKim, would have appreciated that the chateau itself, rebuilt by 1788, looked rather like the north facade of Hoban's White House. The Napoleonic pieces must have been intended to evoke the Monroe furniture, of which a lone pier table survived in the Blue Room.[56]

Marcotte also made a group of white-painted cane-back side chairs, combining English Hepplewhite and Louis XVI designs. Some of the shield-backed chairs were used in the Roosevelt Red Room, along with American-made reproduction mahogany Chippendale tea tables, velvet-covered Renaissance armchairs, and an ormolu-mounted Empire vitrine cabinet. This mixture of styles, with the comfortable tufted sofas, was a palatial swan song of Victorian eclecticism. The use of antiques, or furniture that looked like them, was typical in elegant American homes from New York to California. This quasi-academic baronial taste soon fossilized as "good" in the minds of America's tastemakers and decorators.

Such conscious layering of historical styles was a nod to the White House as a historical place. Esther Singleton's highly successful two-volume work *The Story of the White House,* published in 1907, amplified this new historical awareness.

Boston furniture maker A. H. Davenport was the other major source used by McKim, Mead & White for the White House. Davenport specialized in English and colonial-style furniture but also made the white-painted

Dining room, Henry Phipps house, New York, c. 1901. This grand city dining room was decorated for an English shoemaker turned American steel magnate in the same baronial style as the Theodore Roosevelt State Dining Room.

Franco-English furniture for the Green Room, which reflected American upper-class taste and suited the house's new architectural mélange. In one postcard view, the Roosevelt Green Room still has the circular mahogany center table used in the Hayes Green Room. It must have struck an appropriately "colonial" note. The 1876 Viennese fire screen presented to Ulysses S. Grant after the Centennial Exhibition was also displayed in the Roosevelt Green Room. Undoubtedly considered an atrocity in 1902, its association with a great military hero and Republican president would have justified its presence.[57]

Davenport's furniture for the enlarged State Dining Room was more thoroughly English (and thus colonial by association). Very little was generally known about actual colonial furniture by 1900, and thus differences between English and American forms were not clear (or important) to most people.[58] The huge dining table was neoclassical, mimicking much smaller early 19th-century American tables. Colonial Revival designers used neoclassical models because the drop-leaf tables actually used in colonial America wouldn't have been appropriate for a room

like this. The two styles of chairs selected by McKim, Mead & White were both English but strongly evoked the colonial. The Queen Anne side chairs were of a style long extinct by the time Hoban designed the White House, but Queen Anne would become one of the most beloved of colonial styles in early 20th-century American homes because of its simplicity. The grandiose William and Mary armchairs would have been 100 years out of date in George Washington's dream house, but they set an English tone that appealed to prosperous Americans at the time.[59]

The monumental sideboards and console tables designed by Stanford White were also neoclassical in style, based on European prototypes. These were in the right style for the original White House, but the Roosevelts and their guests would have seen them as one more version of colonial. The State Dining Room as it existed from 1902 through the early Truman administration was furnished like dining rooms in private houses and clubs all over the United States.[60]

Edith Roosevelt inadvertently introduced the first modern-style furniture to the White House with the 1904 purchase of a pair of china

Theodore Roosevelt's temporary executive office, with green burlap walls, 1902, was functional and followed a restrained Colonial Revival taste that suited its administrative purpose. The self-consciously European grandeur of the residential interiors contrasted with the no-nonsense American-businessman look of the executive wing.

First Oval Office in the finished west wing, with green burlap walls, c. 1909, for William Howard Taft. The shape of the new office echoed the oval rooms in the residence, in particular the second-floor oval room, which had served as both sitting room and presidential study. This repetition provided design continuity with the original Hoban building.

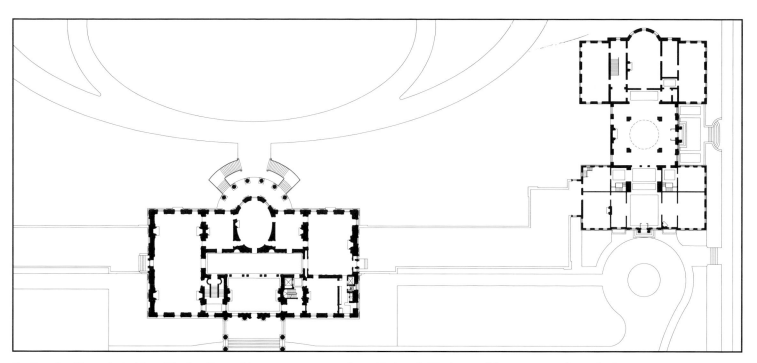

For President Taft, who had been Theodore Roosevelt's secretary of state, architect Nathan C. Wyeth expanded McKim, Mead & White's executive office wing (right) in 1909 and built the first oval office.

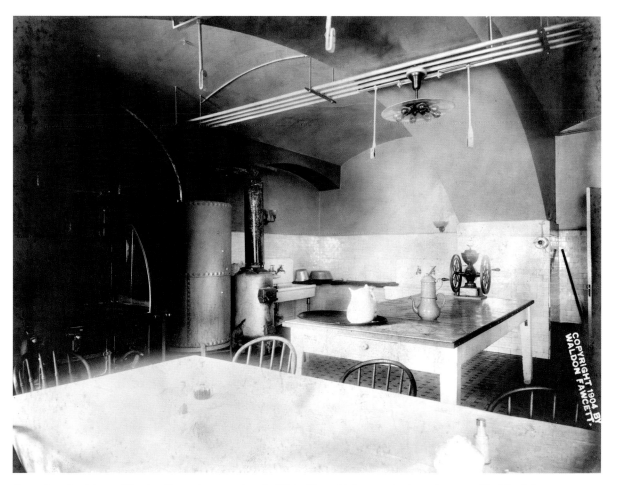

Even after the elaborate Theodore Roosevelt renovation, the White House kitchen remained merely serviceable. Until changes in immigration laws reduced the availability of domestic help and technological innovations brought new efficiencies later in the century, the American kitchen remained the domain of servants who were expected to live and work in modest spaces, 1904.

Left: Wilson east hall, looking northeast. In the space that had been the president's office lobby until 1902, Ellen Wilson arranged old objects in modern ways that were clean and uncluttered. Right: West hall, where Ellen Wilson's use of old pieces in the modern decor recalls museum furniture installations of the time. She gives pride of place to things that must have been ugly to her but that deserved respect because of their presumed history; photographs, c. 1916.

cabinets made by Gustav Stickley's furniture shop in Eastwood (Syracuse), New York. The cabinets held pieces of White House porcelain that Caroline Harrison had begun bringing together in the 1890s. They were placed in the newly remodeled ground-floor entrance corridor, where their appeal was functional, not aesthetic. Stickley's Mission -tyle furniture was aimed at an intellectual middle-class audience, who chose to lead simple lives in well-crafted but modest houses. Mrs. Roosevelt did not have this in mind and may never have known who made these cabinets, because later versions were made to order by a local shop. From this point forward there was little place for modern-style decorative objects within the historic structure. As the 20th century progressed, historical, not modern, style interested the families who lived in George Washington's dream house.

The only conspicuous addition to the furnishings of the White House under Helen Taft was the custom-made white grand piano she purchased for the Blue Room. Echoing its associations of feminine culture back to Dolley Madison's days, Mrs. Taft's piano was also a clever tool to transform the somewhat useless and forbidding Blue Room into an elegant music room—a constant feature in Beaux-Arts palaces in the early 20th century.

Both Ellen and Edith Wilson continued the new "tradition" of using antiques and reproductions to furnish the state rooms and the private rooms upstairs at the White House. The second Mrs. Wilson ended the hegemony of French and English ceramics that had kept American porcelain off the president's table. The Theodore Roosevelts chose Wedgwood over any American firm in 1902, because no American name came to mind. Mrs. Wilson, however, ordered her porcelain from the Washington department store Dulin & Martin in 1917. The Wilson service was produced by Lenox China in its Trenton, New Jersey, factory, where it had made fine porcelain since 1889. Lenox was the first American manufacturer to compete successfully with Wedgwood, Haviland, and Meissen. With a richly gilded border and restrained design, the Wilson Lenox was perfectly suited to McKim, Mead & White's aesthetic.

When all finished, Ellen Wilson had moderated the formal interiors of the palace-era White House with romantic ideas of an imagined past. In its white splendor, the renovated house was poised for the tumultuous 20th century, when the building's historic importance would shape the decorating ideals of presidential first ladies.

❖ ❖ ❖

In the upstairs hall, Ellen Wilson used Oriental rugs on hardwood floors, as did most affluent Americans by this period. Light colors and spare, functional arrangements made even the old furniture seem less fussy. The 1829 Jackson East Room tables, by Anthony Quervelle of New York, can be seen in the central hall, c. 1916.

The Wilsons' second-floor oval room was used as an informal living area and music room. Top: Contemporary American paintings distinguished the Wilsons' living quarters. The furniture arrangement focused on the fireplace, which was no longer used for heating but was a reminder of the nation's colonial past. Bottom: With a piano, a colonial-style bookcase, and plain carpeting, the room purposely offered the kind of comfortable family retreat first established in the same room by Abigail Adams, c. 1916.

Top and bottom: The Wilson's sitting room, c. 1916, was called the Blue Mountain Room after its blue-and-white textiles and carpet woven by Appalachian craftswomen. It retained its 1850s mantelpiece and the Lincoln bed. The combination of homespun craft and old-fashioned Victoriana made the room an homage to pre-industrial America. The adjoining Wilson bedroom had modern twin beds.

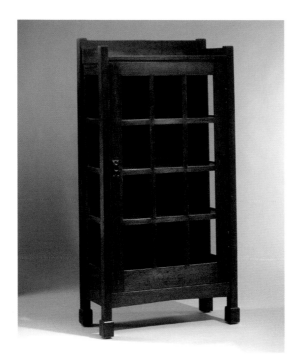

Top: Mission-style cabinet, Gustav Stickley, Syracuse, New York, purchased by Edith Roosevelt to display the collection of White House china that she was gathering, c. 1902. Neither the style nor the philosophy of Arts and Crafts furniture fit the newly palatial White House. Bottom: Gilded Steinway piano, patriotically decorated with shields of the original 13 states by Thomas Wilmer Dewing. New York. Donated to the Theodore Roosevelt East Room in 1902, it was first played January 22, 1903.

Top: Ground-floor China Room, seen here in 1931. The White House's first museum-like space was created for Edith Bolling Wilson, Woodrow Wilson's second wife, in 1917. Bottom: Service plate, Lenox Incorporated, Trenton, New Jersey, from the Wilson service, 1917. Edith Wilson chose Lenox china because it was the most prestigious porcelain made in America at the time, available exclusively through the finest department and jewelry stores. Lenox competed successfully with foreign imports.

AMERICAN SUBURBAN HOMES

Top left: Sunset Hill, Eugene D. Stocker house, Richfield Springs, New York, 1923. Dwight James Baum, architect. Top right: Swan House, Atlanta, Georgia, 1928. This residence was designed by Philip Trammel Schutze with Henz, Adler & Schutze, architects. Owner Edward H. Inman inherited a cotton brokerage fortune made after the Civil War and became a Georgia investor. Bottom left: Casa Encantada, the Hilda B. Weber house, Bel Air, California, 1938, architect James E. Dolena. Bottom right: The house designed by John F. Staub in 1938 for Mr. and Mrs. Dan J. Harrison of Houston, evoked the White House with its painted brick and columned portico, but inside it was pure Andrew Jackson Downing villa seen through a Colonial Revival / Beaux-Arts lens.

Suburban Home
1921–1961

A house is the core of your family life, in which you live, relax, and bring up your children. Its plan is pointed to suit your own specific routine of living, so it is functional according to your own ideas and demands of functionalism.

—Royal Barry Wills, *Houses for Good Living*, 1940

For the past eight years the White House has been my home.... I have always looked on it with a reverence and a pride which I am sure all Americans share. But now it has become part of my life.

—Mamie Eisenhower
From her introduction to "Inside the White House," *National Geographic*, 1961

KEEPING UP WITH THE CLEAVERS

The years following World War I saw an unprecedented boom in the suburbanization of America, a process that had first begun in the 1840s. The genteel suburban middle-class villa imagined by Andrew Jackson Downing in 1850 had almost been realized by 1920. It could be a three-bedroom, one-bath house on one-eighth of an acre, or a six-bedroom, three-bath house on two acres.

The suburban house always had a living room and a dining room, a den for Father, or, if the family was especially prosperous, a library with built-in bookcases. Starting in the 1930s, something called a rumpus room or family room began to appear, offering casual living in a world with fewer servants. Kitchens became increasingly important from the 1920s on, as housewives and their families spent more and more time in them. Whatever the style of the house itself, the kitchen was always modern and glittered with the latest technology. The suburban house initially had hardwood floors, but linoleum in myriad colors began to be used by the 1940s, both in and outside the kitchen. As the century progressed, ceilings got lower, windows got bigger, and modern designs in furnishings and textiles competed with colonial and other traditional styles. Modest or grand, the suburban house was deeply infused with the spirit of family and community, twin pillars of American democracy.

All through the hard years of the Great Depression, movies supported the maturing American vision of the suburban home. The film industry's portrait of this type of dwelling, neat and tidy on its neatly mowed lawn, was exemplified in the 1948 comedy *Mr. Blandings Builds His Dream House*, starring Cary Grant and Myrna Loy. After World War II, with the birth of commercial television, the suburban dream house was further enshrined in the American consciousness through situation comedies. The idealized vision of suburban families dealing with the small events of everyday life, and morally benefiting from the experience, was seen in programs such as *Leave It to Beaver* (1957–63), *Dennis the Menace* (1959–63), and *Hazel* (1961–66). In these weekly broadcasts, the houses helped define the families that inhabited them.

The White House might seem a far cry from TV's cozy domestic scenes, but America's presidential families, from the Coolidges to the Eisenhowers, did their best to transform the palatial White House into something approximating an American home, where the president and his family tried to lead suburban lives in interiors of unpretentious simplicity. The emphasis was on comfort and practicality, and the grandeur of the White House rooms became a problem to be dealt with rather than an asset to be showcased. This was particularly true for the more private rooms on the second floor, where ceilings were dropped dramatically during a drastic renovation and numerous modern bathrooms and closets chopped up the lofty spaces of the original house. In its intentional blandness, the postwar White House sought to represent the first family as reflecting American culture at large. Images of presidents sitting on President Truman's 1947 second-floor south porch or flipping burgers on the roof assured Americans that the social distinctions of the Gilded Age were far behind and that their leaders were, indeed, just folk.

The suburbanization of the White House succeeded only partially. The lasting popularity of the Colonial Revival movement, manifest in the success of John D. Rockefeller Jr.'s 1930s recreation of Williamsburg, and the sheer weight of presidential history overwhelmed the everyman incarnation of the President's house. By the late 1940s, the impact of these cultural forces was evident as the White House moved inextricably into the expanding world of the historic house movement.

Dwight Eisenhower, like businessmen on their patios after a day at the office, could grill up some steaks on the third floor terrace and put aside national concerns. The space outside the sunroom was furnished with rattan furniture meant to be dragged outdoors. Harry S. Truman's 1947 porch on the second floor was not sufficiently private.

HOMEMAKERS

GRACE AND CALVIN COOLIDGE with their sons, John and Calvin Jr., seated on the south portico, June 1924.

J. Calvin and Grace Goodhue Coolidge on the south portico with their sons Calvin Jr. (left) and John (right). Just days later, Calvin Jr. died on July 7, 1924, from a blood infection developed after playing barefoot on the White House tennis court with his brother. Sociable and engaging, in contrast to her more serious husband, Mrs. Coolidge added the 1927 third floor to the White House, replete with suburban comforts and a modern "sky parlor" furnished with wicker. During her White House years, the state rooms began to be taken more seriously as historic spaces, although she still relied more on department-store reproductions than on antiques for a period effect.

LOUISE HENRY HOOVER stands under a topiary arch along the president's walk in the rose garden, planted for Ellen Wilson in 1913; photograph, c. 1930.

Always known as Lou, the 1906 Stanford University graduate came to the White House in 1929. She modernized the private quarters in a style more linked to contemporary taste than to any colonial authenticity. Yet she commissioned and personally funded reproductions of historic objects from the Monroe years and created some of the first "period" settings in the White House.

1923–29

1929–33

ELEANOR AND FRANKLIN D. ROOSEVELT in the second-floor Oval Sitting Room, 1933.

The aristocratic Franklin Roosevelts were comfortable with modest changes to the White House during the tumultuous 12 years of FDR's administration, from the Depression to World War II. Mrs. Roosevelt, the niece of Theodore Roosevelt, was more interested in social causes than in decorating. The president hired landscape architect Frederick Law Olmsted Jr. to draw up a comprehensive plan for the White House grounds, still in use today.

1933–45

HARRY S. TRUMAN at his presidential library, c. 1955.

When the leg of his daughter's piano pushed through the ceiling of the second floor, President Truman undertook a drastic rebuilding of the White House interior to make it safer and more comfortable. His 1949–52 renovation was driven more by time and budget than by preservation; the house's historical integrity was sacrificed to modernization, with only a broad attempt to make it look the way it had in 1800. New York department store B. Altman & Company provided suburban colonial decoration for the newly built interior.

Here Truman stands with the mantelpiece and firescreen that he appropriated for his Missouri library from Theodore Roosevelt's 1902 State Dining Room, designed by Charles F. McKim and Stanford White.

1945–53

A SUBURBAN HOME

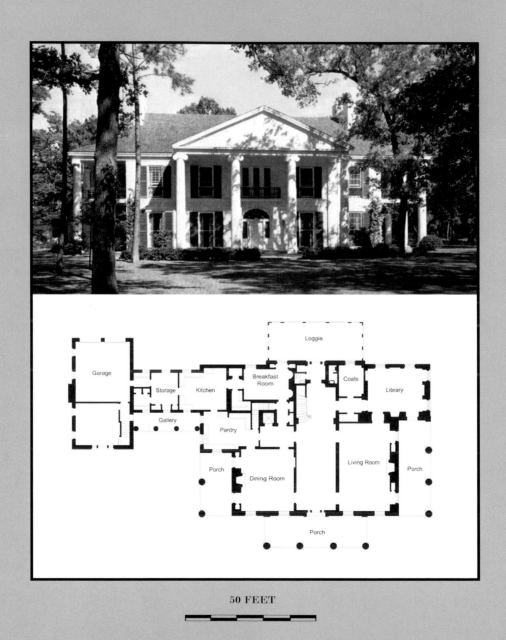

50 FEET

DAN J. HARRISON HOUSE, 1938

First-floor plan of the Houston, Texas, house built for oilman Dan J. Harrison in 1938. It was designed by Tennessee-born John F. Staub, who apprenticed with New York country house architect Harrie T. Lindeberg. Staub brought restrained Colonial Revival architecture to fashionable developments in the lean Depression years. The entrance to the 9,700 square foot house evokes the north portico of the White House, and its overall plan mimics southern design. The interior layout, with a prominent kitchen and attached garage, is completely suburban, devoted to the convenience of life with few servants.

THE WHITE HOUSE AS
A SUBURBAN HOME

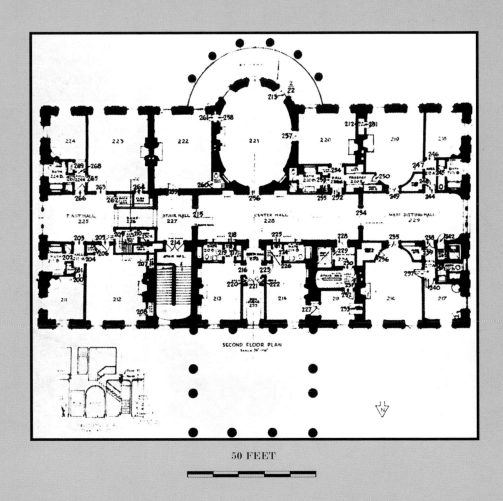

50 FEET

WHITE HOUSE, 1952

Second-floor plan, after the Harry S. Truman renovation, 1949–52. Across America modesty replaced Robber Baron splendor in the 1930s and '40s. The White House itself evolved from a family house to a building with public and residential spaces. The first floor, except for dining, was devoted to state functions. The second floor became a 14,000-square-foot apartment, as large as a house in a wealthy subdivision. Suburban amenities included bathrooms, closets, and air-conditioning.

For all the efforts by presidents and first ladies to make the White House a private home, the media has used the north and south porticos to signify the public American presidency. The White House appeared dignified and safe on the cold night of December 7, 1941, when Japanese pilots bombed Navy ships in Hawaii's Pearl Harbor.

HOUSE

By the time post–World War I social and economic changes rendered palace building largely obsolete, the Colonial Revival was firmly entrenched in America's suburbs. A. J. Davis's Gothic villa did survive as the hugely flexible Tudor house, but every possible variation on American colonial house forms thrived all across the nation. The White House hardly seems to be an appropriate model for the suburban dwelling, yet it had its incarnations. The Magnolia, a precut house sold by Sears, Roebuck & Company between 1915 and 1920 for slightly over $5,000, is the most striking suburban echo of the White House. Its romantic name might suggest the antebellum South, but its advertising text referred to the Longfellow House in Massachusetts. Its pillared entranceway could not have failed to evoke the White House for many.

Although the White House itself did not see changes as significant as those instituted by architect Charles McKim in 1903, it did experience improvements and renovations that functionally brought the house up to

the current standards of modern American life. The Army Corps of Engineers' 1923 discovery of structural problems in the house's roof set in motion a rebuilding of the entire third-floor attic. Ulysses S. Grant III, the corps's officer for public buildings and grandson of the president, oversaw the project and hired architect William Adams Delano, of the well-known New York–based firm Adams & Delano.

As completed in 1927, the redesigned third floor, previously used for storage, was expanded to contain modern guest bedrooms and servants' quarters. Slanting walls were removed, and new rooms had full-height ceilings. Grant and Delano sought to minimize the visual impact of the new construction on the exterior of the house. Reflecting the increased interest in and knowledge of U.S. architectural history, they consulted Hoban's north elevation of the house, drawn in 1793. Donated to the Maryland Historical Society in 1912 by Thomas Jefferson Coolidge Jr., a descendant of Thomas Jefferson, the drawing was attributed to Hoban by Fiske Kimball, who

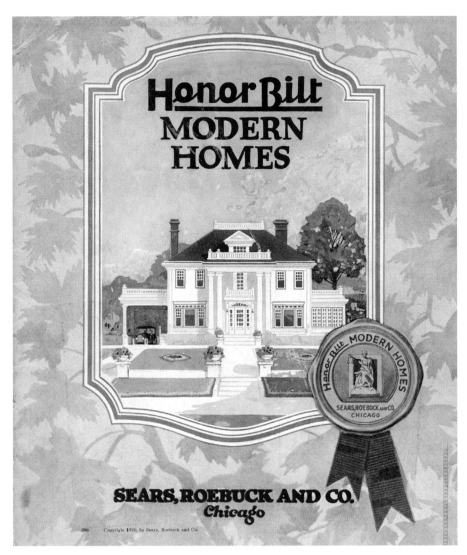

The Magnolia, a Sears, Roebuck & Company mail-order house available from 1915 to 1920.
Middle-class Americans could live in a suburban White House of their own.

reproduced it in 1919 to accompany his essay "The Genesis of the White House."[1] Inspired by the high roof that appeared in Hoban's drawing, Grant and Delano significantly increased the roof's pitch.

In contrast to the main house, the temporary office wing underwent numerous changes. In 1909, seven years after the completion of McKim's building, William Howard Taft called for its expansion by 80 percent and instituted a national competition for the commission. The winner, Nathan C. Wyeth, designed a building that housed the president's main office, modeled on the White House's Blue Room and identified as the Oval Office, as well as space for his staff. Three tall windows on the office's south wall faced a fireplace on the north side. The room was Colonial Revival, with pedimented doorways and simple wood trim throughout. When Herbert Hoover took office in 1929, he immediately increased the size of his executive staff from 40 to 70. Ulysses S. Grant III was responsible for refitting the offices. Additional

office space was created in the basement and attic, and air-conditioning was installed in some offices.

In 1933, Franklin D. Roosevelt asked Grant to prepare drawings for an indoor swimming pool that the president sought to use for physical exercise intended to mitigate his polio-induced pain. Following Roosevelt's rejection of initial proposals, Grant passed the job on to the Army Corps's civilian architect, Lorenzo S. Winslow, who later became the official White House architect. Collaborating with Major Douglas H. Gillette, Winslow designed a pool that could be steam heated and used year-round. The pool was built in the wing Jefferson had added to the west of the house. In an additional accommodation to Roosevelt's health, air-conditioning units were installed in the president's living quarters in 1933. Working with Roosevelt and Winslow, the architect Eric Gugler redesigned the executive office building to accommodate the president's enlarged staff, now numbering 120. Gugler hid a new second story behind a parapet and created a basement that

Top: South facade, 1946, with awnings that interrupted the line of the columns but were necessary before central air-conditioning. Bottom: South facade with Harry S. Truman's controversial second-floor porch, 1947.

extended beyond the building's perimeter; subterranean offices were illuminated with natural light entering from a sunken, landscaped court.

Hours after Japanese forces attacked Pearl Harbor on December 7, 1941, Roosevelt met with Winslow to discuss the design and construction of temporary buildings on the south lawn to house staff required to aid the war effort. The following morning, Roosevelt decided instead to go forward with an extension to the east wing, which Winslow had been sketching for the president for at least four years. Replacing McKim's loggia, the plan called for a rather blocky two-story building facing east with a single-story porte cochere defined by a row of paired columns. Though Roosevelt had hoped the wing would contain a museum of presidential memorabilia, something he had long sought to establish, the new building contained extensive offices, as well as a secretly constructed bomb shelter. The extension's facades were articulated in a reductivist manner that reflected the revivalist architects' prevailing taste for stripped-down classicism in the wake of modernism.

When Harry S. Truman became president upon Roosevelt's death in 1945, he inherited a staff that had grown from 140 before World War II to 225. Truman quickly sought to quadruple the size of the west wing, adding 15,000 square feet of office space, as well as a cafeteria and an auditorium to be used for press conferences and other purposes. The proposal, designed by Winslow, furthered the simply detailed classicism the architect had pursued earlier. Congress strongly opposed the plan, and it was never realized. Truman advocated another architectural modification of the White House two years later. This time, he called for a balcony to be inserted into the south-facing colonnade and entered from the house's second-story oval room, located directly above the Blue Room. Though the Commission on Fine Arts initially opposed this insertion of a suburban porch into a historic facade, it later recommended that William Adams Delano design the balcony. Delano ultimately assisted Winslow in the design of a concrete-and-metal structure that was completed in 1948.

While only the balcony significantly altered the exterior of the White House during the Truman administration, the president's rebuilding of the interior was the most radical alteration to the house since its reconstruction in the aftermath of the War of 1812. In late 1947 the president sensed that floors in the White House were not only creaking with age, but sagging. At his instigation, in 1948 the commissioner of public buildings, W. E. Reynolds, oversaw tests that revealed structural weaknesses in the White House. Congress approved additional funds for a more extensive survey and the creation of a plan to rebuild and fireproof the house. It was discovered that the McKim State Dining Room and the Coolidge 1927 attic and roof rebuilding had put stress on the entire wood structure of the original White House. In August 1948 the legs of Margaret Truman's Steinway piano came through the ceiling of the family living room (today's Family Dining Room), dramatizing the need for rebuilding.

The Truman family left the house in November 1948, taking up temporary residence in nearby Blair House, the presidential guest house, and work began the following year. Collaborating with Winslow and Reynolds, and working under Truman's watchful eye, were Major General Philip F. Fleming, architectural engineer Edward F. Neild, and architect Harbin S. Chandler. Delano served as design consultant.

Much of the house was stripped down to its stone walls. Within the existing envelope, a concrete-and-steel structure was erected. The basic arrangement of the house's principal rooms was left the same, though numerous smaller rooms and service spaces were added. On the third floor, reconfiguration resulted in the creation of 35 rooms, including nine guest rooms. The rooms, with low ceilings and, in some cases, linoleum-tile floors and fluorescent lighting, employed the same sort of materials being used in contemporaneous suburban houses.

The approach to demolition and rebuilding was far from archaeological. Although the preservation of historic homes in the United States had been undertaken since 1853, when Ann Pamela Cunningham founded the Mount Vernon Ladies' Association and worked to preserve George Washington's house as a national symbol, architectural preservation as a movement had yet to develop either a broad mandate or an ethos.

◆ ◆ ◆

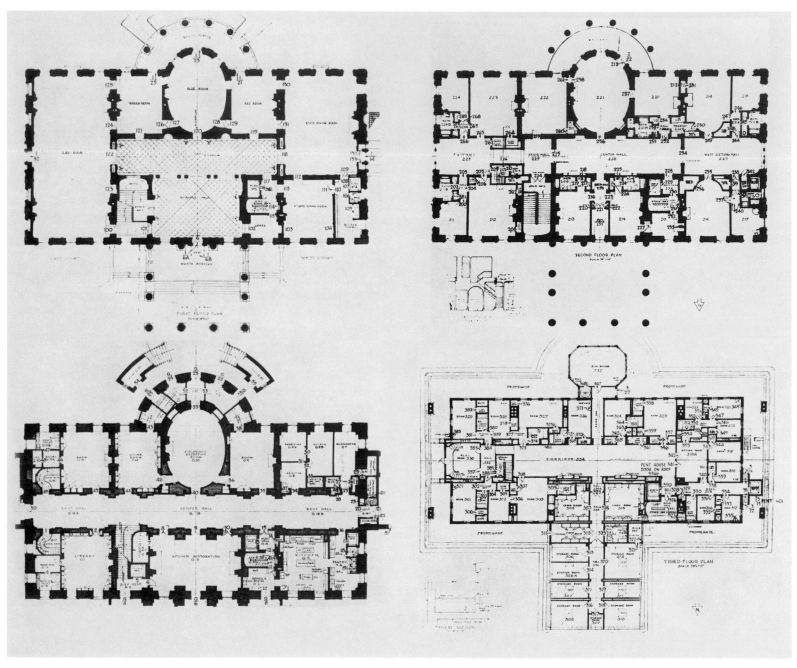

After the Truman renovation of 1949–52, the state floor of the White House (top left) looked relatively unchanged from the renovation of 1902. The second floor (top right) was modernized with additional bathrooms. The basement level (bottom left) and the third floor (bottom right), were drastically different. What had been Jefferson's cellars was now a modern corporate reception area, with up-to-date technology and false period rooms that were part of the public function of the house. The third floor had the feeling of a small hotel, its design, materials, and proportions entirely based on postwar suburban standards.

After a century and half, the White House that greeted Harry S. Truman in 1945 was not up to the standards of new American houses. Here reconstruction architect Lorenzo S. Wilson and engineer C. W. Barber stand next to a brace that kept the East Room ceiling from collapse. This and construction flaws were repaired during the 1949–52 renovation that brought comfort and security at the expense of historical accuracy. Photograph, 1948.

Aerial view of the White House in 1919, before the Coollidge 1927 third floor addition; the garden was much the way Frederick Law Olmsted Jr. found it in 1934. Lafayette Park was still planted in the Gardenesque style of A.J. Downing.

GARDEN

When Eleanor and Franklin Delano Roosevelt arrived at the White House, the south and north lawns showed signs of age, and random trees and bushes planted over many administrations interrupted the south river view. The poetic east and west gardens of Mrs. Wilson had been efficiently, though unimaginatively, maintained. Their fading continental sophistication was at odds with the gentility of the Colonial Revival, reinvigorated when America turned to its past for reassurance after the Crash of 1929. At that time, federal funds were allocated to energize the national landscape-preservation movement, and women led the restoration of early colonial boxwood gardens. Architect Eric Gugler outlined a new west garden for Roosevelt's expanded executive office, but the president was unimpressed. Instead, he engaged Frederick Law Olmsted Jr. to prepare the first comprehensive plan for the White House gardens since Andrew Jackson Downing.

Olmsted was the éminence grise of American landscape architecture and had overseen from 1902 the erratic implementation of the ambitious McMillan Plan. His presence alone symbolized the White House's return, once again, to the traditions of the revered founding fathers.

Olmsted's historicist approach to the White House gardens reflected the national spirit. He hired Morley Jeffers Williams, historian of both the Mount Vernon and Stratford Hall gardens, to prepare a study of the White House grounds. Informed by Williams's work and scouting photographs of the present-day conditions, Olmsted presented a report to FDR in October 1935. His recommendations were democratic in spirit, balancing the public right to enjoy the White House from the street with the president's need for increased privacy. The naturalism of Downing's plan, though without its moral imperatives, guided Olmsted's preservationist approach.

The language of Olmsted's extensive report rings with pride in the history of the presidential grounds. He disdained the "planless" way in which the gardens had evolved since the 1880s. Nonetheless, Olmsted believed they were still "characterized by many long-established qualities

Scouting photographs of the south lawn, for Frederick Law Olmsted Jr., spring 1934. The view from the south portico to the Ellipse was interrupted by shrubs and trees planted over a century of presidents.

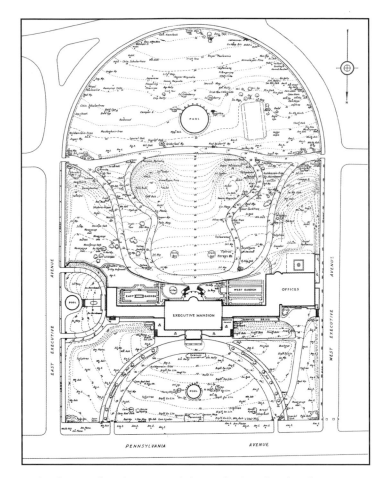 

Frederick Law Olmsted Jr. surveyed the president's park and garden in January, 1935 (left), and then presented a landscape plan to President Franklin Roosevelt in October (right). Olmsted recommended a selective thinning of trees to preserve the public's view of the south and north facades. Additional planting close to the rose garden would increase the president's privacy. Olmsted's plan enshrined the landscape of the White House and continues to guide its curators.

of great dignity and appropriateness…. It is of the utmost importance to perpetuate these qualities."[2] Olmsted sought to "strengthen and perfect" the historical aspects of the north and south grounds by removing "deliberate or accidental alterations" from prior administrations. Harmony in the garden design could be achieved by balancing tree-shaded spots with open views.

Olmsted recommended a selective thinning of the trees on the south lawn to form a naturalized allée from the south fence up to the White House, much as the allée at Mount Vernon framed the view to Washington's house. Olmsted warned that any new planting should be done "without choking up and frittering away any of those open spaces which are as vital to the character of the landscape as are the foliage masses adjoining them." In the English tradition of the ha-ha, a ditch used to separate gardens from fields without intrusive fencing, Olmsted called for lowering the road south of the fence to extend the visual sweep of the lawn from the south portico across to the Ellipse. This change, not carried out, would have unified the presidential garden with its southernmost reaches as originally envisioned by L'Enfant and then reinterpreted by Downing.

Thirty years after his work with Charles McKim, Olmsted still found the gardens east and west of the south portico "admirable as to location and appropriate enough as to the general conception of their design." Like his father, Olmsted believed that flowers were a distraction from the inspiring tranquility of parks. Although a "greater richness and perfection of floral display than in the past" would be appropriate along the south facade, Olmsted thought that these "formal garden areas, however, cannot be very greatly extended without doing violence to the historically long-established, and in its own way admirable and dignified informal landscape of a simple and large-scale character which is the dominant characteristic of the general design." In his report to Roosevelt, Olmsted called for a return to the balanced symmetry of the McKim plan and parterre gardens. The flower plantings on the north side of the White House were to be "simplified into a more dignified and less restless and self-assertive appearance."

With Olmsted's plan, the evolution of the White House gardens ceased and the presidential grounds became a park and garden that synthesized 100 years of White House landscape design. Formative elements of

Aerial view, c. 1940, of the White House after Eric Gugler shifted the oval office in 1934; with Wilson rose and southeast gardens preserved and mature trees groomed to frame the south facade.

Olmsted's recommendations were carried out in the years after 1935. Trees were planted to screen the east and west gardens from public view. Grant's carriage path, which Olmsted had wanted to remove in 1903, was replaced with grass, and a new, simplified drive to the south portico was created. The rose-covered, lacy fence along the south facade, what Olmsted's report called a "trivial feature," was finally carted away. The south-facing east and west flower gardens remained largely as they had been designed for Mrs. Wilson.

At the end of the Truman renovation in 1952, the north driveway was repaved and smoothed. Like front yards throughout postwar suburbs, the new north lawn of the White House was well fertilized and mowed, unornamented, and open to the street. At President Truman's suggestion, *Buxus sempervirens* "Suffruticosa" ("Truman Boxwood") was planted along the base of the north portico as a rolling hedge that suggested the house's colonial traditions.[3] From the street, the north facade, with its distinct portico, was framed by mature shade trees. The house appeared as stately and serene as many manor houses built in the Colonial Revival era. An example of suburban propriety was Graceland in Memphis. Built in 1939 for Dr. Thomas and Ruth Moore, a newspaper heiress, the estate was sold to rock star Elvis Presley in 1957.

In 1943, before renovation fervor swept away the old White House, the Truman administration commissioned a detailed landscape plan to preserve the Ellen Wilson gardens designed by Beatrix Farrand and George Burnap. The plan was drawn by government landscape architect Irving W. Payne, who had studied the White House grounds since the 1920s and landscaped the 1922 Lincoln Memorial on the Mall.[1] It was abandoned after the Truman renovation devastated the grounds immediate to the house. In outline the Truman south gardens echoed the landscape plans of the Wilson era, but with the bland lifelessness of much tradition-based design of the postwar period. Rows of low, clipped hedges framed roses in the west garden, and in the east, border plantings surrounded a lawn no longer animated by the lily pool. The restored south portico faced what Olmsted called the "in-look," the public view from the White House fence that he insisted be maintained "in perpetuity." The Ellipse was now an open lawn for public gatherings. Across the river, on axis with the White House, was John Russell Pope's Jefferson Memorial, finished in 1943. This alignment, echoing the placement of classical revival temples in 18th-century British aristocratic gardens, recalled the importance of English design in the early planning of the White House and its park.

West garden during the Truman administration, 1952. It was a ghost of Ellen Wilson's 1913 rose garden.

The southeast Truman garden was no more than a southern suburban lawn bordered with boxwood. The garden's privacy was lost when the 1942 office block replaced the 1902 east wing. The east and west gardens were now symmetrical as Frederick Law Olmsted Jr. had recommended in 1935.

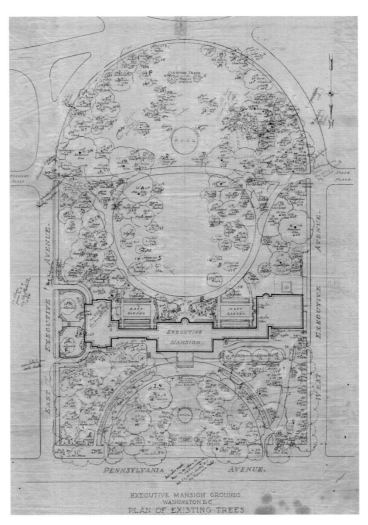

Plan of the president's garden during the Truman administration, as of August 1952; after the 1935 Olmsted plan became official, President Grant's path was finally planted with grass. The house, now a private residence with a separate home office, had a private garden visible from the street but closed to the public. Its trees had been preserved as part of White House history.

The American porch has been at the intersection of American house architecture and landscape design since the 18th century. George Washington entertained guests on the piazza at Mount Vernon, with its river view of the Potomac, and Thomas Jefferson initiated the tradition of first-floor terraces at the White House. For A. J. Downing, the covered veranda was an improvement over open terraces because it provided a sheltered outdoor experience. Downing and his colleagues believed that nature, composed through landscaping and studied through observation, inspired thoughtful reflection and moral improvement in an increasingly urban world.

Nature as a source of inspiration and a relief from the stress of city life was behind Harry Truman's justification for his porch at the White House. Even though the south portico had been a porch since it was finished in 1824, Truman wanted a "breath of fresh air" in a private place, away from the public view and state room floor. The president got his balcony and the moral benefits of observing the natural world followed. One afternoon he looked south from his new porch to the Ellipse and there was democracy at work. "A ball game goes on in the park south of the lawn. Evidently a lot of competition, from the cheers and calls of the coaches…A mocking bird imitates the robin, jays, redbirds, crows, hawks—but has no individual note of his own. A lot of people like that."[5]

America returned to the tradition of the open-air terrace when patios replaced porches at suburban ranch houses. At the White House the south portico was put to use again. On the third floor outside the Truman sunroom and behind the roof balustrade, Dwight Eisenhower barbequed. Barbeque was authentic American cooking, with a history that reached back to roasting over an open spit on cattle drives in the American West. In shirt sleeves, the president, at least for an evening, could be the man of the house, not the president of a nation.

Top: North facade after Truman renovation, with "Truman" Boxwood, 1952. The north lawn and drive had been simplified. Bottom: Graceland, Memphis, Tennessee, Furbinger & Erhman, architects, built in 1939 for newspaper heiress Ruth Moore and purchased by rock star Elvis Presley in 1957. The north entrance to the White House and the drive of this Colonial Revival estate shared a simplicity characteristic of Colonial Revival gardens after the Depression, when lawns and shade trees replaced flower displays.

Patio dining set in the shade of the south portico with a view to the Thomas Jefferson Memorial, 1948. That year President Truman built himself a porch upstairs, outside his second floor office, to enjoy, as Time Magazine *reported, "an evening, as he used to back in Independence, listening to the whir of the sprinkler on the lawn and the sound of the neighbors' voices...."*

Hoover oval room, 1931. Despite her interest in history, Lou Hoover followed suburban decorating ideas in her private quarters. Here the oval room boasts a black and light green color scheme and an eclectic mix of objects typical of American interiors of the 1930s.

INTERIORS

The palace-building era in America was brief, and World War I forever changed the way people—even rich people—lived. Between the advent of the income tax in 1913 and the onset of the Great Depression in 1929, the Gilded Age vanished, and with it evaporated the American desire to live in a palace. With its new office and entrance wings, the White House had, for a brief window of time in the late Gilded Age, seemed just the right size. Now it was once again bizarrely grand for an American family and too old-fashioned for the duties of the president. The 20th-century American suburban dream house represented a rebirth of the genteel villa of the 1850s. The suburban house could be modest or grand but always expressed the shared American values of comfort, good taste, and suitability for family life.

The white painted brick house designed by John F. Staub in 1938 for Mr. and Mrs. Dan J. Harrison Sr. of Houston, evoked the White House with its paint and columned portico, but inside it was pure Downing villa seen through a Colonial Revival/Beaux-Arts lens. For all its classical grandeur, the three basic markers of the genteel villa—parlor (by now renamed living room), dining room, and library—are arranged asymmetrically as in a home of the 1840s. Large porches provide transition from the house to the extensive gardens. The main departure from the villa model is the sine qua non of modern suburbia, the attached garage. Unnecessary fireplaces make a nostalgic nod to the past, and modern technology (including nine toilets) assures the family every possible comfort. In light of these suburban developments, the White House began to seem increasingly disconnected from the reality of even presidential lives. As the 20th century progressed, first families abandoned the state floor in favor of the more suburban comfort of the private quarters. Even as they tried to carry on the patterns established by the

Theodore Roosevelt Blue Room, as seen virtually unchanged in the Coolidge White House in 1929.

Theodore Roosevelts, the families in the White House during the second quarter of the 20th century tried to make it work as a home appropriate for their American way of life. At the same time, the house had already started down a path toward its ultimate destiny, that of museum and shrine.

After Woodrow Wilson's tenure, the White House's palatial state rooms were increasingly alien to the daily life of the presidents. The main floor became more and more a purely ceremonial stage for presidential performance, after which the family retreated (with a sigh of relief) to the spacious comfort of the second floor. As the novelty of the Theodore Roosevelt overhaul receded into the past, the historic roots of the White House began to reassert themselves in the minds of its occupants, and this impulse was fostered by such historical undertakings as the massive restorations in Williamsburg, Virginia, and the growing interest in Americana in major East Coast museums. Powerful collectors of American antiques emerged all over the nation, including several who created their own museum collections, such as Francis P. Garvan in New York, Henry Ford in Michigan, Ima Hogg in Texas, and Henry Francis du Pont in Delaware. In this national context, decorating at the White House was refocused, with the influence of the Colonial Revival becoming ever more pronounced.

The Coolidges had never completely settled down in Washington, and they approached the White House as their first real homemaking project. Starting in the fall of 1924, Grace Coolidge decorated the second-floor rooms in the prevailing suburban colonial style, choosing from the plentiful offerings of American manufacturers. Mrs. Coolidge had envisioned her second-floor home in the White House as comfortable modern interiors that would not go out of fashion and would also be appropriate to the history of the house. She followed the same model for the new rooms on the new third floor, rebuilt and expanded under Colonel Ulysses S. Grant III, eldest grandson of the president.[7]

That same fall, the Metropolitan Museum unveiled its American Wing, the first in any U.S. museum, full of authentic period rooms from colonial and Federal America, decorated and furnished accurately according to current scholarship. Inspired by the American Wing, and sanctioned by a 1925 congressional act, Mrs. Coolidge put together the first advisory committee to help in seeking donations of appropriate art and objects for the White House interiors. The committee included important architects, art experts, and two prominent antiques collectors, R. T. Haines Halsey (mastermind of the American Wing) and Luke Vincent Lockwood. The committee saw the Roosevelt-era state rooms as too imperial and too foreign, resulting in a push to redecorate them in a more colonial vein. Assisted by Ulysses S. Grant III, who mediated between the not-always-harmonious factions of the committee, Mrs. Coolidge proceeded with a redecorating plan for the Green Room. Grant simply renewed the Red room's 1902 velvet and damask with similar materials, but he replaced the Green Room's cut velvet with green brocade chosen to match a carpet bought by Mrs. Coolidge, ordered "colonial" window hangings of the same silk, and had the

Top left: The colonial style furnishings shown in an upscale model "ideal home," decorated by L. Bamberger & Company, Newark, in the 1920s, were the sort of thing that Grace Coolidge looked for in furnishing the private quarters, including her new third-floor guest rooms (top right). Bottom left: The modern wicker used by Mrs. Coolidge in her new Sky Parlor in 1927 (left) was also paralleled by the casual sunroom furniture promoted in Bamberger's model home (bottom right).

Left: This sleek kitchen, pictured c. 1935, was one of the few dramatic modernizations undertaken during FDR's years. A dream kitchen for any suburban housewife, it was highly publicized; but only the staff dined here. The Roosevelts lived on the second floor; the ground-floor kitchen was a world away. Right: Franklin Roosevelt's swimming pool in the west wing, 1933. Although not interested in spending money for redecoration, Franklin Roosevelt added new, modern comforts to his White House.

Franklin Roosevelt East Room, 1938. Generally indifferent to decorating, Franklin Roosevelt did order new red silk damask draperies and a concert grand piano designed by architect Eric Gugler. The state rooms were important to the Roosevelts as a setting for the presidency, but as family rooms, they had lost most of their meaning.

furniture upholstered in yellow brocade. The committee completed the room as they imagined John Adams or Thomas Jefferson might have done, making it the first official attempt at an authentic interior in the house. By the end of the 1920s, both the Red and Green rooms had new custom-made rugs with the great seal of the United States, commissioned from Tiffany Studios, still owned by the retired Louis Comfort Tiffany.[8]

Herbert and Lou Henry Hoover entered the White House in March 1929 and brought a cosmopolitan mixture of historicism and suburban domesticity to the second-floor quarters. Mrs. Hoover transformed the west hall into a whimsical tropical room complete with palm trees, cages of canaries, and green-and-white sisal matting. The oval living room got a black and pale green color scheme, the upholstered and reproduction Chippendale sofas covered in black and gold brocade, with lettuce green taffeta draperies tucked inside the window casings. The black velvet pile rug and pale green walls completed a look that was very much of the 1930s and had little conscious reference to the history of the house. Although they were the first presidential family to see the second floor as a self-contained apartment, the Hoovers always dressed for dinner and ate their meals in the State Dining Room, even when alone.

On the other hand, Mrs. Hoover loved to place relics and antiques in the rooms of the house, although she was not interested in re-creating "period rooms" as such. She oversaw the advisory committee's completion of the Green Room with an antique crystal chandelier, but the Monroe Room she created on the second floor above it (where the cabinet room, and then the president's study, had been) was decorated with soft rose walls and boxy fabric valances, colors and textiles that were as contemporary as the scheme in the adjacent oval room.

Franklin and Eleanor Roosevelt were not intimidated by either the size or the history of the White House. Other than its scale, it was not all that different from the sprawling Roosevelt estate on the Hudson River. Although not hugely rich, the Roosevelts were very grand and felt at home in the president's residence. They valued comfort over style, a preference that resonated across the nation as the depression deepened. Relatively indifferent to decorating compared with other first ladies, Eleanor Roosevelt economized and made do. She did change the state rooms a little, bringing the Red Room into the 1930s (sort of) with a quasi period overhaul to coordinate with the Green Room. Deep red damask covered the walls and was used for curtains and the upholstery on the new

Early American furniture, Val-Kill, New York, 1930s, for the Franklin D. Roosevelt second-floor hall sitting room. With its plain furniture, Oriental rug, and slipcovered sofa, the Roosevelts' sitting room had the same kind of modest, vaguely colonial furniture seen in most surburban houses in the 1930s. Eleanor Roosevelt lived at Val-Kill after she left the White House.

reproduction furniture. The Blue Room fabric was also updated in the 1930s, and McKim, Mead & White's gold damask draperies in the East Room were changed to red damask.

Although the Roosevelts installed a widely publicized modern kitchen that would have appealed to American housewives, it was a kitchen used only by servants. The swimming pool created for the president from old ground-floor service areas was perhaps a more characteristically privileged Rooseveltian gesture. On the other hand, the private quarters were decorated with informality and an eye to personal taste that made the Roosevelts seem more suburban than they really were. In the 1934 watercolor of the Roosevelt family in the upstairs oval room, its great height and size are minimized by the composition. Mr. Roosevelt's nautical pictures, the model battleship on the mantel, and the pile of papers by the president's chair speak of a house well lived in. If you didn't know who they were, the people portrayed could be any upper-middle-class American family relaxing in their colonial-style living room before dinner.

By the Roosevelt years, the Fillmore library in the upstairs oval room had long since been displaced, and President Roosevelt commissioned a new library on the ground floor, across from Edith Wilson's China Room. The design of the room reflected the enthusiasm for colonial paneled rooms engendered by the reconstructions in Colonial Williamsburg. The Diplomatic Reception Room gained new importance as the location of Roosevelt's Fireside Chats during World War II, but aside from the reopening of a 19th-century chimney flue to make the fireplace function, the room didn't change significantly.

Harry and Bess Truman had always lived modestly in Washington in rented apartments, and their model for home was the 19th-century Missouri villa in which Bess Truman had grown up. This villa had been modernized during the new century and took on the aspect of a good-size suburban house: comfortable and modestly stylish, but neither grand nor luxurious. The Trumans approached the White House from a very different perspective than the Old-World Roosevelts.

By the time of Franklin Roosevelt's death on April 12, 1945, the interiors were shopworn after years of depression and war. Eleanor Roosevelt had spent nothing on the second floor, and the shabbiness that had been a sort of aesthetic noblesse oblige to the Roosevelts just looked

FRANKLIN ROOSEVELT FAMILY, *John C. Johnson, watercolor, 1934. The second-floor oval room, with informal furnishings and the president's nautical pictures, looked like any affluent American's living room of the 1930s. The painting suggests that the family had all but ceased using the state rooms except for official purposes, the second floor having become a suburban home. It was there that relative Joseph W. Alsop recalled Mrs. Roosevelt serving scrambled eggs from a family chafing dish during Sunday evening get-togethers when the staff was off work.*

The Cleaver family, as seen on television in their Colonial Revival living room, 1950s. The landscape paintings and reproduction early American furniture were suburban middle-class versions of those used in the White House from the 1920s through the 1950s.

Red Room, as decorated for Harry S. Truman, pictured c. 1960. The color chosen for the Red Room by B. Altman &
Company in 1952 reflected the brighter colors of the post–World War II years. Like the other state rooms, the Red Room's
conventional upper-middle-class Colonial Revival decoration reflected neither the taste of the first family nor the true history
of the house. The White House was ceasing to be a home and was decorated instead as an institution.

seedy to the Trumans, for whom freshness was essential to a comfortable home. New curtains came from a Kansas City decorating firm, which also helped Bess Truman pick out new paint colors: soft, conservative hues for the grown-ups' rooms (lavender, gray, blue, green) and the oval living room (tan), with stronger, more modern colors for her daughter Margaret's rooms (Wedgwood blue and raspberry pink). Unlike the Roosevelts, who had removed a trainload of their own furniture and art, the Trumans moved in with only their personal effects and a piano. Their most significant alteration to the house was the addition of the second-floor balcony, which made their upstairs living room infinitely more pleasant—and suburban—by giving them a back porch from which to watch the world.

The Green Room was the only state room to get new textiles in the late 1940s, before the massive renovation of 1949–52, using a brighter postwar green adaptation of an 18th-century damask. The Roosevelt-era deep crimson damask was in the Red Room, and McKim, Mead & White's dark blue silk twill was still on the walls in the Blue Room. By the end of the 1940s, all three parlors also had glittering English crystal chandeliers, which would come back to the rooms in 1952. The State Dining Room got new gold damask draperies, but other than Lincoln's

portrait replacing Teddy Roosevelt's moose over the fireplace, it looked much as it had since 1903.

Unlike the 1902 Roosevelt renovation, the Truman renovation was structurally necessary, to a point. Today's preservationists might have found a less drastic solution than gutting the interior and would have been far more careful to preserve details that had survived the decades since 1814. But this was the 1940s, and historic preservation barely existed, certainly in the view of the government. The primary concerns were for the safety and comfort of the first family. Modern bathrooms, closets, air-conditioning, wiring, security, and structural steel were more important than any architectural details. These values reflect a truth that runs deep in America: new is better than old, and nothing is more important than convenience. This preference for newness is the reason historic houses are torn down every day to be replaced with high-tech replicas in ersatz period styles. For all the talk of history, the final result was a simplified version of the White House of 1902 and an eerie modernized avatar of what had risen from the ashes in 1814. In addition to the massive new internal framework of the house, all of the surviving Victorian mantelpieces from the upstairs rooms were discarded in the wholesale rethinking of the interiors. A large portion of the surviving details—including the last of

Blue Room as decorated for Harry S. Truman. B. Altman & Company installed the bright royal blue silk with brocaded gold medallions for the Trumans in 1952, reusing the Roosevelt furniture from 1903. Elegant and vaguely evocative of the Monroe oval room, it had all the personality of a luxury hotel salon. Photograph, c. 1960.

Hoban's ornamentation and the McKim, Mead & White East Room woodwork and mantelpieces—was ultimately disposed of. In the entrance and cross halls, the ornate Beaux-Arts classicism was stripped down, and in the East Room a less robust version of the 1902 interior was put in place. In simpler spaces, such as the Family Dining Room, changes were fewer, although virtually every upstairs room was modified in some way to accommodate modern systems and conveniences. As long as the house looked more or less like it had, the fine points were irrelevant.

The interiors for the new state rooms were based on what was thought to be appropriate, in consultation with the Trumans and a select list of others, by Charles T. Haight, chief decorator for New York's B. Altman & Company. The tradition of using high-end retail furnishers for the White House dated back to the 1820s, although no one involved knew that in 1950. It was without doubt the biggest job a department store ever had gotten from a single client, but the need for cost-cutting that had been part of White House decoration since the Madisons was in force here. If the scope of the job was imperial, the attitude was suburban housewife. Altman's did the restoration on old furniture considered good enough to reuse and also provided new furniture and textiles for all three floors.

In the Blue Room, a brocade like that used on the 1902 furniture, but of a richer royal blue, was applied to the walls. The Green Room got the same treatment it had before the renovation, and the Red Room received a matching scheme in a bright cherry red. The dark paneling in the State Dining Room, which had looked colonial in 1902, now looked Victorian and was painted a pale "colonial" green (which now looks "fifties"). Four ground-floor rooms, including the library and the China Room, were dressed in colonial-style knotty-pine paneling made from salvaged 18th-century structural timbers. This romantic use of unpainted pine, unheard-of in colonial times, reflected the parallel popularity of knotty-pine paneling in dens and rumpus rooms that swept the American suburbs from the 1930s through the 1950s.[9]

A subtler result of the renovation was the isolation of the family quarters as an independent residence. Now the first family did not even pretend to use the downstairs rooms, except the Family Dining Room, for anything other than formal functions. If the echoing spaces on the first floor had the feel of a splendid country club, the second floor was now like a vast hotel suite. No bright hues here as in the state parlors, only soft neutrals favored by homemakers across the country from ranch house to mansion. The rebuilt third-floor solarium had the colorful floral chintzes and marbled linoleum

Model living room on display at B. Altman & Company on New York's Fifth Avenue, 1944. The bland, affluent suburban colonial style promoted by the elegant department store appeared in the much larger-scale interiors that the firm created for the Truman White House.

flooring of suburban family rooms, while the design for the president's bedroom had a tailored, masculine look, its bland elegance enlivened only by an 1850s gilt mirror from one of the state rooms. Throughout the seven bedrooms and nine sitting rooms on the second floor, pale plush wall-to-wall carpeting muffled sound, and pretty, vaguely historical fabrics proclaimed an unimaginative style that reflected America's deeply conservative postwar sense of good taste. Only the Lincoln Bedroom, a sacred—if historically erroneous—shrine to the martyred president, attempted to reflect the interiors that had dominated the largest part of the White House's past. This was a moment in American taste when Dolley Madison's ravishing red velvet walls would have been considered vulgar, and the less anyone said about the Victorian White House, the better.

Dwight and Mamie Eisenhower left the Truman renovation largely untouched, and it was up to America's first Roman Catholic president and his glamorous wife to transform the White House one last time.

FURNISHINGS

Both Lucy Hayes and Caroline Harrison helped the Colonial Revival take root in the late Victorian White House, as the style was spreading throughout the eastern United States in the wake of the Centennial Exposition. The Roosevelts' palace renovation gave the Colonial Revival added momentum as the 20th century began. However, the Roosevelt renovation also helped codify a reality that dominated the White House from this point on: a more complete divorce of the "historical" state floor from the private, "modern" second floor. Even as furnishing choices for the state rooms began to turn in a museum-like direction, those for the family floor looked to suburban houses for cues. The White House started a split into two separate but linked dream houses.

Grace Coolidge, energetic and stylish, took the Colonial Revival in the White House to its next stage. Inspired by increasingly sophisticated department stores, as well as the opening in 1924 of the first galleries in

Green Room, as decorated for the Truman administration. The only state room redecorated before the 1949 renovation, the Green Room reflected high-bourgeois Colonial Revival taste as it had been embraced since the Coolidge years. No longer quite appropriate for an American home, the state rooms had taken on the aspect of a plush country club, with only a faint sense of the building's history permeating the standardized upscale decor. Photograph, c. 1959.

New York's Metropolitan Museum of Art dedicated to early American decorative arts, Mrs. Coolidge began to transform the presidential palace into a new postwar dream house. To furnish the state rooms, Mrs. Coolidge assembled a short-lived advisory board that solicited gifts of antiques and artwork from donors. She was the initial first lady to seek out gifts of appropriate American objects for the White House. By means of a 1925 congressional resolution, the first step in turning the White House into a museum, the White House was allowed to accept such gifts. Mrs. Coolidge acquired enough antiques and "appropriate" reproductions to refurnish the Green Room. During the Coolidge years, the neoclassical aspect of the colonial style became established as appropriate for the public parts in the house, through the influence of important figures in the antiques-collecting world.[10] From this time on, aesthetic control of the state rooms tipped in favor of a museumesque committee of quasi curatorial advisors, although the concept of museum-quality furnishings had not yet taken hold.

Mrs. Coolidge added the third floor to the White House, with guest rooms, bathrooms, and a sun parlor, in what was essentially a functional suburban space on top of the Rooseveltian palace, and then furnished it with modest, off-the-rack Colonial Revival furniture. The two original third-floor guest rooms of the Coolidge White House were furnished with plain maple furniture in the colonial style; these furnishings could have been in any American suburban home in the 1920s and 1930s. Maple was typically used for less formal furniture in the Early American mode of the Colonial Revival, both because of its appealing color and because it cost less than mahogany and walnut.

The Sky Parlor, which became the Coolidge family sunroom, was furnished with bamboo rolling blinds, modern wicker furniture, and Oriental scatter rugs. Wicker or rattan furniture, long used for bedrooms and as conversation pieces in Gilded Age interiors, was widely employed for informal indoor–outdoor living spaces in suburban America. The Sky Parlor's wicker furniture was almost the only modern-style new furniture in the White House.

Lou Henry Hoover was essentially the first curator of the White House, the first person systematically to document the origins and histories of all

Top: Reproduction colonial furniture and grand piano, American, in the Truman second-floor oval study, 1948. There was nothing distinctive or historical about the furniture Harry S. Truman used in his study. Only the piano departed from the generic taste of the objects and hinted at President Truman's passion for music. Bottom left: Truman Family Dining Room, looking northwest, 1952. Most of the 1902 Theodore Roosevelt decoration of the Family Dining Room survived the drastic 1949 renovation, but the tasteful, generic colonial style that permeated the other state-floor rooms had taken hold here, as well. Bottom right: Reproduction and modern upholstered furniture, American, for the Truman west sitting hall, 1952.

Top: Truman ground-floor library, 1952. Knotty-pine paneling was not used in colonial America, but it was fashionable for upscale homes in the 1930s and gradually became a standard feature of suburban interiors right into the 1950s. Bottom left: Reproduction colonial furniture and TV set in the Truman west sitting hall, 1952. The tasteful reproductions and modern television set Bess Truman selected for the White House could just as easily have been chosen by any suburban housewife. Bottom right: Truman China Room, ground floor, 1952. New pine cases made from wood salvaged from the renovation replaced Edith Wilson's original cabinets in the China Room. The cozy quaintness of knotty pine exuded a quality of "American-ness" that had little to do with historic authenticity in a nation anxious about the future.

Top: Design for the president's bedroom as proposed by the staff of B. Altman & Company to the Truman administration, 1951. The only thing that differentiated the Truman bedroom design from any expensive suburban bedroom is the 1850s gilded mirror that somehow survived the purge of the first-floor state rooms. Bottom: Truman rose guest room, as decorated by B. Altman & Company, 1952. Soft colors and plush modern carpeting gave the Truman guest rooms the comfort and personality of luxurious hotel rooms.

Truman solarium, third floor, 1952. Looking like a suburban Florida room, Truman's solarium was replete with bright floral chintzes and pale rattan furniture. Americans—including the Trumans—were now living in informal rooms that served multiple functions.

its objects. Mrs. Hoover created the Lincoln Bedroom by gathering many of the remaining Victorian pieces in one room. In this undertaking she echoed a brief flurry of interest among museums in Victorian period rooms in the 1930s.[11] Significantly, she did not put any Victorian objects in the public rooms. Mrs. Hoover also was the first to create a nostalgic evocation of the White House's early years, in her assembling of the "Monroe" room in the former cabinet room. Using old pieces that she had either borrowed from the Smithsonian (such as a pianoforte) or located in the White House collections (such as some of the Polk dining chairs), Lou Hoover also commissioned reproductions of French furniture owned by the Monroes, from Morris Dove, a local cabinetmaker, in 1932. From photographs of the room, it is clearly not a period room in the strict sense, but an assemblage of relics arranged in a completely modern setting to evoke an imagined past.

Eleanor and Franklin Roosevelt were American aristocrats, but during the Depression they lived a comfortable suburban life upstairs at the White House. During Eleanor Roosevelt's many years as first lady, the influence of the Commission on Fine Arts grew stronger, and a sharper line was drawn between the state floors and the private quarters. Springwood, the Roosevelt estate in Hyde Park, New York, was a Victorian villa turned colonial mansion; it had never been palatial, and it was furnished with the same sort of hodgepodge of old and new furniture that had long filled the White House.[12] The Roosevelts' low-key Lenox porcelain, ordered in 1934, was custom designed but not luxurious, with a narrow band of cobalt blue and discreet gold striping and stars. To save money, the state seal was a colored decal rather than hand painted, a new technology developed by Lenox in the 1920s to make fine china less expensive to

Mamie Eisenhower, like many affluent suburban women in the 1950s, embraced the historical value of objects that had survived the aesthetic purges of the early 20th century. In the Eisenhowers' west sitting hall, Andrew Jackson's Quervelle center table from the 1829 East Room had pride of place as an "antique," even as a reproduction mirror hangs above a built-in television set.

The ground-floor, oval diplomatic reception room, seen here in the Truman Administration, 1948, with cast-offs from the state rooms. This room was created by Teddy Roosevelt for official visitors; in the Depression it was the setting for Franklin Roosevelt's Fireside Chats. In the 1950s, the White House inched towards its role as a museum when Mrs. Eisenhower transformed the room from a repository of leftovers into a showcase for authentic American antiques.

produce. Mrs. Roosevelt's controversial decision to use the rose and feathers of the Roosevelt family crest as part of the gold decal border was the only betrayal of a sense of entitlement to life in the White House.

The Roosevelt family quarters were furnished in the Early American style, with pieces from the Hyde Park, New York–based Val-Kill workshop, which Mrs. Roosevelt supported. These were not custom-made nor particularly expensive pieces. In a view of the upstairs living hall during the Roosevelt years, only the high ceilings distinguish the room from any comfy middle-class living room of the era. The china cupboard and two occasional tables visible in the picture are undoubtedly Val-Kill products, and these exemplify the Early American mode that had been popularized since World War I in trade magazines such as *Good Furniture*.[13] The slipcovered pieces reflected a modern emphasis on comfort over elegance. Imported Oriental rugs became all the rage in American mansions during the Gilded Age, replacing wall-to-wall carpets by the

1890s. Such rugs were later mass-produced in American factories and had become part of the ready-made Colonial Revival by the early 20th century.

The Franklin Roosevelt Red Room used reproductions of Hepplewhite and Sheraton furniture purchased from W. & J. Sloane, a high-end furniture retailer on New York's Fifth Avenue. The overall style was colonial, including Federal designs from the early 1800s, as well. This decor, together with the Green Room similarly furnished in "period" style by Lou Henry Hoover, was the start of a conscious museum-like separation of the state rooms from the private rooms.

Harry and Bess Truman were proudly average Americans who brought their unpretentious middle-class style to the White House. President Truman had grown up relatively poor on a midwestern farm, while Mrs. Truman was raised in a genteel villa in Independence, Missouri. Their Lenox service with a wide celadon brim, the third made for the White House, was ordered through B. Altman in New York and was meant to

Top: President Eisenhower's Oval Office, commercially furnished, was as efficient as a corporate executive's suite. On the left a painting of a restored colonial boxwood garden foreshadowed the design of the Kennedy gardens. Bottom: It was fitting that NATO flags and an American rifle were combined in the office of America's modern general-president. Photographed January 14, 1961, just days before the president's term ended.

Reproduction French desk, Morris Dove, Washington, D.C., 1932. Mrs. Hoover, seated here, was increasingly intrigued by the history of the White House. She borrowed antiques and commissioned reproductions of pieces associated with President Monroe.

harmonize with the newly painted State Dining Room. European and American antiques were being donated for the main floor and for the new rooms under way in the basement, but images of the renovated family quarters from 1952 show B. Altman reproductions that would have been at home in any postwar suburban development. The second-floor sitting hall featured a bland mixture of Chippendale and Queen Anne reproductions, along with a modern entertainment center (television, hi-fi, and radio) in a vaguely colonial mahogany cabinet. The oval room was still a family sitting room, as it had been since Adams's time. Its reproduction Federal furniture, acquired by the Roosevelts in 1943, included a pair of lolling chairs, called "Martha Washington" chairs, and a sofa. The modern notes are the television set to the left of the fireplace and the shiny black piano, President Truman's passion. By this time pianos were too domestic to be appropriate in the state parlors and were played solely by visiting professionals in the East Room. Truman was the only president to have a piano in his personal study.

A new third floor was built during the Truman renovation of 1952, and the Coolidge Sky Parlor was upgraded and furnished with a mixture of colonial reproductions and light-colored rattan. It reflected the rise of informal living spaces in the American home after World War II and the increasingly casual living–dining rooms that were standard in the postwar American ranch house. The north portico, with the Trumans' wrought-iron patio furniture, paralleled suburban porches. An offspring of 19th-century cast-iron garden furniture, such suites appeared on patios and in sunrooms all over America in the 1930s and 1940s.

Absent from the White House in the postwar years was the modern style in furniture and decorative arts championed by such American manufacturers as Herman Miller and Knoll Associates. Although many Americans began to embrace modernism after the war, the White House became irrevocably locked into historical styles, except for its utilitarian spaces. Millions of Americans likewise rejected modern designs and continued to build colonial-style houses and furnish them with a wide range of Early American and other colonial-style decorative arts. Colonial Williamsburg had influenced American suburban taste since the 1930s, despite museums' efforts to celebrate modern design through exhibitions and publications. The iconic Cleaver family of TV's *Leave It to Beaver* had its 1950s colonial home furnished along the same lines as the private quarters in the Truman and Eisenhower White House.

Left: Dinner plate, Lenox Incorporated, Trenton, New Jersey, from the Franklin D. Roosevelt service, 1934. Mrs. Roosevelt chose porcelain featuring decals rather than hand decoration, to save money during the Depression. Right: Service plate, Lenox Incorporated, Trenton, New Jersey, from the Truman service, 1952. But for its gold presidential seal, the plain Truman service could have graced the dining table of any affluent home in the 1950s. The subdued "colonial" green of the wide brim reflects the conservative, muted colors favored in the postwar years.

Dwight and Mamie Eisenhower made no significant shift from the suburban pattern of furnishing the White House. Their second-floor West Sitting Hall was a carryover of the room created for the Trumans by B. Altman's designers. The reproduction red-and-white toile slipcovers recalled the Roosevelts' use of informal upholstery and reflected a growing interest in authentic reproduction textiles. The use of one of the Quervelle tables from the Jackson East Room of 1829 hints at the ongoing interest in objects with White House histories. Since day one, presidential families had retreated upstairs to relax. Early presidents gathered with their families in the oval room, Harriet Lane found solace in her conservatory, President Grant retired to his billiard room and, from the Coolidge years onwards, presidents found complete privacy, away from public scrutiny, in the third-floor sunroom and on its adjoining roof terrace. A color snapshot of the late 1950s shows President Eisenhower barbequing outside the sunroom on the roof of the south portico, with light-colored rattan patio furniture nearby. Here the president becomes Ward Cleaver, the wise father in *Leave It to Beaver*, embracing the comfortable suburban domesticity into which the White House and its occupants had quietly slipped.

In vivid contrast to the suburban lives led by the presidents of the 1940s and 1950s, a bequest from Margaret Thompson Biddle of European gilded silver in 1956 was one more step toward the White House's becoming a museum. A longtime friend of the Eisenhowers, Mrs. Biddle saw her collection as an ideal addition to the White House. The aristocratic French and English vermeil mirrored the taste of America's museums and millionaires in the 1950s and was clearly intended as a link to the opulent French objects acquired by the Monroes and by Andrew Jackson. The basement space next door to the China Room became the Vermeil Room. Mrs. Biddle, who used these pieces, would have understood that she was giving them to a place that was as much a museum as a house. Whether or not she expected the president and his wife to use the vermeil for state dinners, she felt that the White House was the right place for them. Her bequest was a foretaste of the renovations of the 1960s.

Another move toward museumhood was the redecorating of the basement oval room, furnished since Theodore Roosevelt's day as a secondary reception room with leftovers from earlier presidencies. This room in 1960 was decorated through a collaboration of Mrs. Eisenhower and the National Society of Interior Designers. Collectors and antiques dealers donated Federal-period furniture that reflected upper-middle-class suburban taste as much as it did the history of the house. The Diplomatic Reception Room was a fantasy of what life in the Adams White House should have been and established a model for the final presidential dream house.

AMERICAN HOUSE MUSEUMS

Top left: Boscobel, Garrison, New York. This 1808 neoclassic house, built for early Dutch descendent States Morris Dyckman, was relocated and restored with money from the founders of The Reader's Digest. When it opened in 1961 the public discovered a fantasy of colonial life and landscape design, not an archaeological restoration. Top right Bayou Bend, Houston, Texas, 1927, by John F. Staub, architect. The home of oil heiress and art collector Ima Hogg was donated to the Houston Museum of Fine Arts in 1957 and opened to the public in 1966. Bottom left: The Port Royal entrance to the Henry Francis du Pont Winterthur Museum in Wilmington, Delaware. Winterthur, the 1839 home of Henry Francis du Pont, was renovated beginning in 1929 and opened to the public in 1951; this photograph was taken c. 1931. Bottom right: The Governor's Palace in Williamsburg, Virginia, opened to the public in 1934. The building is a re-creation from period documents, including a drawing by Thomas Jefferson, of the 1720 British governor's house, which burned in 1781.

SHRINE
1961–PRESENT

Yet the significance of the President's House goes beyond its historical meaning. It suggests a way of life in which we all take pride. We want it to be an example of excellence.

—John Walker, *The White House: An Historic Guide*, 1962

KEEPING UP WITH THE MUSEUMS

The changes made to the White House in the first half of the 20th century reflected a broad cultural dynamic. As the nation went through two wars and a depression, Americans simultaneously embraced a modern world freed from the inequalities of the Gilded Age and continued to look back to their early democratic heritage for reassurance in the face of an unknown future. The struggle intensified as post–World War II urban renewal leveled old neighborhoods in the face of an expanding preservation movement.

At the White House itself, the conflict between wanting to be new and to preserve the past manifested itself in Harry Truman's radical renovation. The president himself signed into existence the National Trust for Historic Preservation in 1949 and considered historic issues before gutting the frame of the president's house.[1] But Truman, and then Dwight Eisenhower, saw the White House first in practical terms, and only second as a historic building—just as all their precursors, except James Madison, had done.

The longing for America's past was reflected in the movement to preserve 18th- and 19th-century houses. American museums participated by installing period rooms. The Brooklyn Museum, the Philadelphia Museum, and the Metropolitan Museum all created groups of American period rooms in the 1920s that became immediately popular. John D. Rockefeller Jr. funded the reconstruction and restoration of numerous buildings and interiors at Colonial Williamsburg in the 1920s and 1930s. This work was done with a loose mixture of scholarship and upper-class ideas of good taste, encouraged by private collectors of American antiques.

Antiques collecting accompanied building preservation. It began as a craze in the wake of the Centennial Exhibition of 1876. In the early decades of the 20th century emerged a powerful community of rich and socially prominent collectors, from Boston to Houston, from Detroit to Los Angeles. At a more modest level, suburban middle-class Americans also collected antiques, having embraced museums as arbiters of taste. These collectors ignored cultural leaders who were antihistorical and pro-modernist. In 1944, designer Thomas Robsjohn-Gibbings published a sly little polemic called *Good-bye, Mr. Chippendale.*[2] On the surface it appeared to be a humorous overview of America's obsession with antiques, but in fact it was an uncompromising manifesto calling for Americans to throw out anything and everything old—architecture, gardens, interior decoration, and furnishings. The book singled out traditional decorator Elsie de Wolfe as the villain who had turned Americans away from respect for everything modern and toward a perverted love of the antique.[3]

In this world of revering antiques and preserving old houses, Jacqueline Bouvier Kennedy came of age. With a deep attachment to the legacy of America's historic ruling class, Mrs. Kennedy ignored modernism and took up the preservation of the White House using the curatorial approach of the house museum movement. In the

In the postwar years, television came to living rooms coast to coast. Harry S. Truman understood its power to shape public opinion and in May 1953 he led 30 million Americans on a CBS tour of his refurbished White House. On Valentine's Day, 1962, Mrs. Kennedy showed over 50 million TV viewers her White House, recently redecorated in the style of an imagined colonial past that associated the Kennedys with early presidents. On January 15, she stood in the State Dining Room during the filming of the broadcast.

tradition of the melting pot, the first Roman Catholic first lady, wife of the first Irish American president, reinvented the White House, which had been the domain solely of America's Protestant majority.

The Kennedy vision forever changed 1600 Pennsylvania Avenue into a museum dedicated to an imagined American past. Consequently, the president's house today no longer evolves with the times and, like Disneyland's "Main Street, U.S.A.," seems to be authentic without precisely reflecting anything other than Mrs. Kennedy's world of the 1960s.

SHRINE KEEPERS

JACQUELINE AND JOHN KENNEDY in the second-floor oval room, 1963.

Aided by prominent social figures and wealthy connoisseurs, Jacqueline Bouvier Kennedy swept away 40 years of suburban interiors and oversaw the transformation of the White House into a shrine to upper-class taste. Mrs. Kennedy's museum-like vision of the state floor and the private quarters dominates today.

CLAUDIA TAYLOR JOHNSON, known as "Lady Bird," in 1968, posing in the upstairs living hall of the White House, decorated with two lacquered Chinese screens brought to the White House by Mrs. Kennedy.

Mrs. Johnson introduced southern hospitality to White House after the formality of the Kennedy administration, but dutifully maintained the elegance of the early 1960s. Like presidents in the 19th century, Mrs. Johnson devoted herself to improving not just the White House garden, but the capital city grounds as well. When she completed the east flower garden along the south facade in 1964, Mrs. Johnson dedicated it to Jacqueline Kennedy.

1961–63

1963–69

NANCY AND RONALD REAGAN in the second-floor oval room, 1984.

Nancy Davis Reagan, like all first ladies since Jacqueline Kennedy, carried on the tradition of high-style decoration and elegant comfort throughout the second-floor residence of the White House. Here, the Reagans, dressed like royalty, wait for the president of Mexico, Miguel de la Madrid, in the room that Abigail Adams first furnished as a "ladies' parlor" with second-hand furniture from President Washington's Philadelphia house.

WILLIAM AND HILLARY RODHAM CLINTON with American-born Queen Noor and King Hussein of Jordan, August 7, 1998, on Harry and Bess Truman's porch built in 1947.

Mrs. Clinton tried to bring change to the White House, but was criticized for her Victorian-inspired second floor interiors. In contrast to the White House reverence for tradition, she created in 1994 a temporary exhibition of modern sculpture in the east garden.

1981–89

1993–2001

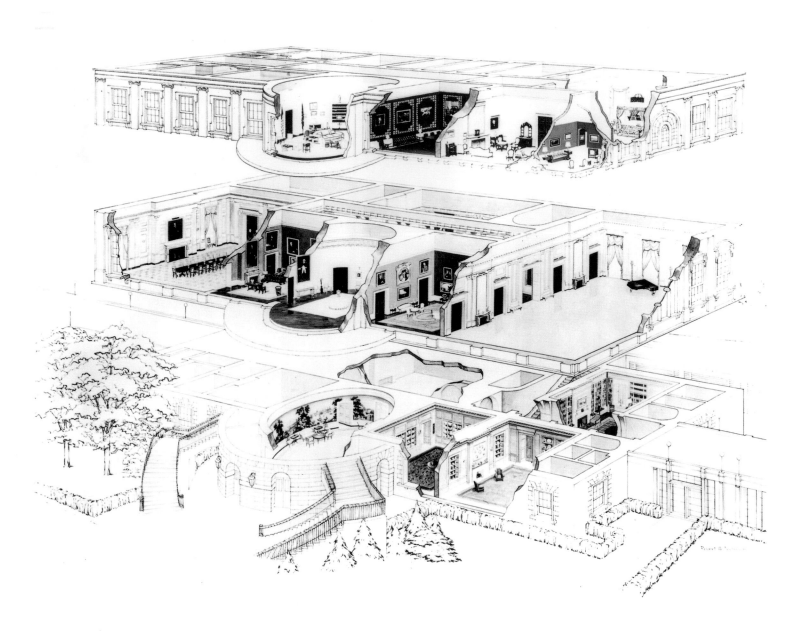

An isometric drawing of the John and Jacqueline Kennedy White House. Though still seen by the public as an historic house in a garden, the White House inside had become a museum with a private apartment for the first family.

HOUSE

As early as the 1950s, the White House had become so ingrained in the popular imagination and so redolent of American history that it had taken on the quality of a national shrine. Jacqueline Kennedy's nationally televised tour of the White House in 1962 secured the house's near-mythic status.[4] In a comparatively young country, absent a monarchy or a state religion, the role of a building having such powerful associations with shared national experience and values was, and remains, defining.

Since Truman's rebuilding, the White House has seen few important architectural changes, other than new "period rooms" constructed in the basement story that have complemented the house's increasingly museum-like identity. In 1969, Richard Nixon covered over Franklin Roosevelt's indoor swimming pool and replaced it with facilities for the media, including television broadcasters. Internal changes to the west wing have been ongoing.

View from Oval Office, April, 1963, to the new rose garden. Like the early agrarian presidents who had first planted the president's park, John F. Kennedy was directly involved with the redesign of the southwest parterre.

GARDEN

Guided by the 1935 Olmsted plan prepared for Franklin D. Roosevelt, the White House staff had already enshrined the president's garden as an Anglo-American landscape when President and Mrs. Kennedy arrived. The gardeners had shaped and refined the plantings of the 19th century. The south park had matured, with shade trees and shrubs framing the iconic view of the Ellipse from the columned south portico. The north and south drives, the east and west entrances, and the panorama of the Potomac River, Washington Monument, and Thomas Jefferson Memorial were preserved.

When John F. Kennedy stood in his Oval Office for the first time, he could see the west flower garden, planted with a nursery assortment of roses bordered by low privet hedges. The east garden was similarly uninspired, with an open lawn and beds of annuals. Romanticism has been an inevitable part of White House history; by the Kennedy administration, a trite sentimentality had crept into the south gardens. Arthur Schlesinger Jr. complained to White House social secretary Letitia Baldrige that a sign with Dorothy Frances Gurney's poem "God's Garden"

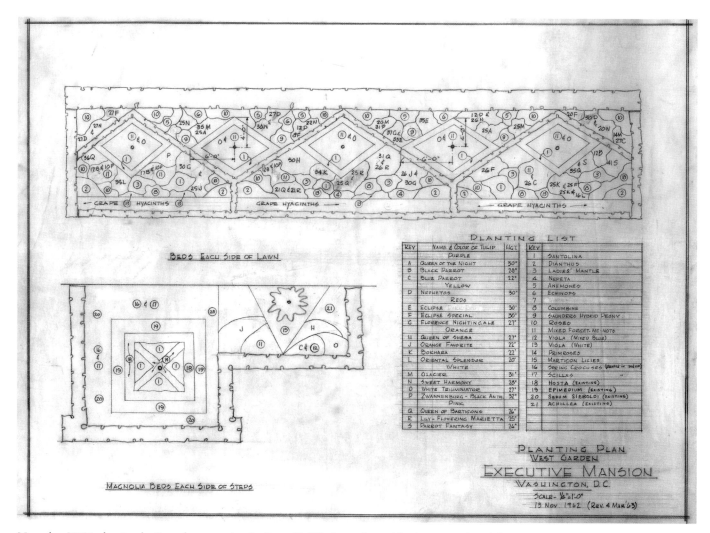

November 1962 plan for the Kennedy rose garden, by Perry H. Wheeler, influenced by American colonial design.

was "doggerel of an exceptional mawkishness beginning: 'The kiss of the sun for pardon.' . . . I shudder," wrote Schlesinger, "every time I bring an eminent foreign statesman or writer over to the west wing and watch him wince as he observes these bloodcurdling sentiments."[5] Clearly this was not a garden suitable for the Kennedy Camelot presidency.

President Kennedy embraced the restoration spirit of the interiors and continued the Jeffersonian tradition of democratically elected presidents' being inspired by the splendor of aristocratic parks. After returning from a state visit to Europe in 1961, he persuaded Rachel Lambert Mellon, wife of National Gallery patron Paul Mellon, to oversee the redesign of the south terrace gardens. The president shared with his colonial predecessors the Enlightenment belief that nature guides sound judgment. A member of Jacqueline Bouvier Kennedy's Fine Arts Committee, Mrs. Mellon recalled that JFK wanted a garden that would "endure and whose atmosphere, with the subtlety of its ever changing pattern, would suggest the ever changing pattern of history itself."[6] She redesigned the garden as both the president's private refuge and an outdoor room for public receptions.

Just as Mrs. Kennedy enlisted professionals for her redecoration of the White House interiors, Rachel Mellon turned to landscape architect Perry Wheeler. Wheeler was well known in Washington for his work at the National Cathedral and as a designer of private Georgetown gardens for the capital's elite. He eventually landscaped the John F. Kennedy grave site at Arlington National Cemetery and continued working with Mrs. Mellon on the White House gardens in the Johnson administration. The design for the Kennedy White House gardens began in the spring of 1962, and the planting was completed in the Rose Garden the following year.

The Kennedys' desire for a house reflecting East Coast establishment values brought to the White House contemporary ideas of what a period house and garden should be, not what they in fact had been. Mellon and Wheeler's south gardens were not historic re-creations of early 18-century American gardens, but upper-class 1960s interpretations of colonial designs.

Like Edith Roosevelt before them, Mellon and Wheeler ignored the mid-century, gardenesque world of A.J. Downing and returned to the formal traditions of southern colonial plantations. After substantial soil

The ballroom garden at the Governor's Palace, Williamsburg, Virginia, was a 1930s re-creation of an 18th-century colonial garden. Southern Virginia gardens like this inspired the Kennedy rose garden, c. 1945.

and structural preparations, the White House staff, under the direction of horticulturalist Irwin Williams and White House operations chief executive J. B. West, created geometric flower beds framed in boxwood and planted with historic American flowers and trees. "The divisions gave the garden its own pattern, not unlike an early American garden in southern Virginia, in which the earth could be left bare if need be and the garden would still have form," wrote Mrs. Mellon.[7] The Ballroom Garden of the Governor's Palace at Colonial Williamsburg, a 1930s homage to the 18th century, is a fine example of a southern garden with patterned boxwood parterres like those in the president's Oval Office garden.

President Kennedy requested that roses be planted again on the site of the original 1878 Hayes rose house and 1913 Wilson garden. "Red roses are often the most beautiful of all roses, but they are better planted together, or with flowers related to them," wrote Mrs. Mellon. "Here we planted them with large red cabbages, blue thistles, and heliotrope."[8] Because the president wanted to see flowers from his desk, Mellon and Wheeler planted a spring spectacle of 2,000 tulips and 8,000 grape hyacinths. They fulfilled Frederick Law Olmsted Jr.'s recommendation that the president's garden be a rich "floral display" symmetrically conceived.[9]

Mrs. Mellon recalled that Kennedy envisioned a garden that would "appeal to the most discriminating taste, yet [be] a garden that would hold a thousand people for a ceremony."[10] At the president's direction, a stone platform in the steps outside the Oval Office was built so he could stand above assembled guests. Kennedy, a modern-day orator, brought his

On the site of Edith Roosevelt's 1903 colonial parterre, Rachel Mellon and Perry Wheeler planted their version of an 18th-century Virginia garden, with an open lawn to accommodate guests of a modern presidency; photograph, April 1963.

renowned charisma and sense of occasion to the White House gardens, just as Abraham Lincoln had done by speaking from the window above the north entrance door a century before.

A month before his death, at a tribute to Robert Frost, America's poet of the wilderness, Kennedy articulated his hope for the preservation of historic buildings and landscapes: "I look forward to an America which will not be afraid of grace and beauty, which will protect the beauty of our national environment, which will preserve great old American houses and squares and parks of our national past, and which will build handsome and balanced cities for our future."[11] The president's call was an eloquent summation of the goals of America's preservation movement, reflected in the new White House interiors and gardens he left to the nation on November 22, 1963.

Today the Kennedy gardens are preserved by curators, architects, and the National Park Service, charged by Kennedy with the ongoing maintenance of the grounds. Their combined oversight has preserved the 1935 Olmsted plan while accommodating unobtrusive public-spirited changes

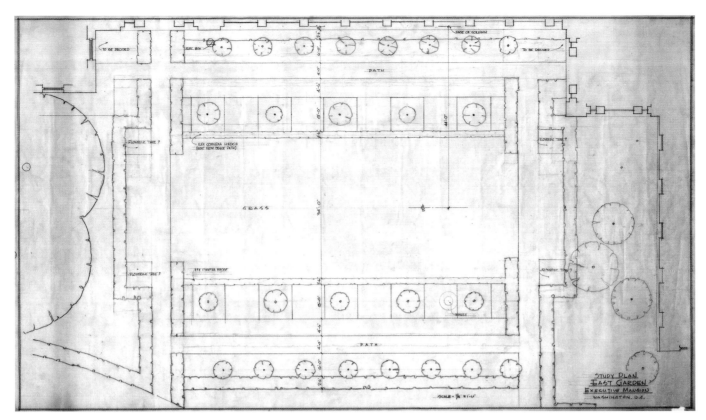

Working plan for the Kennedy east garden, by Perry H. Wheeler, 1962. It called for American flowers and trees associated with the gardens of early presidents.

The Kennedy southeast garden, shown here in July 1963, was completed by Lady Bird Johnson the following year. The faux-bois suite from the Wilson garden was preserved.

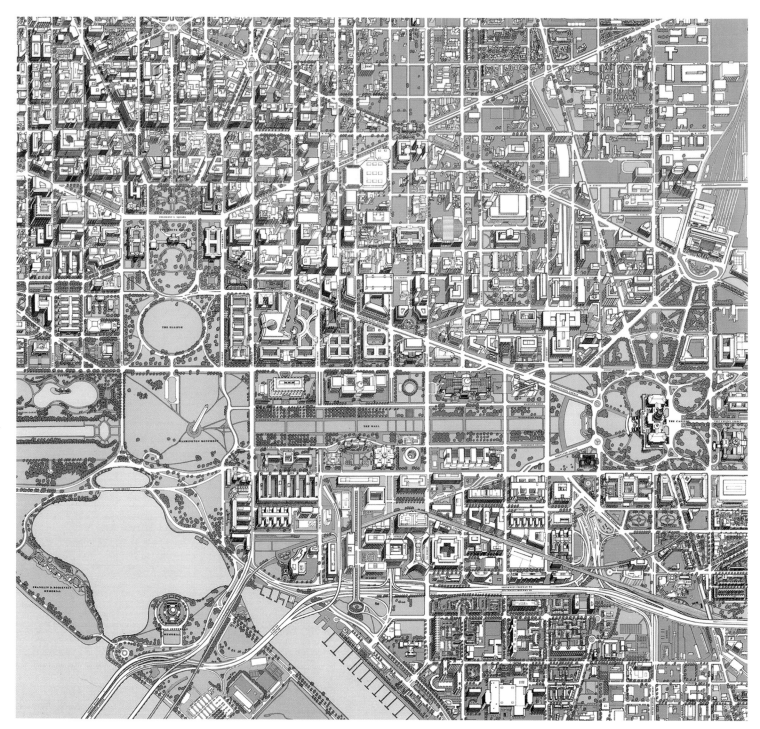

Map of Washington, D.C., 1996. The open spaces envisioned by Pierre-Charles L'Enfant have been preserved. Unlike the Capitol, a public building in an open park, the White House, after two centuries of being home to presidents, is a city house in a private garden overlooking public parks.

consistent with the national park ideals of a century earlier. In 1964 Lady Bird Johnson, assisted by Mellon and Wheeler, completed the southeast garden after the assassination of President Kennedy in 1963 and dedicated it to Jacqueline Kennedy. On Christmas Day 1969, President and Mrs. Lyndon Baines Johnson dedicated a children's garden on the south lawn, and in 1973 President Richard Milhous Nixon planted a permanent Christmas tree on the Ellipse. Downing's call for the educational labeling

of trees has been heeded both in the grounds and in tourist maps that identify the presidential trees by name and species.

Vegetable gardening at the president's house has followed national trends. Until the end of the 19th century, the White House, like other American estates, was self-sustaining, with a vegetable garden southwest of the house. During World War II, Eleanor Roosevelt planted a Victory garden to support federal efforts to mitigate food shortages. Today

252

Aerial view of Washington, D.C., during the Kennedy administration, 1962. The White House had a garden of its own visible from the public Ellipse.

Michelle Obama has planted a vegetable garden to support sustainability and self-sufficiency, values held by the early farming presidents.

Security and privacy continue to define planning at the White House, but these have been ensured through structural changes to entrance gates and access to streets, not through substantial changes in the historic planting.

If George Washington were to visit Washington, D.C., today he would find that the White House and its garden have been developed with ongoing respect for the defining Potomac view, despite the complexity of 21st-century urban life. A consistent and protected vision of pre-urban America has ensured that today's capital city map remains much as L'Enfant envisioned when he presented his plan to the first president two centuries ago. At the heart of the city, for the pleasure of the public and the president, remains the city's Reservation No. I, the president's garden and park.

253

Kennedy second-floor dining room, decorated by Sister Parish, assisted by Henry F. du Pont, 1963. Fine antiques chosen by du Pont, the heir to a vast chemical fortune, complemented by rare scenic wallpaper installed by a high-society decorator, made the White House's new second-floor dining room a shrine to museum-quality taste. The creation of this room and its adjacent kitchen also permanently transformed the second floor into a self-sufficient house within the White House, separate from the museum-like shrine of the state rooms.

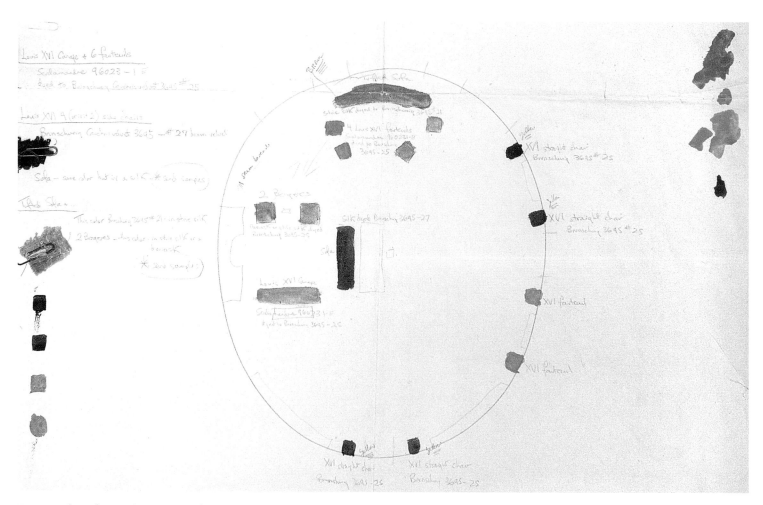

In a furnishing plan for the upstairs oval sitting room, Mrs. Kennedy and Sister Parish followed precedents set in motion by Edith Roosevelt, who reclaimed the space in 1902 as a family drawing room. Unlike the Blue Room below, designed for formality, the upstairs room was for comfort. As it had been in the Wilson and Franklin Roosevelt administrations, the main seating furniture was clustered around the largely ornamental fireplace in the manner of a suburban living room. A seating area by the windows to the Truman porch created a second grouping. For all its 18th-century French antiques, the design was distinctly 19th-century, following patterns established by American villas back to the 1840s. Though this organization had been introduced to America by French design publications, it was embraced by collectors of colonial antiques and Americana in the 20th century.

INTERIORS

By the early 20th century, a new type of decorator had replaced the retail furnisher–upholsterers of the Gilded Age.[12] Edith Wharton (an upper-class New York novelist) and Ogden Codman (an upper-class New England architect) published *The Decoration of Houses* in 1897. Elsie de Wolfe, considered the founder of modern interior decoration, established the use of 18th-century European period furniture and objects by 1913 with her own book, *The House in Good Taste.*[13] These new decorators were selectively historicist in the manner of Beaux-Arts designers such as McKim, Mead & White, basing their canon of good taste on a rejection of anything Victorian. They were assisted in their promotion of 18th-century-style interiors by the Metropolitan Museum's American Wing and Colonial Williamsburg.[14]

Although their work was widely popularized by magazines aimed at suburban housewives, their clientele was self-consciously upper-class (or at least rich).

America's reverence for its own history, burgeoning since the 1876 Centennial in Philadelphia, was accompanied by a paradoxical purge of architectural and aesthetic history to accommodate the comforts and conveniences that came with industrial progress. By the 1920s, city dwellers saw rows of Gilded Age houses replaced by skyscraper apartment buildings suitable for modern living and yet filled with reassuring period-style details. On the outskirts, historic farms gave way to 1920s and 1930s suburban developments populated with Colonial and Tudor Revival houses.

The Baltimore Parlor at Winterthur, 1965, arranged by Henry F. du Pont. His credentials of good taste and scholarly expertise were well known from his Delaware mansion. Rooms such as this parlor, painted pale celadon green, were models for the Kennedy White House.

America's struggle with the present and the past was most clearly expressed in the movement to preserve old houses, both public and private. In the 19th century, Americans had torn down old houses or entirely remade them into something better, something new. The Colonial Revival as a movement went hand in hand with the growing respect for old American houses. Richard Pratt's 1949 coffee-table book *A Treasury of Early American Homes* was so popular that a second volume came out in 1953.[15]

In the 1950s, two influential house museums full of colonial antiques appeared on the American scene: Bayou Bend in Houston, Texas, and Winterthur in Delaware. Bayou Bend was a grand, neoclassical pink stucco house in Houston's exclusive River Oaks neighborhood, built for oil heiress and philanthropist Miss Ima Hogg. The collection, begun in 1920 and the only major accumulation of Americana in the Southwest, was accepted as a gift by the Houston Museum of Fine Arts in 1958 and was transformed into a house museum during the early 1960s.

Winterthur was already legendary among antiques aficionados by the late 1950s. Henry Francis du Pont inherited his family's vast Delaware estate in 1926 and transformed the enormous 1906 French hunting lodge into a rambling colonial palace, packed with the best possible colonial woodwork, furniture, and decorative objects. Du Pont established a graduate program for the connoisseurship of American decorative arts at Winterthur in the early 1950s, creating a professional field of study that existed nowhere else in the nation.

John and Jacqueline Kennedy were young, rich, and glamorous. They were not, however, part of the old-guard Protestant establishment that had occupied the White House since the Adamses first moved in. The academic Wilsons, the frugal Roosevelts, and the bourgeois Trumans and Eisenhowers had left the White House a cavernous old barn, vaguely palatial, vaguely colonial, blandly grandiose in a comfortable suburban way. It had always been buffeted by budgets and politics, filled with odds and ends from past

Kennedy Green Room, showing Stéphane Boudin's green moiré silk walls, as well as furniture selected by Henry F. du Pont, 1963. A French decorator for international jet-setters, Boudin brought his aristocratic eye to the Green Room. Du Pont brought his scholar-connoisseur's eye to the selection of objects. Together they created a plausible historical fantasy for the space Thomas Jefferson had used as a "common dining room."

regimes; but the house itself had survived intact since 1814. The brutal Truman renovation and redecoration had left the White House sterile, an ersatz colonial palace stripped of its historic layers and filled with an uneasy mixture of relics, inappropriate antiques, and soulless new interiors.

Jacqueline Kennedy's dream house was a 1960s fantasy of how an upper-class family would live, using an authentic Georgian house as the background. Her taste, with its preference for "period rooms" and antiques, meant a return to the French glamour of the Monroes, the Gilded Age luxury of the Grants, and the imperial splendor of the Theodore Roosevelts. She abandoned forever the department store and ready-made, by turning to high-profile decorators favored by America's upper crust.

Disheartened by the White House's undistinguished decoration yet simultaneously moved by its history, Mrs. Kennedy brought in two important interior designers, each representing a related but distinct style. Mrs. Henry Parish II, known to her high-society clients as Sister Parish, had been raised in rural New Jersey, in houses filled with "good" old things and layered, understated interiors. Her style combined elegance and comfort in a cozy way that particularly suited America's elite.[16] Stéphane Boudin, longtime principal in the Parisian decorating firm Maison Jansen, was both European and aristocratic in his taste and clientele. He brought a scholarly French glamour to everything he designed and was a favorite of the wives of American power brokers.[17]

Kennedy Red Room, 1962. Stéphane Boudin consciously returned to the glamour of Malmaison, Emperor Napoleon Bonaparte's country house outside Paris, in his redecoration of this room. Re-creating a historical reflection of the "best parlor" of generations of first ladies was less important than making the room look as it "ought to have looked" when it was new.

Every first lady has a hand in furnishing the White House, upstairs and downstairs, but the process of restricting her role, begun with the creation of the first Fine Arts Committee in the 1920s and strengthened with the Commission on Fine Arts in 1941, was completed by a different kind of committee in 1962. From this point on, the presidential family's personal wishes were overshadowed by history, authenticity, and officially sanctioned good taste. Unlike the advisory committees with which Grace Coolidge, Lou Henry Hoover, and Eleanor Roosevelt had worked, Mrs. Kennedy's Fine Arts Committee consisted of uniformly rich and powerful people who shared her vision. Aside from validating the upper-class taste Mrs. Kennedy sought, this committee had the ability to network with other, similar people

to leverage financial and material support for her dream house. Henry Francis du Pont was one of the few members with any scholarly credentials, although his participation largely arose from his unwillingness to lend Winterthur's treasures; his chief curator, Charles F. Montgomery, suggested du Pont's presence on the committee would make up for the absence of his objects in the White House.[18] Du Pont also provided the White House with its first curator, Lorraine Waxman Pearce, a recent graduate of the fledgling master's program in early American culture created for Henry Francis du Pont at his Winterthur estate in Delaware.[19]

Jacqueline Kennedy finally clarified the upstairs/downstairs dichotomy that had existed in the White House since it was built. By

Kennedy Blue Room, 1961. Stéphane Boudin initially softened the Truman-era silk walls with paintings, and Sister Parish added the yellow-silk-covered table. Making the room historically accurate was irrelevant; making it chic (or at least less dowdy) was the point.

installing a family dining room on the second floor, complete with its own kitchen and elevator entrance, she severed the last link between the state floor and the private quarters, transforming the second floor into the kind of elegant Park Avenue apartment she had known as a girl.[20] The state floor finally became strictly a public space.[21] With the Kennedy restoration, the tripartite nature of the house—offices, state rooms, family quarters—permanently supplanted the two-part division created by the 1902 office wing.

The main goal of the Kennedy redecoration was twofold. The first was to create on all four floors stylish, distinctively upper-class interiors that appealed to moneyed donors and had just enough scholarly underpinning to validate them as period rooms according to museum standards of the day. The second was to fill her interiors with a museum-quality collection to encourage donations from wealthy patrons interested in preserving America's material heritage. The advisory committee's comment that "no other residence reflects so meaningfully the struggles and aspirations of the American people"[22] would have resonated with almost every first lady

since Abigail Adams, each of whom had her own interpretation of those struggles and aspirations and tried to make the White House reflect her understanding of the broader values of American society. In this way, Jacqueline Kennedy was no different than all the first ladies who had battled budgets and public opinion to make the White House accommodate their needs.

The state rooms in the Kennedy White House were dominated by Stéphane Boudin's French elegance, which Mrs. Kennedy and her friends felt (not incorrectly) was appropriate to the scale and original style of the house. The reemergence of such strong French influence recalls Madison's 1817 decoration and the reverence for French culture that seems to have infused America ever since. Sister Parish, who jostled for influence on the state floor, was more involved in the private quarters, although Mrs. Kennedy gave Boudin extensive work upstairs, as well. For both floors' interiors, Parish and Boudin deferred to Henry du Pont because of his unerring eye and knowledge of American decorative arts. Mrs. Kennedy handled all three of these intelligent, opinionated people with a mixture

Kennedy Blue Room, with Stéphane Boudin's completed decoration, 1963. The finished room more closely reflected the taste of rich collectors in New York and Paris than any decoration the Monroes would have known.

of diplomacy and ruthlessness, relying on her curatorial staff to apply professional museum standards to the project.

Mr. du Pont's academic approach to interiors was seen in the Green Room, which resembled the many Federal interiors he had designed and furnished at Winterthur. From the pale French brocades to the muted colors of the carpet to the arrangement of the furniture, the Kennedy Green Room was more a reflection of 1930s aristocratic taste than of the White House of 1800. Du Pont's historically correct insistence that draperies be placed inside the window casings, as at Winterthur, only exaggerated the height of the room, which had long been mitigated by Victorian-type draperies hiding the woodwork. The furniture arrangements favored by du Pont reflected Victorian customs dating back to his childhood at Winterthur (although one suspects that he would have been horrified to realize this). Boudin, who had no respect for American objects, ultimately dominated this room by using a muted deep green silk moiré for the walls, replacing the bright green Truman damask of 1952.

In her remarks on the Red Room for the 1962 White House guidebook, Lorraine Pearce noted that the space was "very reminiscent of the Red Music Room at Malmaison . . . which was furnished in the antique style after the designs of Percier and Fontaine."[23] This similarity was no accident, as Boudin, whose role was being kept low profile because he wasn't American, had worked on the restoration of Malmaison, Napoleon's favorite country house. Although Boudin provided an appropriate period document for the French silk and trimming in the Red Room, his use of straight side panels to frame the windows without draped valances indicates that style trumped history when it contradicted his preferences. Sister Parish also played a significant role in the Red Room, mostly by finding donors for the objects and textiles.

The Blue Room, like the Green Room, was not entirely redecorated by the time the 1962 guidebook appeared. Paintings were hung on the Truman-era deep blue walls to make the room less forbidding. Sister Parish, to break up the huge empty space, added a round center table covered in a ruffled yellow silk cloth, which Boudin referred to as a "fat

Kennedy State Dining Room, 1961. Truman painted McKim, Mead & White's baroque banquet hall green to look like a suburban colonial dining room. When Stéphane Boudin wanted it to be a Louis XVI salon, he painted the paneling and consoles white and gilded the silvered lighting fixtures to coordinate with existing gold silk draperies.

Spanish dancer." When completed, the Blue Room was Boudin's most dramatic White House space and his greatest departure from the 20th-century precedent established by McKim, Mead & White in 1902. The continuous blue drapery frieze and white-on-white striped walls, again inspired by Napoleonic interiors, were not inappropriate for the room, which had seen such pale walls in the course of the previous century. Dolley Madison had used a drapery frieze in her yellow parlor (now the Red Room). The yellow silk tablecloth was replaced with a shimmering blue velvet one and a French carpet. The result was, without question, a room that fulfilled Mrs. Kennedy's desire for a "sense of state, arrival, and grandeur."[24] It had little bearing on American historical interiors but beautifully embodied aspirations of the American elite in 1962.

In the State Dining Room, Boudin opted for a gold and white color scheme, which meant painting Truman's celadon green walls and dark green marble mantelpiece ivory, gilding the silver-plated Roosevelt sconces and chandelier, and giving the McKim, Mead & White sideboard and console

tables a gold and white finish. To provide pattern and color in this toned-down room, Boudin ordered a reproduction carpet based on one he had put in the dining room at Leeds Castle in Maidstone, England. Similarly, in the East Room, Boudin had the red marble mantelpieces (themselves reproductions of the discarded McKim, Mead & White versions) marbleized white, reducing the room to a chilly, monochromatic concert hall. On the ground floor, Boudin provided chic designs for the Library and Vermeil rooms, inspired not by American history but by interiors he had done for Lady Baillie at Leeds Castle.

In addition to asserting her skill at obtaining donations (something Boudin could not do), Sister Parish staked out her own territory in the massive project. The informal period-based style she brought to the Kennedys' private quarters could be found in the glamorous houses and city apartments she decorated. This style was imitated by many decorators (as well as by countless housewives, who saw such interiors in shelter magazines) and influenced affluent suburban interiors across the country,

Kennedy East Room, c. 1961. The Truman administration stripped the room of its Beaux-Arts vigor. Stéphane Boudin went further and marbleized the 1952 reproduction red mantelpieces white to eliminate any strong color contrast reminiscent of Gilded Age excess. The room, finished by Andrew Jackson to impress the nation, now impressed the elite.

with success determined by the skill of the decorator and the quality of the objects.

Parish's largest project was the upstairs oval living room, which became the Yellow Oval Room for good under the Kennedys. The most French room in the house, it was Mrs. Kennedy's favorite because it embodied perfectly her vision of elite chic. In 1965, style critic and *Harper's Bazaar* editor Russell Lynes included this space in his book *The Finest Rooms by America's Great Decorators,* classing it with others that "epitomize a kind of well-bred ease, a concern with objects that have quality . . . and a delight in comfortable (not just ostentatious) luxury."[25] But even in this room— and throughout the family quarters—Boudin's influence was present, in the choice and placement of the furniture and even in the design of the draperies. Sister Parish threatened to resign over Boudin's interference.[26]

Mrs. Parish decorated both the state-floor Family Dining Room and the new second-floor President's Dining Room. Parish collaborated with Mr. du Pont on the latter, using Federal furniture and hanging French scenic

wallpaper of a type produced for the American market in the early 19th century. Such wallpaper was hugely expensive and considered a prize for elite Colonial Revival interiors of the 1930s and 1940s.[27] What had been the first-floor private dining room for presidential families for generations was now used by the president as a smaller State Dining Room. The Roosevelt-era moldings of 1902, which had miraculously survived the Truman renovation, were eventually stripped off the walls by Sister Parish, and the neutral 1960 color scheme was replaced with a vivid yellow and a bright floral carpet.

Sister Parish decorated both the president's bedroom and Mrs. Kennedy's suite with off-white walls and unthreatening blues and greens, perfectly in line with the received canon of refined taste that dominated the early 1960s. What rescued the rooms from dullness was their grand scale and Mrs. Parish's deft use of drapery and fine objects. The quiet neutrality of the private rooms underscored the public nature of Boudin's dramatic state parlors (and his pseudo-Victorian Treaty Room on the

American Federal furniture chosen by Henry F. du Pont, in the Kennedy first-floor Family Dining Room, 1961. During the 1962 redecoration of the White House, fine antiques replaced reproductions. Chinese screens, like the one seen here, had been a symbol of class since they first appeared in 19th-century mansions.

second floor). These were rooms for living in, not for public display. Boudin later redecorated Mrs. Kennedy's suite, feeling it was not grand enough for the space.

Today the White House, for all its changes, remains a shrine to the taste of Jacqueline Kennedy, much as Winterthur is a shrine to the taste of Henry Francis du Pont. Both hold collections of exceptional American period objects preserved in architectural settings decorated in the taste of privileged Americans of the mid-20th century. Although the White House is officially a museum, overseen by the permanent Office of the Curator

and the Committee for the Preservation of the White House, it is not like any house museum in the country, because it does not attempt to present history accurately.

Because the Office of the Curator, working in the spirit of the Kennedy renovation, continues to oversee any changes to the state rooms, these rooms no longer reflect contemporary American taste. The first floor remains palatial and aristocratic, embodying our place in the world—or at least our imagined place. Even though documentary evidence survives to restore any one of the state rooms to a specific

Jacqueline Kennedy bedroom, decorated by Sister Parish, 1962. The decorator's skilled use of antiques and deft arrangement of furniture saved the Kennedy private rooms from blandness. The soft tones and 18th-century furnishings of this bedroom reflect a period when intense color was considered vulgar and 19th-century furnishings were seen as ugly.

Federal furniture, United States, 1795–1810, chosen by Henry F. du Pont, and two paintings by Paul Cézanne, chosen by Jacqueline Kennedy. Mrs. Kennedy trusted Mr. du Pont to use only the best American antiques in the Green Room, but her love of French art led her to select the inappropriate landscape paintings, which were soon moved upstairs to the oval yellow room. Kennedy Green Room, 1961.

historic period, they bear little resemblance, in their artifacts or their decoration, to their appearance at any given moment in history. They do not look like the rooms of the Monroe White House, although they evoke them, and they certainly do not simulate any of the rooms that began with Andrew Jackson and ended with Edith Roosevelt. The only

space in the White House that honors its Victorian heritage is the so-called Lincoln Bedroom (originally Lincoln's office). Since 2005 it has been decorated to reflect the way Mary Todd Lincoln decorated her Prince of Wales room, although with colors more acceptable to modern taste than Mrs. Lincoln's light purple walls and vivid floral carpet. The

Green Room, 1971, as redecorated by the Nixons. Long after the Kennedy era, the style set by Jacqueline Kennedy remained enshrined. The Nixons and their successors continued to upgrade the collections according to museum standards but maintained the strongly French-accented style for the decoration. Nothing but the best would do for the state rooms of the president's house, nor would historical accuracy override received notions of status and taste.

White House is forever frozen in a style that, although seemingly appropriate, is only marginally linked to anything real.

The second-floor rooms, because they represent the first family personally, change with each administration. Ironically, they seem more subject to public scrutiny and criticism than the state rooms. Although

Nancy Reagan was vilified for being too imperial in her redecoration, she in fact was faithful to the upper-class establishment spirit of Jacqueline Kennedy.[28] Hillary Clinton's decorator, Kaki Hockersmith, a prominent Arkansas interior designer (with roots as a staff decorator at Dillard's department store) was ridiculed for not adhering to the canon of good taste (i.e., soft colors and 18th-century aesthetics) in her vivid, Victorian-inspired interiors; yet the private rooms were as luxurious and comfortable as the Kennedys' had ever been.[29] Although neither born nor accustomed to such luxury, the Clintons carried on the Kennedy model of expensive custom interiors for their private space.

Weighed down by two centuries of tradition and Jacqueline Kennedy's revered model, today's first ladies are no longer free to experiment and change the White House to be what they and their friends admire.[30] Not quite a private house and not quite a museum, the White House is now a national dream house, a monument to conservative ideals of taste and refinement. As Michelle Obama takes on the role of first lady, this dual burden of history and establishment good taste will confront her. Her 10-year-old daughter Malia can redecorate her room in the private quarters any way she wants, but her mother does not have the freedom that Dolley Madison or Julia Grant—or even Jackie Kennedy—had to make the White House *her* house.[31]

FURNISHINGS

Jacqueline Kennedy assumed a new role for a first lady: that of curator and lady of the manor, with television interviews and personal tours that gave the American public a glimpse of an unknown, cosmopolitan world. The 1962 guidebook *The White House: An Historic Guide* was the first "official" report on the White House, and Mrs. Kennedy's voice opens the book in a facsimile letter with her distinctive signature. John Walker, director of the National Gallery of Art, wrote the guidebook's introduction, although he had no particular qualifications to talk about the White House. His position in the museum world gave him the authority to sanction the "restored" White House as a museum worthy of receiving gifts of money and objects. In his brief introduction, Walker compares foreign monarchs of the past, who "ordered" craftsmen and artists to fill their palaces with art, to America's president, who "welcomes the generosity of private citizens who provide the works of art whose beauty he shares with all his fellow Americans."[32] Walker effectively swept away 160 years of presidents and first ladies' behaving like house owners, furnishing the White House rooms as their needs, their budgets, and the caprices of fashion and politics dictated.

The museum aspect of the White House was not a new idea, dating back to Edith Bolling Wilson's creation of the China Room in 1917, but Jacqueline Kennedy's guidebook memorialized her as an innovator and established the president's house as a museum.

The author of the guidebook's tour of the new Kennedy rooms was Lorraine Waxman Pearce, the first White House curator. She was part of the tight du Pont–Kennedy inner circle that had overseen two years of redecorating. Despite Mrs. Kennedy's self-proclaimed interest in historic objects from earlier administrations, Pearce favored objects recently acquired for the restored rooms over the Victorian things that had actually filled those same rooms for more than a century. Mrs. Pearce's curatorial wording was careful but made the point that the White House of 1962 was, at long last, *right,* both in its style and in its collections.

The guidebook, wrote Pearce, was "not intended to be a comprehensive survey of White House furnishings, but rather a careful survey of objects chosen for their quality as great furniture rather than for their historic associations."[33] The surviving Monroe pier table made the cut for the "great furniture" section in the book because Mrs. Kennedy discovered the beaten-up table in storage and had it restored, which resulted in the donation of an armchair by Bellangé.[34] The Monroes' round mahogany French table was placed in context with American furniture in this style, along with a French Empire pier table from Joseph Bonaparte's New Jersey estate. Well-known names of neoclassical America—Samuel McIntire, Duncan Phyfe, and Charles-Honoré Lannuier—were featured prominently, although their furniture was not present in the original White House. The Biddle vermeil collection was duly noted as a masterpiece, with no attempt to have its inclusion make any historical sense, other than the logical connection between it and the Monroe ormolu.

Mrs. Kennedy had grown up in a world where antiques and period objects were always present, a world that was as self-consciously aristocratic as the palace world of the Roosevelts. Expressing her desire to have period rooms in the White House, she commented that the White House "was still mainly B. Altman 1948." Good-quality reproductions that had been adequate for previous presidents did not meet the standards of her vision.[35] Although seemingly concerned with American history, Kennedy, du Pont, and their acolytes were more interested in quality. One sees this preoccupation in a comment Mrs. Kennedy wrote to Mr. du Pont in one of many brief notes: "I think the mirror should be accepted if you like it. As long as it has the eagle, it doesn't matter if it's French. There are so many places it could go . . . one can always use a good mirror."[36]

Every part of the house was to share in this "fine antiques" vision, including nonhistoric areas, such as the ground-floor entrance corridor. For this efficient but lifeless entrance, Mrs. Kennedy encouraged a gift of antique lighting fixtures from the Society of Colonial Dames, because "to me, [they] do more than anything to give the feeling of an historic house—as it is where everyone comes in—instead of a dentist office bomb shelter."[37]

Mrs. Kennedy's interest in using museum-quality objects was also driven by a sincere desire to fill the rooms with things that could have been there when the house was young. Thus Mrs. Kennedy's choices for furniture for the state rooms (or "period rooms," as she called them) were driven equally

The Monroes' French marble-topped center table, c. 1817, graces the middle of Nancy Reagan's Blue Room in 1983. This piece reflects Mrs. Reagan's support of the Kennedy legacy.

by a sense of history and a sense of correctness. She borrowed a Chippendale mirror from Mount Vernon because it came from President Washington's Philadelphia house. President Kennedy's bedroom was furnished with Chippendale furniture because "this vigorous style is well-suited to the apartment of the Chief Executive."[38] Mrs. Kennedy placed a fine Empire sofa in the Red Room, not because of its quality, but because it had belonged to Dolley Madison.[39] The Gilbert Stuart portrait of Washington was a sacred relic, the only surviving object from the Adams White House. The Monroe ormolu was called "[t]he greatest historic treasure of the White House,"[40] while the de Tuyll silver purchased by Jackson, and the surviving Vollmer causeuse, or love seat, from the Buchanan era, became cherished artifacts. Edith Roosevelt got credit in the guidebook for saving the Lincoln bedroom furniture, and Caroline Harrison was lauded for preserving the presidential porcelain.

The redecoration of the White House deeply favored the pre-1840 period. Since the turn of the century, the public had developed an antipathy to every phase of 19th-century design after 1840. This antipathy had led to the final dispersal of White House furnishings in 1903. Henry du Pont, who had grown up in the 1880s in a very Victorian Winterthur, shared the general horror of Victoriana.[41]

Only in the late 1960s did collectors and museums began to reappraise the decorative arts that had dominated the greater part of the White House's history.[42] In 1963, the Newark Museum in New Jersey mounted an exhibition called "Classical America, 1815–1845." The first museum survey in America to study 19th-century art and decorative arts, it focused on the styles for which the White House had been designed.[43] This early 1960s surge in interest in the decorative arts of the early 1800s gave Mrs. Kennedy's restoration project added momentum.

The White House lent one of the Monroe-era East Room armchairs by William King to this exhibition, breaking with recent congressional legislation restricting such loans. This bending of the rules is explained by the fact that Newark's exhibition was underwritten by New Jerseyans

In 1962 Sister Parish replaced frumpy reproductions in the second-floor oval sitting room with museum-quality French antiques; seen here in the Reagan yellow oval room, 1983.

Charles and Jane Engelhard, major contributors to the Kennedy restoration project.[44]

Despite her use of Victorian objects in the Treaty Room and Lincoln Bedroom, Mrs. Kennedy shared the public's distaste for Victoriana. "If there's anything I can't stand," she noted to a staff member, "it's Victorian mirrors—they're hideous. Off to the dungeons with them!"[45] Perry Wolff, who wrote a 1962 book on the celebrated televised tour of the White House, commented that "between 1860 and 1900, for instance, the White House was glutted with the worst of machine-made Victorian."[46] Mrs. Kennedy was more diplomatic, acknowledging that history sometimes trumped taste. In a letter to Henry Francis du Pont regarding the replacement of an inappropriate mantelpiece, she noted, "I don't really mind it, as it has that rather ugly charm that so many White House objects had (i.e., furniture in the Treaty Room). . . . We always have to make concessions to history."[47]

The Kennedy Green Room was furnished as the Federal period rooms at Winterthur and various American museums were. An emphasis on key forms of the 1790s and early 1800s from major Federal style centers—New York, Salem, Baltimore, Philadelphia—paralleled current scholarship on regionalism in American furniture spearheaded by Charles

Montgomery, du Pont's curator. These pieces represented the Adams and Jefferson years in both their style and (inadvertently) their too-small scale. Two paintings by Paul Cézanne that in 1962 had been placed over a Federal card table in the northeast corner of the Green Room were soon relocated to the second-floor oval living room. They represent Mrs. Kennedy's taste's trumping history. The Victorian presidents would have hated Cézanne's work for its radical modernism, but the Impressionists were revered by elite collectors and museums in 1962.

In the Blue Room the Bellangé armchair and pier table were joined by a large number of reproduction side- and armchairs. The Red Room was arranged with American Empire furniture of the 1810–20 period, still a novelty in the early 1960s, when accepted good taste still focused on colonial and Federal pieces.

But for its size, the Kennedy Family Dining Room could have stood in for many upper-middle-class dining rooms in America. With the exception of two Severin Rosen still-life pictures from the mid-19th century that stood in for all the Victorian objects long since purged from the house, the objects approved by the Fine Arts Committee related closely to the Roosevelt renovation of the room in 1902. Authentic Federal furniture replaced the Roosevelt-era mixture of reproduction Chippendale pieces

The collection of silver-gilt, French and English, 18th and early 19th centuries, donated in 1956 was a harbinger of the White House's transformation from residence to museum in the 1960s. Ground-floor Vermeil Room, Reagan administration, 1983.

and a sideboard apparently made out of the surviving East Room pier table from Jackson's era. Both the massive Oriental rug and the Chinese coromandel screen again reflect elite taste rather than historical accuracy. By 1962, it was known that Oriental carpets were not used in colonial or Federal houses, but such rugs had become entrenched as good taste since the time of Teddy Roosevelt. Chinese folding screens were introduced during the Gilded Age as exotic accessories in mansion parlors. By the 1920s, coromandel screens had become standard features of upper-class "period" rooms.

The second-floor oval room became a glamorous drawing room full of French and American antiques. For the family quarters on the second floor, furniture was chosen the same way that Americans had "always" furnished their homes—with bits and pieces handed down from previous generations. All first ladies had done this to some degree, but Mrs. Kennedy approved objects that were not merely lying around and useful, but could be called antiques.

Since the Kennedy years, two parallel tracks of collecting for the White House—objects associated with presidents, and American masterpieces— have continued, both appropriate to a presidential residence and an accredited house museum. In addition to the state room and family

quarters, ground-floor rooms intended for servants in Washington's dream house have become museum rooms full of treasures in the post-Kennedy dream house. The Vermeil and China rooms, the Library, the Diplomatic Reception Room, and the Map Room, made over for Richard Nixon in 1970, were furnished with objects better than any the house had known in its early years. Gone were the days when the first lady had to shop at department stores for ready-made goods. Freed from the constraints of congressional furnishing appropriations, the White House could leverage a combination of patriotic feeling and high-society networking to bring in a flood of amazing treasures—finer in quality than any first lady could have otherwise afforded—without ever costing the public a penny.[48] Even Mrs. Ronald Reagan's 4,372-piece Lenox service, commissioned in 1980 and banded in her favorite bright red, was a tax-deductible gift.[49] One of the most aggressive collectors for the White House collection was Clement Conger (1912–2004), appointed curator in 1970. A State Department official with no curatorial training, Conger vigorously raised funds and solicited increasingly fine examples of (non-Victorian) American objects. White House history was not his central concern, although American history from the pre-industrial era was. Conger lost his post as a result of aesthetic disagreements with Mrs. Ronald Reagan

Pier table, France, c. 1800, borrowed by Jacqueline Kennedy, 1962. Mrs. Kennedy was as interested in historical association as in fine quality, and she selected antiques that she felt reflected the original style of the White House. She chose this table because it had come from the New Jersey country house of Napoleon's exiled brother Joseph Bonaparte.

Turned wood bowl, Edward Moulthrop, United States, and iron candlesticks, Albert Paley, United States, 1993, for the Clinton White House. Hillary Clinton brought important contemporary objects to the White House, but its museum decor made them seem out of place. The 1902 portrait of Edith Roosevelt seated in her west colonial garden is by Théobold Chartran. Clinton Family Dining Room, 1993.

President Monroe's splendid 1817 ormolu plateau by Jean-François Denière and François Matelin is the grandest survivor of nearly two centuries of changing taste at the White House. Purchased as appropriate for a great country manor, the centerpiece is now a revered treasure of a house museum; seen here in the State Dining Room, 2000.

in 1986, but he left a legacy of continual searching for ever-finer objects for an ever-more-rigidly elegant White House.

For all the importance of American designers in the decorative arts of the 20th century, there is virtually no trace of their influence within the historic confines of the present-day presidential dream-house-as-museum. Once the idea of the house as a museum was planted in the early part of the century, the notion of introducing modern-style objects became unimaginable. The one exception was the assembling in 1993 of the White House collection of contemporary American crafts under Hillary Rodham Clinton. Intended to provide a document of the thriving craft movement in the world's most industrialized nation, the 72 modern works of glass, clay, wood, metal, and fiber by American craft artists were assembled by Michael Monroe, then curator in charge at the Renwick Gallery.[50] Initially, the objects were displayed all over the White House. They were placed with a very clear sense of the historic nature of the interiors, which defined their aesthetic and scale. In the Family Dining Room, for example, a pair

of wrought-iron candlesticks by Albert Paley and a turned wooden vessel by Edward Moulthrop was positioned on a Federal sideboard beneath a famous portrait of Edith Roosevelt. The collection was an exciting gesture and marked the first time since the 1890s that significant modern-style objects had been showcased in the White House at the behest of a first lady. But it didn't last. The Clintons had crossed an unwritten taste boundary established in the Kennedy era. Despite the objects' quality and their historical significance, and despite the fact they represented the first effort since 1902 to bring something new to the White house, the craft collection quickly disappeared into the Smithsonian American Art Museum, where it remains on loan from the White House.

Although she will most certainly bring her personality to the furnishings of the private quarters, it remains to be seen if Michelle Obama, working with California decorator Michael Smith, will want to introduce new objects into the state rooms, objects that reflect American history as she knows it. If she does, one can only hope that she will succeed.[51]

Returning to early American ideals of sustainability, First Lady Michelle Obama and White House chef Sam Kass met with school children in March 2009 to plant the first presidential kitchen garden since the Depression. The private 18 acres of the White House are historic. Seen here are the south pool, first built in 1873 for Ulysses S. Grant; commemorative trees planted since the administration of Rutherford B. Hayes, and one of the two 1855 Jefferson mounds, once thought to have been created for the third president. In the distance is the 1903 East Wing and first-floor terrace.

THE PEOPLE'S HOUSE

When the White House was first completed in 1800, newspaper critics sensed a lingering royalist sensibility in the splendor of the massive Georgian building on its ridge above the Potomac River. They ridiculed it as "a great stone house, big enough for two emperors, one pope and the grand lama in the bargain."[52] But after the "barbarous conflagration" by the British in 1814, public sentiment changed. *The National Intelligencer* called for the White House and capital city buildings to be the "most splendid public edifices in the world—a boast in no way incompatible with the purest principles of Republican government."[53] James Monroe, seeking funds to maintain the restored president's house, wrote Congress in February 1818. He explained that the White House was a public "trust," and its furniture "an object not less deserving attention than the building for which it was intended…." Both were "national objects" representing the United States. Elected officials needed to protect and preserve the people's house for the edification and pleasure of all Americans, then and in the future.[54]

With these words, the fifth president began the now two-century-old tradition of decorating and landscaping the White House to be the nation's finest home, a symbol of democracy's prosperity and stability. At first citizens experienced their national dream house through walks in the president's park or gatherings in the great East Room, decorated by Andrew Jackson as a public reception hall. In the 19th century, as society became stratified by wealth and as White House security increased, visits by invitation superceded political ideals of access. The public came to know the White House in books, written accounts, and, in the 20th century, by watching television. Today more people visit the White House hourly through virtual media than lived in George Washington's America.

At a time of economic struggle, Barack and Michelle Obama have embraced President Monroe's "trust" to reassure all Americans that their way of life will endure. The president and first lady openly describe with wonder the beauty of the first home and recount daily routines familiar to every American family. They eat breakfast with their kids before heading off to work and host after-school sleepovers in the second-floor apartment. Where Archie Roosevelt rode his pony, Algonquin, and Lou Hoover walked her shepherds, Weezie and Pat, the Obama daughters run with their puppy, Bo. Sasha and Malia play on a swing set south of the Oval Office and their dad shoots hoops nearby. The first lady cannot extensively redecorate the White House as presidents' wives did in the 19th century, but she has planted a vegetable garden for organic meals.

To celebrate Black History Month in February 2009, Michelle Obama welcomed invited guests to the East Room. In her speech, posted to the Internet, she complimented staff for making "the White House a warm family home and a great presidential residence commanding pride and respect throughout this country and around the world." Like all first couples, she and the president know they are just "borrowing" the "people's house," but while they are in Washington, they hope Americans will think of them as "just neighbors."[55] With reverence for the White House as America's dream house, the Obamas are making 1600 Pennsylvania Avenue, once again, an American home.

THE MAKING OF AN AMERICAN HOME

COUNTRY HOUSE: 1800–1829

1790: The U.S. Congress, located in New York City, ratifies the Residence Act, calling for the construction of a new capital city; the legislation provides for an official residence for the chief executive of the United States of America.

1791: Major Pierre-Charles L'Enfant presents his plan for the capital city of Washington and the President's Park, Reservation Number 1, to President George Washington.

1792: Thomas Jefferson proposes a national design competition for the president's house; a public call for submissions is issued April 3. President George Washington selects a design by Irish-born architect James Hoban on July 16. Construction on the president's house begins.

1800: John and Abigail Adams move into the nearly completed house, with furniture from the president's house in Philadelphia. The 1796 Gilbert Stuart portrait of George Washington as president is purchased for the new residence.

1806–07: The first landscape plan, attributed to President Thomas Jefferson and Benjamin H. Latrobe, for the president's garden close to the house is created; it shows the emerging influence of the English picturesque movement.

1807: President Jefferson and architect Benjamin H. Latrobe propose an extensive remodeling of the president's house that includes practical as well as stylistic revisions; the complete plan is never realized.

1809: Benjamin H. Latrobe begins refining the house's interior for President and Mrs. James Madison through specially designed furniture and textiles. The first custom-made furniture for the White House, for the oval drawing room, is designed by Latrobe and made by John and Hugh Findlay of Baltimore. The state floor is furnished and decorated in line with the most fashionable American country houses of the day.

1810: The first sale to dispose of used and outmoded White House furnishings is ordered by President Madison.

1814: On August 25, during the administration of President Madison, British troops occupy the president's house and set it on fire. Except for the Gilbert Stuart portrait of Washington from 1800, rescued by Dolley Madison, all of the original furnishings and interiors are lost.

1817: President James Monroe purchases both American and European furnishings to create the first White House interiors intended to evoke the elegance of palaces lived in by European heads of state. The newly decorated oval room includes gilded furniture from Pierre-Antoine Bellangé; a strong French accent in the decorative arts with French ormolu and porcelains prevails. William Worthington and William King Jr. serve as American suppliers of furniture.

1817: The White House begins to have a professionally maintained garden when Charles Bizet, the first "gardener to the president of the United States," is hired by President Monroe.

1826: President John Quincy Adams establishes the first ornamental flower garden at the president's house.

VILLA: 1829–69

1829: The iconic north and south porticoes are completed after designs by James Hoban.

1829: President Andrew Jackson oversees completion of the Great Audience Chamber—today's East Room—the first "public" interior designed for large receptions and possibly inspired by the public salons of American city hotels.

1833: President Jackson has the president's house outfitted with running water.

1833: President Jackson sells worn and out-of-fashion furniture, glassware, and china from the White House.

1835: At a time when greenhouses were an essential part of American estate gardens, the first presidential glasshouse is built in the south garden for President Jackson.

1840: During the administration of President Martin Van Buren, the modernization of the White House continues when a central heating system is installed.

1846: Sarah Polk introduces "French modern" villa style to the state rooms with rosewood furniture ordered from J. & J. W. Meeks and Charles Baudouine of New York; she buys Gothic-style chairs from Meeks for her husband's cabinet room on the second floor.

1851: The first comprehensive landscape plan for the capital city, including the president's grounds, is prepared in 1851 by influential domestic house and garden theorist Andrew Jackson Downing for President Millard Fillmore. The plan is never fully realized after Downing dies prematurely in 1852, but its public/private division of the White House's 82-acre park influences post–Civil War improvements.

1851: Abigail Fillmore turns the upstairs oval room into the White House's first permanent library, with built-in bookcases. She purchases a grand piano for the Red Room.

1854: Franklin Pierce auctions off more "old furniture" to make way for new styles.

1859: Gottlieb Vollmer of Philadelphia supplies a large quantity of new furniture for the Buchanan White House, including a French-style gilded Blue Room suite and a now-lost ebonized suite for the Green Room. Cornelius & Baker, also of Philadelphia, supply new gasoliers.

1860: The Buchanan administration sells 50 pieces of old furnishings, including the outmoded 1817 Bellangé suite from the Blue Room.

1861: William and George Carryl, Philadelphia furniture retailers, carry on the White House tradition of ready-made home furnishings. Mary Lincoln buys a large assortment of rosewood bedroom and parlor furniture by different manufacturers for the principal guest room, including several pieces by John Henry Belter of New York.

MANSION: 1869–89

1869: Julia Grant begins to transform the White House from villa to mansion. She replaces the 1817 Hoban grand staircase with a Victorian mansion staircase to create more living space in the upper hall and refurnishes her husband's cabinet room with furniture from New York's Pottier & Stymus.

1872–77: In the prosperous postwar era, President Ulysses S. Grant defines the garden immediate to the White House garden as the president's own; to the north is Lafayette Park and to the south, open grounds.

1873: Mrs. Grant has the 50-year-old James Monroe and Andrew Jackson furniture removed from the East Room when it is dramatically renovated in anticipation of her daughter Nellie's wedding. The 1847 Polk furniture from the Red Room is also sold off and replaced with modern rosewood pieces by New York's Herter Brothers.

1877: For the elaborate garden with carpet beds and fountains, President Hayes hires Henry Pfister, knowledgeable of horticulture, as lead White House gardener; by 1880 he expands the White House staff of gardeners to nine men and one woman.

1879–80: Under President Hayes, the grounds south of the White House wall are finally finished, becoming the public parade grounds known today as the Ellipse. Hayes begins the annual tradition of the public Easter egg roll, but overall he restricts access to the president's garden. The White House as a national shrine begins when President Hayes initiates the tradition of planting trees commemorating presidents.

1880: A greenhouse, dedicated to roses, is built for Mrs. Lucy W. Hayes on the site of today's Kennedy Rose Garden. Improvements in industrial design and international colonialism are reflected in the ongoing expansion of the White House conservatories and horticulture collections.

1882: Socialite President Chester A. Arthur commissions the first custom-made "artistic" interiors in the White House, using New York society decorator Louis Comfort Tiffany to render the residence as glamorous as the mansion of a Gilded Age millionaire. The president sells off the largest quantity yet of old and worn-out White House furnishings: 30 barrels of china and 24 wagonloads of furniture.

PALACE: 1889–33

1889: Caroline Harrison, with architect Frederick D. Owen, conceives the first palace plans for the White House but settles for practical improvements and new gilded interiors. As an early participant in the women's craft movement, which included painting china, Mrs. Harrison begins the White House china collection.

1897: Under President William McKinley, the Army Corps of Engineers, headed by Colonel Theodore A. Bingham, proposes a radical expansion of the White House; delayed by the outbreak of the Spanish-American War; a developed scheme is presented in 1900.

1901: Congress's McMillan Plan for Washington, D.C., as an imperial city is presented to the president and members of Congress.

1902: President Theodore Roosevelt seeks to transform the incoherent century-old White House into a modern Franco-Georgian palace. He selects the New York society architectural firm of McKim, Mead & White to "restore" the interior of the residence in the fashionable Beaux-Arts style; practical considerations include a new ground-floor guest entrance and the first independent office wing. The Diplomatic Reception Room is created in the ground-floor oval room. The massive greenhouse complex is razed to make room for formal gardens along the south facade.

1902: Custom-made furnishings by Marcotte & Company, consciously reproducing antique pieces, are purchased for the renovated Blue, Green, and East rooms; furnishings in the Colonial Revival style, by A. H. Davenport, are purchased for the new State dining room. Paneling produced by Herter Brothers is used in both the East and State dining rooms.

1903: A major post-renovation sale of White House objects takes place under Theodore Roosevelt; this is the last wholesale dispersal of White House furnishings. Edith Roosevelt preserves Victorian pieces for upstairs rooms, including those purchased by Mary Lincoln in 1861. The newly created parterres east and west of the south portico are planted as formal Colonial Revival gardens.

1909: President Taft expands the executive wing and builds the first Oval Office.

1913: Landscape architect Charles Burnap designs for Mrs. Ellen A. Wilson the first exterior rose garden at the White House on the site of Edith Roosevelt's west colonial garden; it is an outdoor room in the Italianate style, just outside the new executive office, with a lattice screen in front of the White House laundry yard.

1913: One of the first women in the professional landscape movement, Beatrix J. Farrand, designs the southeast garden for Mrs. Ellen A. Wilson in a formal Arts and Crafts style.

1917: The second Mrs. Woodrow Wilson (Edith Bolling Galt Wilson), influenced by author Abby Gunn Baker, who believed the history of the White House was being lost, sponsors the White House's first museum-type gallery, the Presidential Collections Room, today's China Room.

1929: Mrs. Herbert Hoover first arranges antiques and custom-made reproductions in the rooms of the White House to evoke past presidencies, leading to the creation of the Lincoln Bedroom (1929) and the Monroe Room (1930).

SUBURBAN HOME: 1933–61

1935: A plan for the White House garden, in the Anglo-American tradition of flower gardens combined with open park lands, is presented by Frederick Law Olmsted Jr. to President Franklin D. Roosevelt. This becomes the final landscape plan for the president's house and is still in use today.

1948: During the administration of President Harry S. Truman, Lorenzo S. Winslow, assisted by William Adams Delano, designs and realizes a second-story balcony in the house's south portico that serves as a suburban porch for the president and his family.

1948: President Truman initiates a study of the structural soundness of the White House.

1949: In a full-scale reconstruction of the interior, with a redefinition of its decorative motifs and modernization of its infrastructure, the White House is gutted and rebuilt with modern structural support and systems.

1952: Continuing the American tradition of shopping at department stores for decorating guidance and furnishings, B. Altman & Company oversees the interior design of the newly rebuilt Truman interiors.

SHRINE: 1961–PRESENT

1961: Society leader Mrs. Rachel L. Mellon and landscape architect Perry Wheeler redesign the south parterre gardens for President John F. Kennedy. They return to the gardening traditions of the early presidents to suggest restoration authenticity.

1961: President and Mrs. John F. Kennedy initiate a plan to furnish the interior with historically significant examples of decorative and fine arts. They create the Fine Arts Committee, Paintings Committee, and Library Committee for advisement; appoint the first curator; and sponsor the creation of the White House Historical Association to promote appreciation and understanding of the residence and its history.

1964: Mellon and Wheeler complete the design of the east garden, which is dedicated by Lady Bird Johnson as the Jacqueline Kennedy Garden.

1969: President and Mrs. Richard M. Nixon adopt a museum-focused philosophy for continuing restoration, basing much of the decoration on work then being done at the New York Metropolitan Museum of Art.

1993: Hillary Rodham Clinton creates the White House collection of American crafts, which are briefly installed in the White House before being transferred to the care of the Smithsonian museums.

2009: Michelle Obama plants a vegetable garden on the president's grounds to support national environmental sustainability.

NOTES

INTRODUCTION

1. William Seale, *The President's House: A History* (Washington, DC: White House Historical Association, 1986), xv.

2. Betty C. Monkman, *The White House: Its Historic Furnishings and First Families* (Washington, DC: White House Historical Association, 2000), 8–9.

3. Michelle Obama, in an interview with Steve Kroft on CBS's *Sixty Minutes*, November 16, 2008, describing her impression after walking through the White House with outgoing first lady Laura Bush.

4. William Seale, *The White House: The History of an American Idea* (Washington, DC: White House Historical Association and the American Institute of Architects Press, 1992), p. 35. It did have its precedents, in the governor's palace at Williamsburg, as well as in Tryon Palace, the governor's palace in New Bern, North Carolina. Both of these were regional, of course, and both were far smaller and less ambitious than the White House.

5. For a discussion of the early planning of the President's Park, see C. M. Harris, "The Politics of Public Building: William Thornton and the President's Square," *White House History* 3 (Spring 1998): 174–87.

William Seale's history of the White House gardens is in *The President's House* and *The White House Garden* (Washington, DC: White House Historical Association, 1996). These histories have informed the overall chronology of the garden history in the following chapters. Additional history of the White House gardens can be found in Eleanor M. McPeck, *The President's Garden: An Account of the White House Gardens from 1800 to Present* (unpublished, 1971), in the collection of the Office of the Curator, the White House, Washington, DC; Barbara McEwan, *White House Landscapes: Horticultural Achievements of the Presidents* (New York: Walker, 1992); and Suzanne Turner, "The Landscape of the President's House: Garden of Democracy," in Wendell Garrett, ed., *Our Changing White House* (Boston: Northeastern Press, 1995), 165–76.

6. As quoted from Thornton's draft for "On National Education," dated to 1795–97 by C. M. Harris in "The Politics of Public Building," 177n5.

COUNTRY HOUSE

1. For an interesting discussion of the president's house in Philadelphia, see Dennis C. Kurjack, "Who Designed the 'President's House'?" *Journal of the Society of Architectural Historians* 12 (May 1953): 27–28.

2. Thomas Jefferson, as quoted in William Seale, *The White House: The History of an American Idea* (Washington, DC: American Institute of Architects Press, in association with the White House Historical Association, 1992), 5. Seale's history is an essential source of information on the White House, as is his two-volume work *The President's House: A History* (Washington, DC: White House Historical Association, 1986). Throughout this volume, William Seale's monumental work has served as a reference for dates and specific interior-decoration details.

For another important historical overview of the house, with a particularly detailed discussion of the extant entries in the design competition, see William Ryan and Desmond Guinness, *The White House: An Architectural History* (New York: McGraw-Hill, 1980). Pointing out that there were no architecture schools in the nation in 1792 and that professional competence was highly variable, Ryan and Guinness note on page 35, "The entrants in the President's House competition covered the entire spectrum of talent and training."

3. Thomas Jefferson to John Page, May 4, 1786, as quoted in Adrienne Koch and William Peden, eds., *The Life and Selected Writings of Thomas Jefferson* (New York: Modern Library, 1944), 392.

4. Marquis de Chastellux, as quoted in William H. Pierson Jr., *American Buildings and Their Architects: The Colonial and Neo-Classical Styles* (Garden City, NY: Doubleday, 1970), 289.

5. Thomas Jefferson, as quoted in Fiske Kimball, "The Genesis of the White House," *Century* 95 (February 1919): 523.

6. For an important discussion of Hoban's scheme, see Egon Verheyen, "James Hoban's Design for the White House in the Context of the Planning of the Federal City," *Architectura* 11, no. 1 (1981): 66–82.

7. Ryan and Guinness have challenged the idea that Hoban was inspired by Gibbs's work. The authors have noted, "A common view, based on [Fiske] Kimball's intense conviction and widely accepted because of his stature as a scholar and critic, is that Hoban used plates 52 and 53 of James Gibbs's *A Book of Architecture* as a model for the President's House. . . . No one really questions that Hoban was familiar with the book, and perhaps owned a copy, but documentary proof does not exist to support any connection between designs in Gibbs and the drawings that

Hoban produced." Ryan and Guinness, *The White House*, 67. The authors contend that one source of Hoban's design was Castletown, a country house designed by Alessandro Galilei and built outside of Dublin in the 1720s.

8. For discussion of the visual effect and meaning of the proposed porch, see Verheyen, "James Hoban's Design for the White House in the Context of the Planning of the Federal City," 72.

9. Jaquelin Robertson, in reference to Monticello, has stated that Jefferson's use of scale seems to say, "Out here in the wilderness, I must exaggerate Classical reference or no one will hear me." As quoted in Robert A. M. Stern, *Pride of Place: Building the American Dream* (Boston: Houghton Mifflin; New York: American Heritage, 1986), 19.

10. Contemporary oval rooms appeared in houses such as Lemon Hill in Philadelphia (1800); Gore Place in Waltham, Massachusetts (1806); and the Nathaniel Russell House in Charleston, South Carolina (1808). All of these are substantially smaller than the oval rooms in the White House.

11. Dimensions obtained from staff at the various historic sites.

12. Abigail Adams to her daughter, November 21, 1800, as quoted in Esther Singleton, *The Story of the White House* (New York: McClure, 1907), 1:11–12.

13. Abigail Adams, as quoted in Kimball, "The Genesis of the White House," 527.

14. Talbot Hamlin, *Benjamin Henry Latrobe: The Man and the Architect* (Baltimore: Maryland Historical Society, 1942), 339.

15. Ibid., 301.

16. Benjamin Henry Latrobe, as quoted in Ryan and Guinness, *The White House*, 67. See also Michael W. Fazio and Patrick A. Snadon, *The Domestic Architecture of Benjamin Henry Latrobe* (Baltimore, MD: Johns Hopkins University Press, 2006), 371.

17. Latrobe, as quoted in Ryan and Guinness, *The White House*, 98.

18. Latrobe, as quoted in Fazio and Snadon, *Domestic Architecture of Benjamin Henry Latrobe*, 371.

19. Dr. William Thornton, as quoted in the *Washington Federalist* (April 26, 1808); see Ryan and Guinness, *The White House*, 409.

20. Kimball, "The Genesis of the White House," 528.

21. Catherine Allgor, "Dolley Madison Creates the White House," in William Seale, ed., *White House: Actors and Observers* (Boston: Northeastern University Press, 2002), 22. For an analysis of Washington as an embodiment of public spaces and democratic ideals, see Michael Bednar, *L'Enfant's Legacy: Public Open Spaces in Washington, D.C.* (Baltimore, MD: John Hopkins University Press, 2006).

22. William Birch, *The Country Seats of the United States of North America with Some Scenes Connected with Them* (Springland, Pa: W. Birch, 1808), n.p.

23. Therese O'Malley, "Art and Science in the Design of Botanic Gardens, 1730–1830," *Garden History Issues, Approaches, Methods* (Washington, DC: Dumbarton Oaks Research Library and Collections, 1992), 294–95.

24. From "Travel Hints," in *The Writings of Thomas Jefferson* (Washington, DC: Thomas Jefferson Memorial Association, 1904), 9:404.

25. For the relationship of man to nature as it evolved from Jefferson's Enlightenment interpretation of nature into the romanticism of 19th-century naturalists and philosophers, see Richard White, "Transcendental Landscapes," in T. J. Jackson Lears, ed., *American Victorians and Virgin Nature* (Boston: Isabella Steward Gardner Museum, 2002), 1–15. Ralph Waldo Emerson, *English Traits,*

1853, as quoted by White, 1.

26. David Stuart to George Washington, Hope Park, Virginia, February 26, 1792, in Philander D. Chase, ed., *The Papers of George Washington* (Charlottesville: University Press of Virginia), vol. 9 (September 1791–February 1792), 600.

27. For Adams as a gardener and the unrealized vegetable garden at the White House, see Corliss Knapp Engle, "John Adams: Farmer and Gardener," *White House History* 7 (spring 2000): 42–51.

28. Benjamin Stoddert to William Thornton, January 20, 1800, as quoted in C. W. Willis, "The Politics of Public Building," *White House History* 3 (spring 1998): 180–81.

29. Abigail Adams to Mary Cranch, November 21, 1800, in Stewart Mitchell, ed., *New Letters of Abigail Adams* (Boston: Houghton Mifflin, c. 1947), 257.

30. For Jefferson's library, which included Robert Castell's *The Villas of the Ancients*, 1783, and Thomas Whateley's *Observations on Modern Gardening*, 1770 (second ed.), see Frederick Doveton Nichols and Ralph E. Griswold, *Thomas Jefferson, Landscape Architect* (Charlottesville: University of Virginia Press, 1973), 76–89. For the English tour, see Edward Dumbauld, "Jefferson and Adams' English Garden Tour," in William Howard Adams, *Jefferson and the Arts: An Extended View* (Washington, DC: National Gallery of Art), 137–57.

31. James P. Ronda, "The Objects of Our Journey," in Carolyn Gilman, *Lewis and Clark: Across the Divide* (Washington, DC: Smithsonian Books, 2003), 15–16.

32. For Jefferson and the Woodlands garden, possibly by English landscape architect George I. Parkyns, see Richard J. Betts, "The Woodlands," *Winterthur Portfolio* 14, no. 3 (Autumn, 1979), 213–34. For Jefferson and Stowe, Thomas Jefferson Memorandum, April 6, 1786, while on tour of England, as quoted in Dumbauld, 146. For Jefferson's association of landscape with Italian culture, first discussed by Fiske Kimball, see George Green Shackelford, "A Peep into Elysium," in Adams, *Jefferson and the Arts*, 262.

33. For a discussion of this plan and Jefferson's contribution to the White House garden, see C. Allan Brown, "Poplar Forest: The Mathematics of the Ideal Villa," *Journal of Garden History* 10 (1990): 121–23; and Dovetone and Griswold, *Thomas Jefferson*, 67–75.

34. The color renderings of the east and west facades by Benjamin Latrobe, which may have begun during the Jefferson administration and continued under Madison, show the axial formality contemplated for the garden but not carried out. For these illustrations and a discussion of the unmarked landscape plan attributed to both Latrobe and Jefferson, see Michael Fazio and Patrick Snadon, "Benjamin Latrobe and Thomas Jefferson Redesign the President's House," *White House History* 7 (spring 2000): 104–21.

35. Letter from Thomas Jefferson to Joel Barlow, May 3, 1802, in *The Writings of Thomas Jefferson*, 9: 453.

36. Charles Bulfinch submitted in 1822 a plan for the undeveloped capital mall. His formal and ordered design for a series of terraced lawns outlined by trees and divided by allées possibly suggests the approach he took with the White House garden. For a color reproduction of this plan, see Richard Longstreth, ed., *The Mall in Washington, 1791–1991* (Washington, DC: National Gallery of Art, 1991), 181.

37. The unsigned watercolors are in the recollections of Anthony St. John Baker, *Mémoires d'un voyageur qui se repose* (Paris: self-published, 1850), in the collection of the Huntington Library, San Marino, California.

38. Charles Francis Adams, ed., *Memoirs of John Quincy Adams* (Philadelphia: Lippincott, 1875), 7:323. For Adams's garden, see Therese O'Malley, "'Your Garden Must Be a Museum to You': Early American Botanic Gardens," *Huntington Library Quarterly* 59, nos. 2 and 3 (1997–98): 207–31.

39. Robert F. Dalzell Jr. and Lee Baldwin Dalzell, "Memory, Architecture, and the Future: George Washington, Mount Vernon, and the White House," in *White House History*, collection 1, nos. 1–6 (Washington, DC: White House Historical Association, 2004), 351–59.

40. Wedgwood was well known in the United States. For example, a blue and white jasperware teapot from 1803 was owned by States Dyckman, who built his neoclassical country house, Boscobel, on the banks of the Hudson River. See Wendy Cooper, *Classical Taste in America, 1800–1840* (Baltimore and New York: Baltimore Museum of Art and Abbeville Press, 1993), 45.

41. Seale, *The President's House*, 1:76. Seale notes that not all of the chosen work was used but that James Hoban continued to place orders with Andrews.

42. The room is now preserved at the Baltimore Museum of Art.

43. Thomas Sheraton, *The Cabinet-Maker and Upholsterer's Drawing-Book* (London, 1793; New York: Dover, 1972), plates 33–36, 61.

44. See Mark Girouard, *Life in the English Country House* (Harmondsworth, UK: Penguin, 1980), 122–26. This suite arrangement also parallels the French use of rooms in country houses.

45. The yellow drawing room in Sir John Soane's House in London, currently preserved as part of John Soane's Museum, suggests which contemporary sources might have inspired the Madison scheme.

46. Betty C. Monkman, *The White House: Its Historic Furnishings and First Families* (Washington, DC: White House Historical Association, 2000), 40. Monkman's great survey of the surviving original furnishings in the White House has supplied this text with many insights into details of the interiors over time. It also has been an invaluable guide to surviving objects from different presidencies, and provenances of those objects, and it contains useful references to furnishings now lost to the White House through the various sales ending in 1903.

47. The rising influence of French taste in the United States is well covered by Dell Upton in "Inventing the Metropolis: Civilization and Urbanity in Antebellum New York," in Catherine Hoover Voorsanger and John K. Howat, eds., *Art and the Empire City: New York, 1825–1861* (New York: Metropolitan Museum of Art, 2000).

48. For a similar example of a figural marble mantelpiece in a Boston house, see William Seale, *The Tasteful Interlude: American Interiors Through the Camera's Eye, 1860–1917* (Nashville, TN: American Association for State and Local History, 1988), 104.

49. Monkman, *The White House: Its Historic Furnishings*, 36.

50. For example, the expatriate John Singleton Copley's full-length portrait of John Adams, painted in 1783 while Adams was stationed in Europe, depicts Adams as far more aristocratic than he in fact saw himself. The intention was no doubt to make the new, raw America appear to match the standards of aristocratic Europe. The painting is now in the collection of Harvard University. Likewise, the heroic portraits of colonial Marblehead merchant Jeremiah Lee and his wife, painted by Copley in 1769 (and now in the Wadsworth Atheneum, Hartford), clearly aim at making the Lees look as if they are English aristocrats.

51. While living in France, their house in Auteuil was perhaps as large, but the Adamses never attempted to furnish it as if it were a national ruler's public residence. See Betty C. Monkman, "John and Abigail Adams: A Tradition Begins," in *White House History*, collection 2, nos. 7–12 (Washington, DC: White House Historical Association, 2004), 63.

52. Ibid., 67.

53. The Bonnin and Morris factory in Philadelphia produced English-type porcelains for only two years, from 1770 to 1772. Competition from English porcelains doomed this early attempt to make porcelain in America. See Alice Cooney Frelinghuysen, *American Porcelain: 1770–1920* (New York: Metropolitan Museum of Art and Harry N. Abrams, 1989), 8–10. The French Sèvres porcelain that the Adamses had brought back from their stay in France was anomalous and stands as a rare appearance of French ceramics in an 18th-century American household. Although Chinese export porcelain was commonplace among elite Americans in this period, it is highly unlikely that this costly tableware would have been included in the White House service. Both George and Martha Washington had their own Chinese export services, which they used during the general's presidency, but these went to Mount Vernon with them.

54. See Barbara McLean Ward and Gerald W. R. Ward, *Silver in American Life* (New Haven, CT, and New York: Yale University Art Gallery and American Federation of the Arts, 1979), 33.

55. Ibid., 168.

56. According to the Inflation Calculator, at www.westegg.com/inflation/infl.cgi

57. LeTellier is known to have worked in Philadelphia extensively, as well as in Wilmington, Delaware. The only other tureen of this early date known to the author is a New York tureen by Hugh Wishart, circa 1795, in the Campbell Soup tureen collection, now at the Winterthur Museum in Wilmington. See Ralph Collier, *Selections from the Campbell Museum Collection*, fifth ed. (Camden, NJ: Campbell Museum, 1983), entry 147.

58. Two sets of such black-painted chairs exist at the Lorenzo State Historic Site in Cazenovia, New York, ordered from this small town's own chair maker in 1808. Likewise, the Dyckman family of Montrose, New York, ordered green-and-gold fancy chairs for their villa, Boscobel, in 1808. See Berry Tracy, *Federal Furniture and Decorative Arts at Boscobel* (New York: Boscobel Restoration and Harry N. Abrams, 1981), 22–23 and 46–47. William Seale, *The President's House*, 1:104. Seale is an invaluable source for references to specific objects and kinds of objects acquired for the White House and the dates they were purchased.

59. For an example of the kind of piano that Mrs. Madison might have had in her parlor, see Charles F. Montgomery, *American Furniture: The Federal Period in the Henry Francis du Pont Winterthur Museum* (New York: Viking, 1966), 439, catalogue entry 448.

60. For Mrs. Taft's piano, see Elise K. Kirk, *Musical Highlights from the White House* (Melbourne, FL: Krieger, 1992), 88–93.

61. The settees with bolsters, as well as the scroll-ended sofas, were attempts to produce archaeologically correct interpretations of ancient Grecian forms. All of them had stylistic relationships to Englishman Thomas Hope's designs. However, Hope was much imitated in his day, and Latrobe's designs for the Madison White House could well have come from other contemporary sources. See Thomas Hope, *Household Furniture and Interior Decoration* (originally published London, 1807; New York: Dover, 1971).

62. The brothers were advertising their "Elegant, Fancy, Japanned Furniture" as early as 1805 and took advantage of their connection with Senator Smith to win what must have been a tremendous coup for their business. See Charles F. Montgomery, *American Furniture: The Federal Period* (Winterthur, DE, and New York: Winterthur Museum and Viking Press, 1966), 243.

63. The suite consisted of two sofas, two bergères, 18 fauteuils, 18 chaises, one pier table, two pier glasses, four tabourets, six footstools, and two screens. The pier glasses remained in place until the McKinley administration; the pier table until the Theodore Roosevelt administration.

64. To better appreciate the restrained glamour of the Bellangé suite compared with truly imperial furniture of this period from royal houses, see John Harris, Geoffrey de Bellaigue, and Oliver Millar, *Buckingham Palace and Its Treasures* (New York: Viking, 1968), 195–98; and for furniture in Napoleon's palaces, see Sacheverell Sitwell et al., *Great Palaces* (London and New York: Spring Books, 1969), 55, 56, and 74.

65. The house built by John and Jeannette Ballantine in Newark, New Jersey, in 1885, contains a gray-marble and gilt-bronze clock and candelabra that are French and probably date from the 1860s or 1870s. The clock features a seated female figure of more generalized "neo-Grec" form. Although the set has always been in this house, it was probably displaced by a new French clock and candelabra set of ormolu and champlevé enamel, purchased in 1885 for the gold-and-white parlor. See Ulysses Grant Dietz, *The Ballantine House* (Newark: Newark Museum, 1994).

66. See Berry B. Tracy, *Classical America, 1815–1845* (Newark, NJ: Newark Museum, 1963), 59, 78.

67. For a table in the French manner by Charles-Honoré Lannuier, who died in 1819, see Wendy A. Cooper, *In Praise of America: American Decorative Arts, 1650–1830/Fifty Years of Discovery Since the 1929 Girl Scouts Loan Exhibition* (New York: Knopf, 1980), 244, image 48.

68. See Charles L. Venable et al., *China and Glass in America, 1880–1980: From Tabletop to TV Tray* (Dallas, TX, and New York: Dallas Museum of Art and Harry N. Abrams, 2000), 193.

69. See Tracy, *Classical America*, 90, 102, for a unique presentation urn from 1816, made for Stephen Decatur.

VILLA

1. For the emergence of the middle-class house, see Gwendolyn Wright, "Independence and the Rural Cottage," in Keith L. Eggener, ed., *American Architectural History* (New York: Routledge, 2004), 142–54.

2. Andrew Jackson Downing, *The Architecture of Country Houses,* with a foreword by J. Stewart Johnson, originally published 1850 (New York: Dover, 1969), 258.

3. William Henry Harrison became the log cabin candidate when he ran for the presidency in 1840, although in fact he had been born at Berkeley plantation in Virginia. On the other hand, Mrs. Ulysses S. Grant worked valiantly to make her husband's log house, Hardscrabble, into a genteel home after the villa model, but she always hated it, proving that the romance of log houses was a masculine one. She preferred the "pretty villa" of Wish-ton-Wish, on her father's farm near Saint Louis. See Julia Dent Grant, *The Personal Memoirs of Julia Dent Grant (Mrs. Ulysses S. Grant)* (New York: G. P. Putnam, 1975), 72, 78–79.

4. For the early development of plant studies and botanic collections in America, see Therese O'Malley, "Art and Science in the Design of Botanic Gardens, 1730–1830," *Garden History Issues, Approaches, Methods* (Washington, DC: Dumbarton Oaks Research Library and Collections, 1992), 279–302.

5. May Woods and Arete Warren, *Glass Houses: A History of Greenhouses, Orangeries and Conservatories* (London: Aurum Press, 1988), 134–36.

6. William Seale, "About the Ogle Speech," and the text of Ogle's April 14, 1840, speech on "The Regal Splendor of the President's Palace," with notes, both in *White House History* 10 (winter 2002): 196–203 and 227–89.

7. For the development of Washington in the years leading to the Civil War, see Therese O'Malley, "A Public Museum of Trees: Mid-Nineteenth Century Plans for the Mall," in Richard Longstreth, ed., *The Mall in Washington, 1791–1991* (Washington, DC: National Gallery of Art, 1991), 61–76.

8. O'Malley, "Art and Science," 302n61.

9. Andrew Jackson Downing, *A Treatise on the Theory and Practice of Landscape Gardening, Adapted to North America; With a View to the Improvement of Country Residences . . . With Remarks on Rural Architecture, by the Late A. J. Downing, Esq.* 6th ed. (Ann Arbor: University of Michigan, University Library, 1859), 35.

10. Andrew Jackson Downing, *The Architecture of Country Houses,* with a foreword by J. Stewart Johnson, originally published 1850 (New York: Dover, 1969), 29–30. For the Greek Revival temple, see the Hosack album of drawings, Thomas K. Wharton, *View of the David Hosack Estate,* c. 1832, pen and ink, accession no. 1994.187.13, Metropolitan Museum of Art, New York.

11. Downing's original plan is lost. The copy of the plan reproduced here from the Library of Congress was prepared by Nathaniel Michler, who was in charge of public buildings, grounds, and works in the capital city, 1867.

12. For Downing's commentary and a history of his capital city plan, see David Schuyler, *Apostle of Taste: Andrew Jackson Downing, 1815–1852* (Baltimore, MD: John Hopkins University Press, 1996), 193–201. Despite the consensus to adopt Downing's plan because of its promise to make Washington a model city, Congress debated the improvements and money expenditures along political lines.

13. As quoted from Andrew Jackson Downing, in Frederika Bremer, ed., *Rural Essays* (New York: Putnam, 1953), 103 and 107, by Therese O'Malley, "A Public Museum of Trees," 67.

14. No mention of these mounds is made in the Jefferson papers, and they do not appear in images before 1860. Records in the National Archives from 1855 note that earth from the extension "was deposited in a mound on the grounds south of the President's House to give an imposing effect to the present flat surface of the lawn." As quoted by Susan Turner, "The Landscape of the President's House," in Wendell Garrett, ed., *Our Changing White House* (Boston: Northeastern University Press. 1995), 181. See also William Seale, *The President's House* (Washington, DC: White House Historical Association, 1986), 1:343, 2:1100n32.

15. Seale, *The President's House,* 1:344.

16. For the place of women in gardening and horticulture, see Ann Leighton, *American Gardens of the Nineteenth Century* (Amherst: University of Massachusetts Press, 1987), 83–91.

17. Downing, *A Treatise on the Theory and Practice of Landscape Gardening,* 386.

18. *Frank Leslie's Illustrated Newspaper* (March 27, 1858): 266.

19. Yellow Wolf died of pneumonia shortly after the picture was taken; War Bonnet and Standing in Water were slaughtered in the Sand Creek Massacre; and Lean Bear, mistaken for a hostile enemy, was killed by troops in the Colorado Territory. Mary

Todd Lincoln has frequently been identified as the woman in the back row at the far right. See Herman J. Viola, *Diplomats in Buckskins: A History of Indian Delegations in Washington City* (Washington, DC: Smithsonian Institution Press, 1981), 101.

20. The extensive Lord & Burnham plans are in folder RG 42, the National Archives, Washington, DC

21. A mantelpiece of this design is in the collection of the Newark Museum, but it is of wood, painted to resemble black marble with gold veining. It demonstrates less expensive alternatives available to those who either did not have access to marble or would not pay for it.

22. Brussels carpeting was less expensive, but also less durable, than cut-pile Wilton carpeting.

23. Richard Guy Wilson, "Nineteenth Century American Resorts and Hotels," in *Victorian Resorts and Hotels* (Philadelphia: Victorian Society in America, 1982), 12, 13. Also see Elizabeth Fitzpatrick Jones, "Hotel Design in the Work of Isaiah Rogers and Henry Whitestone," in the same source, 33.

24. William Seale notes that Polk ordered gilded French figural clocks for Polk Place after his retirement, clearly remembering the White House's ormolu clocks. For references to interior finishes and their dates, see Seale, *The President's House*, 1986.

25. For other references to specific interior work, see Betty C. Monkman, *The White House: Its Historic Furnishings and First Families* (Washington, DC: White House Historical Association, 2000), 103, 115, 125, 130, 135, 292.

26. The monetary calculation is from the Inflation Calculator, http://www.westegg.com/inflation/infl.cgi

27. This description is given in the margin of the drawing done in 1864 by Stellwagen, now in the collection of the Western Reserve Historical Society and illustrated in this essay.

28. This would be over $2 million in 2007 dollars.

29. Ibid., 75.

30. Works patented by Aaron Crane of Newark and licensed to the Year Clock Co., New York. Painted wood, gold-brass mounts, wooden works, circa 1841. Collection of the Newark Museum, accession number 63.115.

31. This interior was one of six featured in an article titled "The President's House," in the third installment of a series of articles on the city of Washington, in *The United States Magazine* 3, no. 3 (September 1856).

32. Frances Benjamin Johnston, inscription on photograph in Library of Congress, LCJ69881359. The figures that Johnston photographed with the clock were actually acquired by Julia Grant for the room in 1869. See Esther Singleton, *The Story of the White House* (New York: McClure, 1970), 1:106–07.

33. The amount of $4,300 in 1833 would be more than $91,000 in 2007 dollars, according to the Inflation Calculator, at http://www.westegg.com/inflation/infl.cgi

34. The history of these pieces is somewhat sketchy, but evidence published by Betty C. Monkman strongly supports the story. Objects from Point Breeze, the Bonaparte estate on the New Jersey side of the Delaware River, were hugely sought-after in the period, always seen as glamorous because of their association with the French emperor's brother and his celebrated sojourn in the United States.

35. Several pieces are known from a large dinner service of mixed classical–rococo style, made for the McKean family of Philadelphia and retailed through Bailey & Kitchen in the late 1830s. Two covered entrée dishes, a tureen, and a large water pitcher with the McKean arms have survived. An entrée dish is in the collection of the Metropolitan Museum of Art, the tureen is in the collection of the Newark Museum, and another entrée dish and the water pitcher are in a private New York collection.

36. Andrew Jackson Downing, *The Architecture of Country Houses*, originally published 1850 (New York: Dover, 1969), 413–14.

37. The basic facts of such furnishings can be found in Betty C. Monkman, *The White House: Its Historic Furnishings and First Families*.

38. Downing, not so surprisingly, mislabels this style as Louis XIV in *The Architecture of Country Houses*, 433.

39. Downing, *The Architecture of Country Houses*, 454.

40. By the 1890s they had been relegated to the Family Dining Room and to other upper-floor rooms, including the oval sitting room and library. The 16 that survive in the White House today were probably those that ended up in the second-floor rooms and thus survived the final furniture purge under Theodore Roosevelt in 1903. Jacqueline Kennedy placed some of them in her restored Treaty Room on the second floor in the early 1960s and incorporated them in the Kennedy-era redecoration of what came to be known as the Blue Toile Bedroom on the third floor. For this room the Baudouine chairs were slipcovered to mask their mid-19th-century form.

41. Downing, *The Architecture of Country Houses*, 292.

42. Ibid., 434–35.

43. William G. Allman, "The White House Collection: From James Buchanan's Time," in *White House History*, coll. 2, nos. 7–12 (Washington, DC: White House Historical Association, 2004), 421.

44. John and Jeannette Ballantine of Newark, New Jersey, owned a similar Japy clock with a cast bronze figure from the 1860s. The Japy clock is currently in the dining room of the restored Ballantine House.

45. The idea of Mary Lincoln as the nation's first homemaker is well covered in Jean Baker, "The Lincoln White House: Stage for the Republic's Survival," in William Seale, ed., *The White House: Actors and Observers* (Boston: Northeastern University Press, 2002), 45–63.

46. Mitchell & Rammelsberg are known to have sold furniture in Newark, New Jersey, from examples in the collection of the Newark Museum. They might even have sold furniture through the wareroom of Newark's own prominent furniture maker John Jelliff & Company, based on the association of some Cincinnati pieces with Jelliff parlor suites.

47. In the Newark Museum collection is a four-piece bedroom suite by Alexander Roux of New York from the mid-1850s, on which all of the carvings, as well as the veneers, are in rosewood. There is another partial bedroom suite, a bed and a chest of drawers, by Mitchell & Rammelsberg of Cincinnati, from about 1860. This set, much more flamboyant in design and larger in scale, combines rosewood veneers with rosewood-grained walnut moldings and carved pieces. Both of these sets were purchased by prominent families in Newark, New Jersey. The Cincinnati bedroom furniture was very possibly retailed by John Jelliff & Company. Known rosewood bedroom furniture by Jelliff does not mix grained wood with rosewood veneers.

48. Monkman, *The White House, Its Historic Furnishing*, 292. Monkman notes that Mrs. Herbert Hoover attributed this piece to the Grant administration, but her evidence for the Johnson purchase seems more appropriate to the style and form of the piece.

MANSION

1. Andrew Jackson Downing, *The Architecture of Country Houses*, with a foreword by J. Stewart Johnson, originally published 1850 (New York: Dover, 1969).

2. E. V. Smalley, "The White House," *Century* 27 (April 1884): 815.

3. Ibid., 809.

4. As quoted from *Annual Report, 1867* of General Nathaniel Michler, the officer in charge of public buildings, by William Seale, *The President's House: A History* (Washington, DC: White House Historical Association, 1986), 1:451.

5. *Report of the Supervising Architect of Treasury Department* (Washington, D.C.: Treasury Department, Office of Supervising Architect, October 31, 1868), 11. The concept of parks democratically bringing together the rich and poor was a fundamental belief of American park pioneer Frederick Law Olmsted.

6. As early as 1851, government plans anticipated a path on the south lawn. See James Keily, surveyor, "Map of the City of Washington, D.C. Established as the Permanent Seat of the Government of the U.S. of America" (Camden, NJ: Lloyd Van Deever, 1851). A version of Mullett's plan of 1868 had been drawn up by 1857; see "Map of Washington City, District of Columbia, Seat of the Federal Government; Respectfully Dedicated to the Senate and the House of Representatives of the United States of North America" (Washington, DC: A. Boschke C. E., 1857). The rounded form the path took closely resembles the outline of the entranceway at Mount Vernon as known from the 1797 plan, drawn by Englishman Samuel Vaughan, which George Washington himself thought was accurate. This plan is now in the collection of the Mount Vernon Ladies' Association, Virginia.

Though left to ruin in the first half of the 19th century, Mount Vernon was saved by the Mount Vernon Ladies' Association, which acquired the property in 1858. The drive of Mount Vernon was reproduced in plan form shortly after the purchase. The property was opened to the public in 1860. See John Lossing Benson, *Mount Vernon and Its Associations* (New York: W. A. Townsend), 154–63. Benson gives a history of the garden with planting plans derived from Washington's own letters and sketches, and he illustrates the sago palm reportedly moved to President Jackson's White House orangery.

7. Ann Leighton, *American Gardens in the Eighteenth Century* (Amherst: University of Massachusetts Press, 1983), 261.

8. Diary entry dated March 31, 1851, in Charles Richard Williams, ed., *The Diary and Letters of Rutherford B. Hayes, Nineteenth President of the United States* (Columbus: Ohio State Archaeological and Historical Society, 1922), 353.

9. The doorway and its brick surrounding block may have come from the stables built when the west wing was reconstructed in 1815–18. William Seale, *The White House: The History of an American Idea* (Washington, DC: American Institute of Architects Press, 1992), 118.

10. See Arnold Lewis, James Turner, and Steven McQuillin, *The Opulent Interiors of the Gilded Age: All 203 Photographs from "Artistic Houses"* (New York: Dover, 1987), 34–37. Oddly enough, the principal guest room in the Stewart house was referred to as the General Grant Room, most likely commemorating a visit by the general.

11. For references to interior details, see William Seale, *The President's House*, 464, 468, 533, 540, 541, 542, 543.

12. Ibid., 468.

13. See Lewis, Turner, and McQuillin, *The Opulent Interiors of the Gilded Age*, 132–35. Louis C. Tiffany's decoration in the East Room was also included in this book.

14. Esther Singleton, *The Story of the White House* (New York: McClure, 1907), 2:183.

15. Ibid., 45, figure 17. Ulysses S. Grant's house on 66th Street in New York City was also included in this book, but more because of Grant's celebrity than the quality of the interiors.

16. See Robert Koch, *Louis Tiffany: Rebel in Glass* (New York: Crown, 1966), 21.

17. Indeed, the sconces were so reflective that they often disappear in photographs. Seale, *The President's House*, 541.

18. William F. Cogswell, 1819–1903, was a close friend of financier Jay Cooke's brother Henry, who lived in Washington. As a result, Cogswell became a friend of the Grants and painted a portrait of the general for Henry Cooke, from whom the U.S. Senate acquired it in the year after General Grant died. Referenced online at http://www.senate.gov/artandhistory/art/artifact/Painting_31_00009.htm

19. Other family portraits of the period express a similarly expansive scale. Lilly Martin Spencer painted a monumental portrait of the children of New Jersey governor Marcus L. Ward in 1858. It was hung more or less floor to ceiling in the family's Greek Revival parlor in Newark. It stands 92 inches high without its massive gilt frame. In 1844 Horace Rockwell painted a group portrait of the Lewis G. Thompson family in Fort Wayne, Indiana. It is only five and a half feet high (without its wide Greek Revival frame), but it is more than six feet wide, to accommodate the nine sitters. Both of these are published in *American Art in the Newark Museum* (Newark: Newark Museum, 1981).

20. For her personal service, in 1868 Julia had ordered from China a 365-piece set of rose medallion porcelain, each piece centered with her husband's monogram within a laurel victor's wreath. It has a ground of dense gold and green scrollwork, with panels of costumed Chinese figures and designs of roses, butterflies, and birds. The overall enameling of this service seems to hover between the lush naturalism of the romantic period and the opulent exoticism of the Gilded Age. Presumably this service was used only in the Family Dining Room of the White House. Many pieces have remained in the family and have also been placed in museums, including the Peabody Essex Museum, the Everson Museum (Syracuse, New York), and the Newark Museum (source: Newark Museum object files).

21. It is interesting to note that in more recent years presidents have used this cabinet table as their personal desk, like a massive corporate executive desk—what once was big enough for the whole cabinet is now suitable for the president alone.

22. One of those sofas survives in the house, which is now a museum in Norwalk. See Katherine S. Howe, Alice Cooney Frelinghuysen, and Catherine Hoover Voorsanger, *Herter Brothers: Furniture and Interiors for a Gilded Age* (New York and Houston, TX: Harry N. Abrams and the Museum of Fine Arts, Houston, 1994), 140–41.

23. See ibid., 167–71. The Goodwin parlor with all its Herter furniture is in the Wadsworth Atheneum in Hartford.

24. Tiffany in fact won the gold medal for its silver, outraging its European competitors. See Ulysses Grant Dietz, "A Gold Standard for the Gilded Age," in Clare Phillips, ed., *Bejewelled by Tiffany, 1837–1987* (New Haven, CT: Yale University Press, 2006), 49–50. An inlaid silver sideboard dish in the Henri II style from the centennial is in the collection of the Newark Museum.

25. Julia herself ordered Gorham medallion pattern flatware from Bailey & Company in Philadelphia in 1865 and acquired an engraved neo-Grec salver from Tiffany & Company at about the same time. At least two examples of the flatware

survive with her descendants, and the salver is in the collection of the Newark Museum, a gift of the author (source: Newark Museum object files and collections of John E. Dietz II and Ulysses Grant Dietz).

26. From original teletype caption, Library of Congress, *New York World, Telegraph,* and *Sun* collection, Geography File, United States, White House, Dining Room, AP photograph taken April 26, 1940.

27. For an exhaustive analysis of the Hayes service and how it came to be, see Margaret Brown Klapthor, *Official White House China, 1789 to the Present* (Washington, DC: Smithsonian Institution, 1975), 97–121. According to Mrs. Baker, Caroline Harrison intended to display the Hayes china in cases built for the State Dining Room. Abby Gunn Baker, "The White House Collection of Presidential Ware," *The Century Magazine* 76, no. 6 (October 1908): 830–31, as noted by James Archer Abbott, *The Presidential Dish: Mrs. Woodrow Wilson and the White House China Room* (Washington, DC: Woodrow Wilson House, 2007), 32n2.

28. The Hayes dining table and sideboard were sold during the Theodore Roosevelt administration in 1903, acquired by the Hayes family, and later added to the Hayes Memorial in Fremont, Ohio, now the Rutherford B. Hayes Presidential Center. For further reference, see Jennifer L. Howe et al., *Cincinnati Art-Carved Furniture and Interiors* (Cincinnati: Cincinnati Art Museum and Ohio University Press, 2003).

29. Thomas Shaw, an enterprising electroplater from Birmingham, England, managed Tiffany's plating works. Tiffany's electroplate was among the costliest in the country, because it boasted the same level of hand chasing as their sterling wares. The compotes cost $35 each in 1882, which was an enormous sum for plated goods. See Monkman, *The White House: Its Historic Furnishings*, 295. This high cost ultimately forced Tiffany to drop its plated line during the Depression in the 1930s.

30. Thomas Shaw's son, Frank, became a specialist in chasing this sort of elaborate overall patterning on plated goods in Tiffany's Newark factory. Frank died of tuberculosis before completing in this manner a silver-plated tea table, which was finished for the World's Columbian Exposition in Chicago in 1893. That table survived and is in the collection of the Munson-Williams-Proctor Institute Museum in Utica, New York. Other examples of the Shaw family's plated work for Tiffany are in the Newark Museum (source: Newark Museum object files).

31. Examples exist in other museums in the United States, including Evergreen House in Baltimore, Maryland.

32. Julia Grant ordered her husband a 365-piece Chinese service in this same general style in 1868. It came with the family to the White House in 1869 (source: Newark Museum object files). Examples of this service are in the Everson Museum, Syracuse, New York; the Peabody Essex Museum, Salem, Massachusetts; the Newark Museum, Newark, New Jersey; and Winterthur Estate and Gardens, Winterthur, Delaware.

33. The Newark Museum owns a custom-made armchair from the George Kemp House in New York, completed by Louis Tiffany in 1879 for his first professional interior. It was manufactured by Tiffany's own furniture-making shop, one of many businesses the enterprising artist created over his long career.

34. It is now known to be from the late 19th century, representing the Colonial Revival interest in Empire forms.

PALACE

1. Letter from Edith Wharton to W. Morton Fullerton, April 26, 1910, in R. W. B. Lewis and Nancy Lewis, eds., *The Letters of Edith Wharton* (New York: Scribner, 1988), 210.

2. Charles Moore, "Restoration of the White House," *Century* 65 (April 1903), 809–11.

3. Leland Roth, *McKim, Mead & White: Architects* (New York: Harper & Row, 1983), 270.

4. Charles Moore, *The Life and Times of Charles Follen McKim* (Boston and New York: Houghton Mifflin, 1929), 215.

5. Charles Follen McKim, as quoted in Fiske Kimball, "The Genesis of the White House," *Century* 95 (February 1919): 527.

6. Moore, *The Life and Times of Charles Follen McKim*, 219–21.

7. Montgomery Schuyler, "The New White House," *Architectural Record* 13 (April 1903): 388.

8. "Washington and Its Vicinity," *Picturesque America; or, The Land We Live In* 19 (June 23, 1894): 455–57.

9. For Olmsted and the McMillan Commission, see David C. Streatfield, "The Olmsteds and Landscape of the Mall," in Richard Longstreth, ed., *The Mall in Washington, 1791–1991* (Washington, DC: National Gallery of Art, 1991), 117–42.

10. Glenn Brown, "The Plan of the City and Its Expanded Growth," *Records of the Columbia Historical Society* 7 (1904): 114.

11. The originals of these drawings are lost. They were reproduced in "The New White House," *Harpers Weekly* 46 (November 22, 1902): 1734, and in *The Restoration of the White House*, Senate Document 197, 57th Congress, 2nd H. doc. (Washington, DC: Government Printing Office, 1903). As noted in William Seale, *The President's House: A History* (Washington, DC: White House Historical Association, 1986), 2:1120n44.

12. Letter from Charles F. McKim to Frederick Law Olmsted Jr., February 16, 1903, 1–3. In the collection of the New–York Historical Society, Collection PR042, Corr. 505, Folder White House, 1968, Misc. M-7. The plan that accompanied this letter is Job 287, Plan #2827–1 in the Frederick Law Olmsted Archive, Brookline, Massachusetts.

13. Mrs. Roosevelt resisted the razing of the greenhouses because they were an affordable source for White House flower arrangements and for the customary bouquets sent to visitors to the capital city. In the end, McKim finessed the concern by arranging for a new greenhouse on the mall to house the conservatory plants, many of which died before the building was constructed. Seale, *The President's House*, 1: 665–69.

14. For an overview of women in the landscape architecture movement, see Mac Griswold and Eleanor Weller, *The Golden Age of American Gardens: Proud Owners, Private Estates, 1890–1940* (New York: Harry N. Abrams, 1991), 16–17, 19–20. Also Dorothy May Anderson, *Women, Design and the Cambridge School* (West Lafayette, IN: P.D.A., 1980).

15. Letter from McKim to Olmsted, 1. Edith Wharton was well known to McKim, who provided editorial suggestions for her influential *The Decoration of Houses*, published in 1897. See Hermione Lee, *Edith Wharton* (New York: Knopf, 2007), 129.

16. For the Roosevelt visits see Harrison Howell Dodge, *Mount Vernon: Its Owner and Its Story* (Philadelphia: J. B. Lippincott, 1932), 126–28.

17. Contemporary scholarship establishes that during George Washington's lifetime, flowers at Mount Vernon were limited, and boxwood, used extensively, was laid out in the flower garden in a fleur-de-lis pattern, not in the maze-and-petal pattern that would have been seen by Edith Roosevelt in her visits to Washington's estate. Symmetrical boxwood parterres thought to be colonial in design were found in many American gardens illustrated in town and city atlases published after the Civil War. For Mount Vernon, see Ann Leighton, *American Gardens in the Eighteenth Century: For Use or for Delight* (Amherst: University of Massachusetts Press, 1986), 260–63. For midcentury gardens, see Patricia M. Tice, *Gardening in America, 1830–1910* (Rochester, NY: Strong Museum, 1984). An archaeological assessment of the Mount Vernon gardens was first carried out in 1935, the year Morley Jeffers Williams was researching for Frederick Law Olmsted Jr. the history of the White House gardens. Thomas E. Beaman Jr., "A Pioneer of Landscape Archaeology: Morley Jeffers Williams and the Restored Historic Landscapes of Stratford Hall, Mount Vernon, and Tryon Palace," accessed online at www.tclf.org/conf_papers/beaman-paper.doc

18. The president's tennis court was moved to its present location on the west side of the south grounds in 1909 when the Executive Office Building was enlarged by President Taft.

19. Theodore Roosevelt, "Professionalism in Sports," *The North American Review* 151, no. 405 (August 1890): 29.

20. Henrietta F. Dunlap, "In the Garden of the White House," *Town & Country Magazine* 330 (March 12, 1910): 31.

21. Ellen Axson Wilson to Florence Hoyt (her cousin), January 1, 1913, as quoted in Ray Stannard Baker, *Woodrow Wilson: Life and Letters* (Garden City, NY: Doubleday, Page, 1927–39), 4:462. For Mrs. Wilson as artist, decorator, and gardener, see Frances W. Saunders, "Ellen Axson Wilson: First Lady and Artist," in Frank J. Aucella and Patricia A. Piorkoski, *Ellen Axson Wilson: First Lady–Artist* (Washington, DC: Woodrow Wilson House, 1993), 5–8.

22. Charles Adams Platt, *Italian Gardens*, reprint of 1894 ed. (Portland, OR: Sagapress/Timberpress, 1993), 6–7.

23. Four photographs of the White House exterior and numerous American colonial buildings appear in Charles A. Platt's photograph album of colonial architecture at the Century Association, New York.

24. Charles Henlock and Margaret Norn, "Flowers for First Ladies," *Saturday Evening Post* 204, no. 22 (November 31, 1930): 12–13, 81–83. Noted in pencil on the plans for the Edith Roosevelt colonial gardens reproduced here is: "Removed Fall 1913." Plan 14.3–4, National Archives, Washington, DC

25. Mrs. Ellen A. Wilson to President Woodrow Wilson, August 20, 1913. As quoted in Virginia Reed Colby and James B. Atkinson, *Footprint of the Past: Images of Cornish, New Hampshire, and the Cornish Colony* (Concord: New Hampshire Historical Society, 1996), 430.

26. For the Slade garden, see Herbert Croly, "A Cornish House and Garden," *Architectural Record* 22 (September 1907): 227. Alma M. Gilbert and Judith B. Tankard, *A Place of Beauty: The Artists and Gardens of the Cornish Colony* (Berkeley, CA: Ten Speed Press, 2000), 121–23.

27. Eleanor Wilson McAdoo with Margaret Y. Gaffey, *The Woodrow Wilsons* (New York: Macmillan, 1937), 237.

28. See Mrs. Schulyer van Rensselaer, *Art Out-of-Doors: Hints on Good Taste in Gardening* (New York: Scribner, 1893). The American Park and Outdoor Art Association, organized in Louisville in 1896, merged with the American League for Civic Improvement to create the American Civic Association on June 10, 1904. President Wilson endorsed the preservation efforts of these groups by supporting the 1916 formation of the National Park Service and signing into law Zion, Sieur de Monte, Capulin, and other federal parks. See Terence Young, "Social Reform through Parks: The American Civic Association's Program for a Better America," *Journal of Historical Geography* 22, no. 4 (October 1996): 460–72.

Before entering private practice in 1916 or 1917, George E. Burnap, as a federal government landscape architect, was responsible for the design and redesign of many capital city parks. He lectured on civic landscape architecture and was the author of *Parks: Their Design, Equipment, and Use* (Philadelphia: Lippincott, 1916). See Deon Wolfenbarger, "Burnap, George Elberton," in Charles A. Birnbaum and Robin Karson, *Pioneers of American Landscape Design* (New York: McGraw-Hill, 2000), 39–43.

29. As quoted from the American Civic Association by William Wilson, *The City Beautiful Movement* (Baltimore, MD: John Hopkins University Press, 1989), 29, in Young, "Social Reform through Parks," 461.

30. As quoted from J. H. McFarland, "Education in Ugliness," printed manuscript, 1908, 856, J. Horace McFarland Papers, MG-85, Pennsylvania Historical and Museum Commission, by Young, "Social Reform through Parks," 461.

31. Robin Karson, *Genius for Place: American Landscapes of the Country Place Era* (Amherst: University of Massachusetts Press, 2007), 133–47.

32. From a 1928 drawing for the Pierpont Morgan Library garden designed by Farrand, it appears that her 1913 garden for banker J. P. Morgan's town house was similar in overall design to the Wilson east garden. For the Morgan garden, see Diane Kostial McGuire, and Eleanor M. McPeck, *Beatrix Farrand's American Landscape* (Sagaponack, NY: Sagapress, 1985), 34–38.

33. Garden furniture was already fashionable at the time of Downing. For the history of the White House limestone suite, believed to be from northern Europe, where such faux-bois work had been popular since the 1850s, see Betty C. Monkman, *Treasures from the White House* (New York: Abbeville Press, 2001), 155; Betty C. Monkman, *The White House: Its Historic Furnishings and First Families* (New York: Abbeville Press, 2000), 200–201. A tinted stereotype of the stools and bench by the south pool, circa 1911, is in the New York Public Library, Dennis Collection, G90F099_080ZF. The stools appear again in the photograph of the Kennedy southeast garden, July 1963, reproduced here.

34. The watercolor published here, p. 169, from the Woodrow Wilson House, relates more closely to the final garden plan, dated 1916, than the rendering with statues in the Environmental Design Collection, University of California, Berkeley. For this reason we date the watercolor to late 1915, early 1916 when Edith Wilson revived the project. A Farrand plan for the west parterre has not been found. The 1913 government plans for the south gardens cited by Jane Brown, *The Gardening Life of Beatrix Jones Farrand, 1872–1959* (New York: Viking, 1995), 101, 108 are prints of the c. 1902 Roosevelt plans reproduced here, p. 164, likely sent to Farrand by Ellen Wilson.

35. As quoted in Edith Bolling Wilson, *My Memoir* (Indianapolis, IN: Bobbs-Merrill, 1939), 68.

36. September 6, 1918, plans for a sheep shed and hay rack are in the National Archives, number 14–2, Washington, D.C. See also Henlock, "Flowers for First Ladies," 83.

37. In 1885, architect George Edward Harney built a house for John and Jeannette Ballantine in Newark, New Jersey, now part of the Newark Museum. The gold and white drawing room of this house was called "Colonial" in the builder's specifications, an early document of this emerging style. See Ulysses Dietz, *The Ballantine House* (Newark, NJ: Newark Museum, 1994).

38. Esther Singleton, *The Story of the White House* (New York: McClure, 1907), 2:223. Electric blue was also the color specified for the drawing-room curtains of the Ballantine House in Newark in 1885; see previous note.

39. Sagamore Hill, designed by New York architects Lamb and Rich in 1884, was the Theodore and Edith Roosevelt country house in Oyster Bay, New York. The Queen Anne house was more villa in scale than mansion, and its decoration echoed the taste of the Victorian White House.

40. Singleton, *The Story of the White House*, 2:279–80.

41. Buckingham Palace in London and the Winter Palace in St. Petersburg come to mind, although both are on a much larger scale.

42. See Michael C. Kathrens, *American Splendor: The Residential Architecture of Horace Trumbauer* (New York: Acanthus Press, 2002), 64, 74.

43. Specifically, the suite of oak-paneled state rooms at Chatsworth, the seat of the Dukes of Devonshire, which surely would have been known to McKim, Mead & White.

44. For example, Elihu Root, Roosevelt's friend and secretary of state, had several mounted elk heads in the entrance hall of his country house in Clinton, New York, as well as leopard-skin rugs framed in bear fur. Root was not a hunter, and these were seen as part of the decor of the time. Root was the author Ulysses Dietz's great-grandfather, and his house remained intact until 1978.

45. Moose also exist in northern Europe and Russia, but they were nonetheless imagined as peculiarly American animals. Ulysses S. Grant signed legislation making Yellowstone the first national park in 1872. Theodore Roosevelt carried on this legacy by putting 230 million acres of wilderness under national protection. See http://www.theodoreroosevelt.org/life/conservation.htm

46. At the turn of the century the Ballantine brewing family in Newark, New Jersey, collected Napoleonic material, some of which is still in the collection of the Newark Museum.

47. Singleton, *The Story of the White House*, 296.

48. Edward F. Caldwell and Company produced all of the new lighting for the White House project. They were the premier manufacturer of high-style electric lighting in the nation.

49. Singleton, *The Story of the White House*, 295–96. Singleton notes the Genoese link for the Green Room, and period images show a similar cut-velvet patterning in the Red Room.

50. See Penny Sparke, *Elsie de Wolfe: The Birth of Modern Interior Decoration* (New York: Acanthus Press, 2005), 86–88, for color images of de Wolfe's 1913 interior designs employing the sort of floral fabrics and light colors used in the White House by Ellen A. Wilson.

51. The Newark Museum began collecting coverlets like this in the late 1910s. These simple handwoven textiles were particularly admired by women who saw them as examples of colonial handiwork, although they originally had been woven in the 1810s and 1820s.

52. See note 1.

53. Aucella and Hobbs, *Ellen Axson Wilson*, 10.

54. See James Archer Abbott, *The Presidential Dish: Mrs. Woodrow Wilson and the White House China Room* (Washington, DC: Woodrow Wilson House, 2007).

55. Interestingly, there are quite a number of important Victorian furnishings from Theodore Roosevelt's parents at Sagamore Hill on Long Island. Perhaps Edith Roosevelt saved these out-of-date objects from the same history-minded impulse.

56. Both Monkman, *The White House: Its Historic Furnishings*, 188, and Seale, *The President's House*, 189, suggest that the architects knew of the Bellangé suite, and Seale further suggests that they would have consciously tried to evoke Bellangé's style.

57. The caption on a postcard of the Green Room reports that the emperor of Austria gave this screen to Mrs. Grant. While this is not true, General Grant's son Frederick was a friend of Theodore Roosevelt's and had been the American minister to the Austrian court under President Harrison from 1889 to 1893. The stories might have become conflated.

58. Irving W. Lyon produced the first scholarly publication on American colonial furniture in 1891, titled *The Colonial Furniture of New England*, reprinted in 1977 by E. P. Dutton, New York. McKim, Mead & White would certainly have known of it.

59. The Symington family of Newark had two pairs of 17th-century William and Mary chairs in their late-Victorian mansion in Newark, New Jersey. These were given to the Newark Museum in 1965 and are currently used in the 1885 Ballantine House.

60. McKim, Mead & White's splendid University Club, built in 1900, on Fifth Avenue in New York City offered rooms very similar to the White House state rooms.

SUBURBAN HOME

1. See Fiske Kimball, "The Genesis of the White House," *Century* 95 (February 1919): 523.

2. For Olmsted's commentary, see the *Report to the President of the White House Grounds by Olmsted Brothers*, October 1935, 1–81, in the Frederick Law Olmsted Archives, Brookline, Massachusetts.

3. For Truman's suggestion, see Margaret Truman, *The President's House: A First Daughter Shares the Secrets of the World's Most Famous House* (New York: Ballantine, 2003), 231. For the boxwood planting, with the notation of "Truman Boxwood," see the plan dated 1.31.52, no. 14.3-151, in the National Archives, Washington, D.C. Also, the 1952 garden plan is reproduced here.

4. A plan of the south lawn, with an axis line drawn to indicate the view from the south portico, dated October 22, 1927, by Irving W. Payne for General Ulysses S. Grant III, director of the Office of Public Buildings and Public Parks, makes clear that the concept of opening the south vista had already been under consideration when Olmsted was hired. A survey similar to Olmsted's, of existing trees, was prepared for Grant on July 7, 1932. Both plans, numbers 14.3–51 and 14.3–48, are in the National Archives, Washington, D.C.

5. For A.J. Downing and the veranda, see Andrew Jackson Downing, *A Treatise on the Theory and Practice of Landscape Gardening, Adapted to North America; With a View to the Improvement of Country Residences . . . With Remarks on Rural Architecture*, by the Late A. J. Downing, Esq. 6th ed. (Ann Arbor: University of Michigan, University Library, 1859), 325-6. For the American villa, a porch was a sheltered entrance, a piazza

and veranda were semi-enclosed outdoor rooms. Truman recorded his observation in an undated note in his daily dairy, quoted in David McCullough, "A House Set in a Landscape," in Frank Freidel and William Pencak, eds., *The White House: The First Two Hundred Years* (Boston: Northeastern University Press, 1994), 205. For caption, p. 219, "Back-Porch Harry," *Time Magazine*, January 26, 1948:17.

6. Howard Barnstone, *The Architecture of John F. Staub: Houston and the South*, Austin: University of Texas Press, 1979: 229–32.

7. Grant (1881–1968) was a 1903 graduate of West Point and had served in Theodore Roosevelt's White House. In 1907 he married Edith, the daughter of Roosevelt's secretary of state, Elihu Root. Mrs. Grant (1878–1963) was a first cousin of Ruth Wales, Mrs. Henry Francis du Pont, who worked with Mrs. Kennedy, and the Grants were familiar with the work Mr. du Pont had begun toward colonializing his father's house in Winterthur in 1926. Author Ulysses Grant Dietz is a grandson of the Grants.

8. Betty C. Monkman and William Seale have documented the details and dates of the decoration of the White House from the Coolidges through the Eisenhowers.

9. There was an upper-class component to this knotty-pine phenomenon, too. Sugar-fortune heiress Electra Havemeyer Webb used knotty pine for her dining room at 740 Park Avenue in the 1930s, and tobacco millionaire Doris Duke installed a Georgian pine drawing room in the Hollywood Wing of her country house in New Jersey in the 1930s.

10. R. T. Haines Halsey, a major instigator of the American Wing, and Luke Vincent Lockwood, an important early collector of American antiques, were both part of the advisory committee established in 1925. For other references to furnishings of this period, Betty C. Monkman and William Seale have documented most of the key details.

11. In 1933, for example, the Newark Museum mounted an exhibition titled "Victorian Vignettes" and was itself beginning to collect pieces of Victorian furniture from local families.

12. Although the large living room/library at Springwood, an 1867 bracketed farmhouse transformed into a Georgian Revival estate by FDR and his mother in 1915, might approach palace scale, the rooms are generally furnished with a prosperous suburban level of style and comfort, with family heirlooms mixed in. In this way, FDR and his family led a life not unlike that of the Theodore Roosevelts at Oyster Bay.

13. *Good Furniture*, (June 1917): 95, Newark Museum library.

SHRINE

1. The National Trust for Historic Preservation was founded in 1949, with an act of Congress signed by President Truman. Among its founding trustees were Ulysses S. Grant III, who built the third floor on the White House and nearly caused its collapse; and Henry Francis du Pont, who would serve on Mrs. Kennedy's Fine Arts Committee.

2. Thomas Robsjohn-Gibbings, *Good-bye, Mr. Chippendale* (New York: Knopf, 1944). The 106-page book was punctuated with comic illustrations by *New Yorker* cartoonist Mary Petty, who specialized in lampooning the old-guard elite and their fussy Victorian interiors.

3. For interiors by de Wolfe, see Penny Sparke, *Elsie de Wolfe: The Birth of Modern Interior Decoration* (New York: Acanthus Press, 2005).

4. The fullest account of this televised event in book form is Perry Wolff's *A Tour of the White House with Mrs. John F. Kennedy* (Garden City, NY: Doubleday, 1962).

5. Memorandum from Arthur Schlesinger Jr. to Miss Letitia Baldrige, January 8, 1962. See also letter from Letitia Baldrige for Mrs. Kennedy to Mrs. James E. McGraw, October 25, 1961. White House Flower Garden, Social File, Box 947, John F. Kennedy Presidential Library and Museum, Boston, Massachusetts.

6. Rachel Lambert Mellon, "President Kennedy's Rose Garden," *White House History* 1 (1983): 9–15.

7. Ibid., 14.

8. Mrs. Paul Mellon, "The White House Gardens, Concepts and Design of the Rose Garden," in Frederick L. Kramer, *The White House Gardens: A History and Pictorial Record* (New York: Great American Editions, 1973), 79.

9. "Report to the President of the White House Grounds by Olmsted Brothers," October 1935, no. 14 in the Frederick Law Olmsted Archives, Brookline, Massachusetts.

10. Rachel Lambert Mellon, "President Kennedy's Rose Garden," 9. For watercolor renderings of the Kennedy garden plans, see also Kramer, *The White House Gardens*, 96–97 and 108–09.

11. As quoted in John Carl Warnecke, "The Rescue and Renaissance of Lafayette Square," *White House History* 13 (summer 2003): 44.

12. Herter Brothers being the most famous of these; see Katherine S. Howe, Alice Cooney Frelinghuysen, and Catherine Hoover Voorsanger, *Herter Brothers: Furniture and Interiors for a Gilded Age* (New York and Houston, TX: Harry N. Abrams and the Museum of Fine Arts, Houston, 1994). Louis Comfort Tiffany had been one of the first individuals who worked as a decorator, but he was also a manufacturer of furnishings.

13. Edith Wharton and Ogden Codman Jr., *The Decoration of Houses* (New York: Scribner, 1897); Elsie de Wolfe, *The House in Good Taste* (New York: Century, 1913).

14. Earlier exhibitions dating back as far as the Hudson-Fulton Exhibition of 1909 strongly influenced the "colonial" aspect of good taste.

15. Richard Pratt, *A Treasury of Early American Homes* (New York: Whittlesey House, 1949) and *A Second Treasury of Early American Homes* (New York: Whittlesey House, 1953); the two volumes were combined in 1967 by Hawthorne Books (New York) with the title *The Golden Treasury of Early American Houses.*

16. For an excellent biography, see Susan Bartlett Crater and Apple Parish Bartlett, *Sister: The Life of Legendary Interior Decorator Mrs. Henry Parish II* (New York: St. Martin's Press, 2000).

17. He had done a French house for Margaret Thompson Biddle, who bequeathed the vermeil collection to the Eisenhower White House in 1956. He also did extensive work for two other White House advisory committee members, Jayne Wrightsman and Barbara Paley. For a detailed history of Boudin's career, see James Archer Abbott, *Jansen* (New York: Acanthus Press, 2006).

18. For the best source of information on the Kennedy redecoration project, see James Archer Abbott and Elaine M. Rice, *Designing Camelot: The Kennedy White House Restoration* (New York: Van Nostrand Reinhold, 1998).

19. Lorraine Waxman received her degree from Winterthur's program through the University of Delaware in 1958, writing her thesis on Charles-Honoré Lannuier, a French-born New York cabinetmaker of the early 1800s.

20. For a sense of the childhood apartment of the Bouvier family, in a building owned by Mrs. Kennedy's grandfather, James T. Lee, see Michael Gross, *740*

Park: The Story of the World's Richest Apartment Building (New York: Broadway Books, 2005). For a survey of this and other upper-class New York apartment buildings by the same architect, see Andrew Alpern, *The New York Apartment Houses of Rosario Candela and James Carpenter* (New York: Acanthus Press, 2001).

21. The White House was formally accredited in 1988 by the American Association of Museums as a house museum, as noted in Betty C. Monkman, *The White House: Its Historic Furnishings and First Families* (Washington, DC: White House Historical Association, 2000), 259.

22. Ibid., 235.

23. Lorraine Waxman Pearce et al., *The White House* (Washington, DC: White House Historical Association, 1963), 101.

24. Abbott and Rice, *Designing Camelot*, 101.

25. Russell Lynes introduction in Katharine Tweed, ed., *The Finest Rooms by America's Great Decorators* (New York: Viking, 1964).

26. Abbott and Rice, *Designing Camelot*, 164–65.

27. In particular, the entrance hall in The Lindens, a colonial house moved to Washington, D.C., in 1935, boasted such scenic paper in its front hall. See Helen Comstock, *100 Most Beautiful Rooms in America* (New York: Viking, 1965), 44–45. The George Read House in Newcastle, Delaware, had a dining room with scenic walls and was published in Richard Pratt's 1949 *A Treasury of Early American Homes* (see note 15). Mr. du Pont himself had such paper installed at Winterthur, for which see John A. H. Sweeney, *Winterthur Illustrated* (Winterthur, DE: H. F. du Pont Winterthur Museum, 1963), 80–81. The Asa Stebbins house at Historic Deerfield, restored by Mr. and Mrs. Henry Flynt in the 1940s, also boasts a room with scenic paper.

28. For more on this, see Ronald Reagan's comments on Nancy's interest in the White House, at "RonaldReagan.com, The Official Site," http://www.ronaldreagan.com/nancy.html.

29. See Patricia Leigh Brown, "A Redecorated White House, the Way the Clintons Like It," in *The New York Times*, Section A, November, 4, 1993: 1. Ms. Hockersmith's Web site can be found at http://www.kakihockersmith.com.

30. Even though a woman will likely be elected president in the coming decades, it will, given our culture, still fall to her to oversee the decoration of the house, just as it did for our first presidents.

31. Malia Obama was widely shown in television news reports, talking about her excitement at redecorating her room in the White House, on November 5, 2008, the day after her father, Barack Obama, was elected as the first African-American president in the nation's history. Her statement was also cited at http://abcnews.go.com/Politics/Vote2008/story?id=5330730&page=1.

32. Lorraine Waxman Pearce, *The White House: An Historic Guide* (Washington, DC: White House Historical Association, 1962), 7.

33. Ibid., 63.

34. Abbott and Rice, *Designing Camelot*, 103

35. Monkman, *The White House: Its Historic Furnishings*, 238.

36. Letter from Jacqueline Kennedy to Mr. H. F. du Pont, November 21, 1962, White House Restoration, White House Social File, Box 947, John F. Kennedy Presidential Library and Museum, Boston, Massachusetts.

37. Ibid.

38. Pearce, *The White House: An Historic Guide*, 64.

39. Ibid., 94.

40. Ibid., 72.

41. Part of the anti-Victorian prejudice was fueled by the misperception that all post-1840 objects were machine made. For images of the Victorian du Pont mansion, see Jay Cantor, *Winterthur* (New York and Winterthur, DE: Harry N. Abrams and the Henry Francis du Pont Winterthur Museum, 1985), 68–72.

42. Not until 1970 did Berry Tracy, who had organized "Classical America in Newark," mastermind the landmark exhibition "Nineteenth-Century America" at the Metropolitan Museum of Art. Its two-volume catalog became a guidebook for the acceptance and revived popularity of Victorian art and decorative arts. Louis Comfort Tiffany had died in 1933, his aesthetic reputation having long since vanished like his White House interiors. It was only in 1958 that the first museum exhibition reevaluating his work was mounted—at the Museum of Contemporary Craft in New York.

43. Henry Francis du Pont, a crucial member of Mrs. Kennedy's Fine Arts Committee, founded the Winterthur Museum at his Delaware estate in 1951. He strongly resisted the later phases of the neoclassical, or Empire, style, preferring the Federal years. Although his aesthetic sense surely had some influence in the White House restoration, Mrs. Kennedy's efforts probably had an equal effect in broadening Mr. du Pont's taste.

44. Charles Engelhard was a trustee of the Newark Museum, and his wife, Jane, was a friend and client of interior decorator Sister Parish, who was instrumental in the Kennedy-era restoration.

45. J. B. West, with Mary Lynn Kotz, *Upstairs at the White House: My Life with the First Ladies* (New York: Coward, McCann & Geoghehan, 1973), 198.

46. Perry Wolff, *A Tour of the White House with Mrs. John F. Kennedy* (Garden City, NY: Doubleday, 1962), 51.

47. Letter from Jacqueline Kennedy to Mr. H. F. du Pont, November 21, 1962.

48. Except, of course, in the tax benefits received by the donors.

49. Given by the Knapp Foundation through the White House Historical Association in 1981. See Susan Gray Detweiler, *American Presidential China: The Robert L. McNeil Jr. Collection at the Philadelphia Museum of Art* (Philadelphia: Philadelphia Museum of Art, 2008), 87. The number of pieces was obtained from http://www.ronaldreagan.com/nancy.html.

50. Michael Monroe, *The White House Collection of American Crafts* (New York: Harry N. Abrams, 1995). The Renwick is the Smithsonian American Art Museum division charged with collecting American craft.

51. David A. Keeps, "Can We Call Him 'Decorator in Chief'?", *Los Angeles Times*, Home section, January 17, 2009: 4.

52. As quoted in Robert V. Rimini, "Becoming a National Symbol: The White House in the Early Nineteenth Century" in Frank Freidel and William Pencak. ed., *The White House, The First Two Hundred Years* (Boston: Northeastern University Press, 1994), 20.

53. *National Intelligencer*, March 30, 1815, as quoted in Rimini, 26.

54. Rimini, 28.

55. "Remarks by the First Lady at Sweet Honey in the Rock Event," March 18, 2009, Release from the White House Press Office at http://www.whitehouse.gov/the_press_office/Remarks-by-the-First-Lady-at-Sweet-Honey-in-the-Rock-event/.

SELECTED BIBLIOGRAPHY

ARCHITECTURE AND LANDSCAPE

Adams, William Howard, ed. *The Eye of Thomas Jefferson.* Charlottesville: University Press of Virginia, 1981.

————. *Jefferson and the Arts: An Extended View.* Washington, DC: National Gallery of Art, 1976.

Balmori, Diana, Diane Kostial McGuide, and Eleanor M. McPeck. *Beatrix Farrand's American Landscapes: Her Gardens and Campuses.* Sagaponack, NY: Sagapress, 1985.

Baron, Robert C., ed. *The Garden and Farm Books of Thomas Jefferson.* Golden, Colo.: Fulcrum, 1987.

Bednar, Michael. *L'Enfant's Legacy: Public Open Spaces in Washington, D.C.* Baltimore, MD: Johns Hopkins University Press, 2006.

Berry, Wendell. *The Unsettling of America: Culture and Agriculture.* San Francisco: Sierra Club Books, 1986.

Betts, Edwin Morris, ed. *Thomas Jefferson's Garden Book, 1766–1824, with Relevant Extracts from His Other Writings.* Philadelphia: American Philosophical Society, 1944.

Birch, William. *The Country Seats of the United States of North America with Some Scenes Connected with Them.* Springland, Pa: W. Birch, 1808.

Birnbaum, Charles A., and Robin Karson, eds. *Pioneers of American Landscape Design.* New York: McGraw-Hill, 2000.

Brown, C. Allan. "Poplar Forest: The Mathematics of the Ideal Villa." *Journal of Garden History* 10, no. 2 (1990): 121–23.

Brown, Glenn. "The Plan of the City and Its Expanded Growth." *Records of the Columbia Historical Society* 7, no. 7 (1904): 114.

Brown, Jane. *Beatrix: The Gardening Life of Beatrix Farrand, 1872–1959.* New York: Viking, 1995.

Bryan, Wilhelmus Bogart. *A History of the National Capital.* 2 vols. New York: Macmillan, 1914.

Caemmerer, H. Paul. *The Life of Pierre Charles L'Enfant: Planner of the City Beautiful, City of Washington.* Washington, DC: National Republic, 1950.

Carter, Edward C., II, John C. Van Horne, and Charles E. Brownell, eds. *Latrobe's View of America, 1795–1820: Selections from the Watercolors and Sketches.* New Haven, CT: Published for the Maryland Historical Society by Yale University Press, 1985.

Colby, Virginia Reed, and James B. Atkinson, *Footprints of the Past: Images of Cornish, New Hampshire, and the Cornish Colony.* Concord: New Hampshire Historical Society, 1996.

Comprehensive Design Plan: The White House and President's Park. Washington, DC: United States Department of the Interior, National Park Service, May 2000.

Dearstyne, Howard, and A. Lawrence Kocher, *Colonial Williamsburg—Its Buildings and Gardens.* Williamsburg: Colonial Williamsburg, 1961.

Downing, Andrew Jackson. *The Architecture of Country Houses.* New York: Dover, 1969, with a foreword by J. Stewart Johnson (orig. pub. 1850).

————. "Explanation Accompanying His Plan Improving the Public Ground of the City of Washington," 1851. Records of the Commissioners of Public Buildings.

————. *Rural Essays.* Edited by Frederika Bremer. New York: G. P. Putnam, 1953.

————. *A Treatise on the Theory and Practice of Landscape Gardening, Adapted to North America; With a View to Improvement of Country Residences.* New York: A. A. Moore, 1850. 6th ed. Ann Arbor: University of Michigan, University Library.

Dunlap, Henrietta. "In the Garden of the White House." *Town & Country Magazine* 33 (March 12, 1910): 31.

Fazio, Michael W., and Patrick A. Snadon. *The Domestic Architecture of Benjamin Henry Latrobe.* Baltimore, MD: Johns Hopkins University Press, 2006.

Gilbert, Alma M., and Judith B. Tankard. *A Place of Beauty: The Artists and Gardens of the Cornish Colony.* Berkeley, CA: Ten Speed Press, 2000.

Griswold, Mac, and Eleanor Weller. *The Golden Age of American Gardens.* New York: Harry N. Abrams, 1991.

Hamlin, Talbot. *Benjamin Henry Latrobe: The Man and the Architect.* Baltimore: Maryland Historical Society, 1942.

Harris, C. W. "The Politics of Public Building: William Thornton and the President's Square." *White House History* 3 (Spring 1998): 174–87.

Honour, Hugh. *The New Golden Land: European Images of America from the Discoveries to the Present Time.* New York: Pantheon Books, 1975.

Karson, Robin. *A Genius for Place: American Landscapes of the Country Place Era.* Amherst: University of Massachusetts Press, 2007.

Kazin, Alfred. *A Writer's America: Landscape in Literature.* New York: Knopf, 1988.

Kimball, Fiske. "The Genesis of the White House." *Century* 95 (February 1919): 524–28.

Kramer, Frederick L., with comments from Mrs. Paul Mellon. *The White House Gardens.* New York: Great American Editions, 1973.

Kurjack, Dennis C. "Who Designed the 'President's House'?" *Journal of the Society of Architectural Historians* 12 (May 1953): 27–28.

Lambeth, William A., and Warren H. Manning. *Thomas Jefferson as an Architect and a Designer of Landscapes.* Boston and New York: Houghton Mifflin, 1913.

Leighton, Ann. *American Gardens in the Eighteenth Century: "For Use or for Delight."* Amherst: University of Massachusetts Press, 1976.

———. *American Gardens of the Nineteenth Century: "For Comfort and Affluence."* Amherst: University of Massachusetts Press, 1987.

McEwan. Barbara. *White House Landscapes: Horticultural Achievements of American Presidents.* New York: Walker, 1992.

McKim, Charles Follen, et al. *Restoration of the White House: Message of the President of the United States Transmitting the Report of the Architects.* Washington, DC: U.S. Government Printing Office, 1903.

Moore, Charles. *The Life and Times of Charles Follen McKim.* Boston: Houghton Mifflin, 1929.

Mullett, A. B. *Report of the Supervising Architect of the Treasury Department.* Washington, DC: U.S. Government Printing Office, October 31, 1861.

Nichols, Frederick Doveton, and Ralph E. Griswold. *Thomas Jefferson: Landscape Architect.* Charlottesville: University of Virginia Press, 1978.

Olmsted Brothers. *Report to the President of the United States on Improvements and Policy of Maintenance for the Executive Mansion* (Brookline, MA, 1935), in the Frederick Law Olmsted Archives, Brookline, MA.

Olmsted, Frederick Law. *Civilizing American Cities: Writings on City Landscapes.* Edited by S. B. Sutton. New York: Da Capo Press, 1991.

O'Malley, Therese. "A Public Museum of Trees: Mid-Nineteenth Century Plans for the Mall." In *The Mall in Washington, 1791–1991,* edited by Richard Longstreth, 61–76. Washington, DC: National Gallery of Art, 1991.

———. "Your Garden Must Be a Museum to You:" Early American Botanic Gardens. *Huntington Library Quarterly* 59, nos. 2, 3 (1997–98): 207–31.

Pierson, William H., Jr. *American Buildings and Their Architects: The Colonial and Neo-Classical Styles.* Garden City, NY: Doubleday, 1970.

Roth, Leland. *McKim, Mead & White, Architects.* New York: Harper & Row, 1983.

Schuyler, David. *Apostle of Taste: Andrew Jackson Downing, 1815–1852.* Baltimore, MD: Johns Hopkins University Press, 1996.

Shelton, Louise. *Beautiful Gardens in America.* New York: Charles Scribner & Sons, 1928.

Seale, William. *The White House Garden.* Washington, DC: White House Historical Association, 1996.

Streatfield, David C. "The Olmsteds and the Landscape of the Mall." In *The Mall in Washington, 1791–1991,* edited by Richard Longstreth, 117–42. Washington, DC: National Gallery of Art, 1991.

Tice, Patricia M. *Gardening in America, 1830–1910.* Rochester, NY: Strong Museum, 1984.

Vaux, Calvert. *Villas and Cottages.* New York: Dover, 1970 (orig. pub. 1864).

Verheyen, Egon. "James Hoban's Design for the White House in the Context of the Planning of the Federal City." *Architectura* 11, no. 1 (1981): 66–82.

"Washington and Its Vicinity," *Picturesque America; or The Land We Live In* 19 (June 23, 1894): 455–57.

White, Richard. "Transcendental Landscapes." In *American Victorians and Virgin Nature,* edited by T. J. Jackson Lears, 1–13. Boston: Isabella Stewart Gardener Museum, 2002.

Woods, May, and Arete Warren. *Glass Houses: A History of Greenhouses, Orangeries and Conservatories.* London: Aurum Press, 1988.

Young, Terrence. "Social Reform Through Parks: The American Civic Association's Program for a Better America." *Journal of Historical Geography* 22, no. 4 (October 1996): 460–72.

DECORATIVE ARTS AND INTERIOR DESIGN

Abbott, James Archer. *Jansen.* New York: Acanthus Press, 2006.

Abbott, James Archer. *The Presidential Dish: Mrs. Woodrow Wilson and the White House China Room.* Washington, DC: Woodrow Wilson House, National Trust for Historic Preservation, 2007.

Abbott, James Archer, and Elaine M. Rice. *Designing Camelot: The Kennedy White House Restoration.* New York: Van Nostrand–Reinhold, 1998.

Burke, Doreen Bolger, et al. *In Pursuit of Beauty.* New York: The Metropolitan Museum of Art, 1986.

Cantor, Jay E. *Winterthur: The Foremost Museum of American Furniture and Decorative Arts.* New York: Harry N. Abrams, 1986.

Dietz, Ulysses Grant. *The Ballantine House.* Newark, NJ: Newark Museum, 1994.

———. *Century of Revivals: Nineteenth-Century Furniture in the Newark Museum.* Newark, NJ: Newark Museum, 1983.

Frelinghuysen, Alice Cooney. *American Porcelain, 1770–1920.* New York: Metropolitan Museum of Art and Harry N. Abrams, 1989.

Gere, Charlotte. *Nineteenth-Century Decoration: The Art of the Interior.* New York: Harry N. Abrams, 1989.

Hope, Thomas. *Household Furniture and Interior Decoration.* New York: Dover, 1971 (orig. pub. London, 1807).

Klamkin, Marian. *White House China.* New York: Charles Scribner's Sons, 1972.

Klapthor, Margaret Brown, et al. *Official White House China: 1789 to the Present.* 2nd ed. New York: The Barra Foundation, in association with Harry N. Abrams, 1999.

Lewis, Arnold, James Turner, and Steven McQuillin, *The Opulent Interiors of the Gilded Age: All 203 Photographs from "Artistic Houses"* (New York: Dover, 1987; reprint of 1883–84 edition).

Monkman, Betty C. *Treasures of the White House.* New York: Abbeville Press, 2001.

———. *The White House: Its Historic Furnishings and First Families.* Washington, DC and New York: White House Historical Association and Abbeville Press, 2000.

Monroe, Michael. *The White House Collection of American Crafts.* New York: Harry N. Abrams and the Smithsonian Institution, 1995.

Schwartz, Marvin D., Edward J. Stanek, and Douglas K. True. *The Furniture of John Henry Belter and the Rococo Revival.* New York: E. P. Dutton, 1981.

Sweeney, John A. H. *The Treasure House of Early American Rooms.* New York: Viking Press, 1963.

———. *Winterthur Illustrated.* Winterthur, DE: H. F. du Pont Winterthur Museum, 1963.

Tracy, Berry B. *Classical America, 1815–1845.* Newark, NJ: Newark Museum, 1963.

Venable, Charles L., et al. *China and Glass in America, 1880–1980: From Tabletop to TV Tray.* Dallas and New York: Dallas Museum of Art and Harry N. Abrams, 2000.

Ward, Barbara McLean, and Gerald W. R. Ward, eds. *Silver in American Life.* New Haven, CT: Yale University Press, 1979.

GENERAL

Aikman, Lonnelle. *The Living White House.* 7th ed. Washington, DC: White House Historical Association, 1982.

Bushman, Richard L. *The Refinement of America: Persons, Houses, Cities.* New York: Knopf, 1992.

Chase, Philander D., and Beverly H. Runge, eds. *The Papers of George Washington.* Charlottesville: University Press of Virginia, 1987–2007.

Colby, Virginia Reed, and James B. Atkinson. *Footprints of the Past: Images of Cornish, New Hampshire, and the Cornish Colony.* Concord: New Hampshire Historical Society, 1996.

Crèvecoeur, Hector St. Jean de. *Letters from an American Farmer.* London: Everyman's, 1912 (orig. publ. 1782).

Daniel, Jean Houston, and Price Daniel. *Executive Mansions and Capitols of America.* Waukesha, WI: Country Beautiful, 1969.

Freidel, Frank. *The Presidents of the United States of America.* Washington, DC: White House Historical Association, 1964.

——— and William Pencak, eds. *The White House: The First Two Hundred Years.* Boston: Northeastern University Press, 1994.

Garrett, Wendell, ed. *Our Changing White House.* Boston: Northeastern University Press, 1995.

Gibbs, George. *Memoirs of the Administrations of Washington and John Adams.* New York: W. Van Norcer, 1846.

Girouard, Mark. *Life in the English Country House.* Harmondsworth, Middlesex, UK, and New York: Penguin Books, 1978.

Harris, Neil. *Winterthur and America's Museum Age.* Winterthur, DE: The Henry Francis du Pont Winterthur Museum, 1981.

Hoover, Irwin Hood. *Forty-Two Years in the White House.* Boston: Houghton Mifflin, 1934.

Hosmer, Charles B., Jr. *Preservation Comes of Age.* Charlottesville: University Press of Virginia, 1981.

Howell, Dodge Harrison. *Mount Vernon: Its Owner and Its Story.* Philadelphia and London: J. B. Lippincott, 1932.

Hunt-Jones, Conover. *Dolley and the "Great Little Madison."* Washington, DC: American Institute of Architects Foundation, 1977.

Hurd, Charles. *The White House Story.* New York: Hawthorn Books, 1966.

Johnson, Marilyn, et al. *19th-Century America: Furniture and Other Decorative Arts.* New York: The Metropolitan Museum of Art, 1970.

Johnston, Frances Benjamin. *The White House.* Washington, DC: Gibson Brothers, 1893.

Leeming, Joseph. *The White House in Picture and Story.* New York: George W. Stewart, 1953.

Lewis, Ethel. *The White House: An Informal History of Its Architecture, Interiors & Gardens.* New York: Dodd, Mead, 1937.

McAdoo, Eleanor Wilson. *The Woodrow Wilsons.* New York: McMillan, 1937.

McCarthy, Kathleen D. *Women's Culture.* Chicago: The University of Chicago Press, 1991.

McConnell, Jane, and Burt McConnell. *The White House: A History with Pictures.* New York: The Studio, 1954.

Mitchell, Stewart, ed. *New Letters of Abigail Adams, 1788–1801.* Boston: Houghton Mifflin, 1947.

Niemcewicz, Julian Ursyn. *Under Their Vine and Fig Tree: Travels Through America in 1797–1799, 1805, with Some Further Account of Life in New Jersey.* Translated and edited by Metchie J. E. Budka. *Collections of the New Jersey Historical Society* vol. 14 (1965).

Parks, Lillian Rogers, in collaboration with Frances Spatz Leighton. *My Thirty Years Backstairs at the White House.* New York: Fleet, 1961.

Pearce, Lorraine Waxman. *The White House: An Historic Guide.* Washington, DC: White House Historical Association, 1962.

Picture of Washington and Its Vicinity for 1848. Washington, DC: William Q. Force, 1848.

Reps, John W. *Washington on View: The Nation's Capital Since 1790.* Chapel Hill: University of North Carolina Press, 1991.

Ronda, James P. "The Objects of Our Journey." Introduction to Carolyn Gilman, *Lewis and Clark: Across the Divide,* 15–49. Washington and London: Smithsonian Books, 2003.

Ryan, William, and Desmond Guinness. *The White House: An Architectural History.* New York: McGraw-Hill, 1980.

Schlesinger, Arthur M., Jr. *The Age of Jackson.* Boston: Little, Brown, 1945.

Seale, William. *The President's House.* 2 vols. Washington, DC: White House Historical Association, 1986.

————. *The White House: The History of an America Idea.* Washington, DC: The White House Historical Association and the American Institute of Architects Press, 1992.

————, et al. *The White House: Actors and Observers.* Boston: Northeastern University Press, 2002.

Singleton, Esther. *The Story of the White House.* New York: McClure, 1907.

Smith, Margaret Bayard. *The First Forty Years of Washington Society.* New York: Charles Scribner's Sons, 1906.

Taft, Mrs. William Howard (Helen Heron). *Recollections of Full Years.* New York: Dodd, Mead, 1917.

Truett, Randle Bond. *The White House: Home of the Presidents.* New York: Hastings House, 1949.

West, James B. *Upstairs at the White House: My Life with the First Ladies.* New York: Coward, McCann & Geoghegan, 1973.

Willets, Gilson. *Inside History of the White House.* New York: The Christian Herald, 1908.

Williams, Charles Richard, ed. *The Diary and Letters of Rutherford B. Hayes.* Columbus: Ohio State Archaeological and Historical Society, 1922–26.

Wilson, Edith Bolling. *My Memoir.* Indianapolis, IN and New York: Bobbs-Merrill, 1939.

Wilson, Richard Guy et al. *The American Renaissance, 1867–1917.* Brooklyn, NY: The Brooklyn Museum, 1979.

Wolff, Perry. *A Tour of the White House with Mrs. John F. Kennedy.* Garden City, NY: Doubleday, 1962.

PHOTOGRAPHY CREDITS

Acanthus Press, New York, NY: 25 (elevations), 28–9 (plans), 71 (bottom), 100, 107 (photo and plan), 149 (plan), 191 (top), 205 (plan)

Architectural Digest, nd [1940]: 198 (bottom left)

Atherton Heritage Association, Atherton, CA: 117 (left)

Avery Architectural and Fine Arts Library, Columbia University, New York, NY: 70

Baltimore Museum of Art, Baltimore, MD: 51 (top)

James Dwight Baum, *The Work of James Dwight Baum*, 1927 (Acanthus Press reprint, 2008): 198 (top left)

John Lossing Benson, *Mount Vernon and Its Associates*, 1859: 114 (right)

William Birch, *The Country Seats of the United States of North America with Some Scenes Connected with Them*, 1808: 42

Boscobel House and Gardens, Garrison, NY: 240 (top left)

Brooklyn Museum, Brooklyn, NY: 85, 98 (top left)

William J. Clinton Presidential Library, Little Rock, AK: 245 (right), 274

Colonial Williamsburg Foundation, Williamsburg, VA: 32–3

DAR Museum, Washington, DC: 63 (right)

Andrew Jackson Downing, *The Architecture of Country Houses: Including Designs for Cottages and Farm-Houses and Villas, With Remarks on Interiors, Furniture and the best Modes of Warming and Ventilating*, 1850: 71 (top)

Andrew Jackson Downing, *A Treatise on the Theory and Practice of Landscape Gardening, Adapted to North America, With a View to the Improvement of Country Residences*, 1841: 64 (top left and right, bottom left), 77 (top left and right)

Dwight D. Eisenhower Library, Abilene, KS: Frontispiece, 201, 234–35, 237

Barr Ferree, *American Estates and Gardens*, 1904: 142 (top left)

Gore Place Society, Waltham, MA: 31

Rutherford B. Hayes Presidential Center, Fairmont, OH: 118–19

Herbert Hoover Presidential Library, West Branch, IA: 197 (top), 220, 238

Historic Hudson Valley, Tarrytown, NY: 54

Historic New England, Cambridge, MA: 72

Lyndon Baines Johnson Library and Museum, Austin, TX: 244 (right)

Frances Benjamin Johnston, *The White House*, 1893: 109

John Fitzgerald Kennedy Library, Boston, MA: 247, 250, 251 (bottom), 253, 254–55, 256, 260, 262, 263

The Family of Robert Knudsen: 258

Library of Congress, Washington, DC: 13, 16 (HABS), 26–7, 30, 34–40, 43, 44 (top), 53, 59 (top left HABS), 59 (middle right, bottom), 62 (top right, bottom right), 67–9, 73 (bottom), 76, 77 (bottom), 82–3, 95 (top left, bottom left), 98 (right), 99 (bottom, HABS), 104–5, 106, 108, 110–11, 120 (top, HABS), 120 (bottom), 122 (left), 129 (bottom), 131 (bottom), 133, 135, 136, 138, 140, 141 (top center, bottom left), 145–47, 151, 156–7, 159, 163, 167, 168 (top), 169 (top), 171, 173 (left), 174, 175, 176, 177, 178, 179 (right), 180–81, 183, 184, 185, 186 (bottom), 187, 188, 190 (top), 191 (bottom), 196 (bottom), 202, 206, 208, 211–12, 228, 243, 246, 252, 269 (HABS), 270 (HABS), 271 (HABS)

Lorenzo State Historic Site, Cazenovia, NY, New York Office of Parks, Recreation, and Historic Preservation: 51 (bottom)

Maryland Historical Society, Baltimore, MD: 56

Massachusetts Historical Society, Boston, MA: 44 (bottom)

Metropolitan Museum of Art, New York, NY: 59 (top right), 79

A Monograph of the Works of McKim, Mead & White, 1879–1915. New York, 1914–20: 153

Joseph West Moore, *Picturesque Washington*, 1884: 103

Munson-Williams-Proctor Arts Institute Museum of Art, Utica, NY: 88

Museum of Fine Arts, Boston, MA © 2009: 57

National Archives, Washington, DC: 114 (left), 115–16, 121 (top), 148, 162, 164 (top), 166 (middle and bottom), 168 (bottom), 217

National Gallery of Art, The Dunlap Society, Washington, DC: 204, 210

National Geographic, March, 1915: 160

National Portrait Gallery, Washington, DC: 50, 75

John Preston Neale, *Views of the Seats, Mansions, Castles & Country Seats of Noblemen and Gentlemen in England, Wales, Scotland and Ireland, and Other Picturesque Scenery,* 1829: 22 (bottom right)

New York Genealogical and Biographical Society, New York, NY: 89, 90

New-York Historical Society, New York, NY: 45 (bottom), 58 (bottom right), 182, 189

New York Public Library, Astor, Lenox and Tilden Foundations, New York, NY, Prints and Photographs: 41, 86 (left)

New York Public Library, Astor, Lenox and Tilden Foundations, New York, NY, Robert N. Dennis Collection of Stereoscopic Views, in the Miriam and Ira D. Wallach Division of Art, Prints and Photographs: 15, 80–1, 84, 91, 93, 112, 117 (right), 122 (right), 123, 124, 126, 127, 128, 129 (top left and right), 130, 134, 137, 173 (right), 179 (left)

Newark Museum, Newark, NJ: 58 (top left, center), 58 (bottom left), 62 (top left), 95 (top right), 139 (bottom left), 197 (bottom), 239

Frederick Law Olmsted Archives, Brookline, MA: 161, 213–14

Pennsylvania State Archive, Harrisburg, PA: 142 (bottom left and right)

Philadelphia Museum of Art, Philadelphia, PA: 62 (bottom left), 97 (top left, bottom left), 141 (top left and right, middle), 272 (top)

Private Collections: 11, 22 (top right, bottom left), 25 (top right three), 45 (top), 64 (bottom right), 73 (top), 100 (top left and right, bottom right), 131 (top), 142 (top right), 150, 154–55, 158, 164 (bottom), 166 (top), 186 (top), 190 (bottom), 198 (top right, bottom right), 215, 218 (bottom), 221, 222 (top left, center right), 222 (bottom), 223, 225 (bottom), 226, 227, 229, 240 (top right, bottom right), 244 (left), 249, 259, 261, 265

Report of the Supervising Architect of Treasury Department. Washington, DC: Treasury Department, Office of Supervising Architect, October 31, 1868: 113

Ronald Reagan Presidential Library and Foundation, Simi Valley, CA: 245 (left)

George Richardson, *Vitruvius Brittanicus,* 2, 1802: 22 (top left)

Franklin D. Roosevelt Library, Hyde Park, NY: 203 (left), 225 (top)

Sears, Roebuck and Co. catalogue, 1920 (Acanthus Press Collection): 207

George William Sheldon, *Artistic Country-Seats,* 1887: 100 (bottom right), 125, 132

Thomas Sheraton, *Cabinet-Maker and Upholsterer's Drawing Book,* 1793. George Peabody Library, Sheridan Libraries, Johns Hopkins University, Baltimore, MD: 52

Louise Shelton, *Beautiful Gardens in America,* 1924: 166 (top)

Esther Singleton, *The Story of the White House,* 1907: 131 (top)

Anthony St. John Baker, *Mémoires d'un voyageur qui se repose.* Paris: Self-published, 1850. Huntington Library and Art Gallery, San Marino, CA, 47–9

Smithsonian American Art Museum, Washington, DC: 272 (bottom)

Smithsonian Institution, Archives of American Gardens, Washington, DC: 248, 251 (top)

Harry S. Truman Library, Independence, MISS: 203 (right), 216, 218 (top), 219, 222 (top right), 230, 231, 232, 233, 236

United States Magazine, 1856: 86 (right)

Washington Historical Society, Washington, DC: 121 (bottom)

Western Reserve Historical Society, Cleveland, OH: 87, 165

White House Historical Association, Washington, DC: 16, 59 (middle left), 60, 61, 75, 95 (middle left, bottom right), 97 (top right), 99 (top), 139 (top, bottom right), 141 (bottom right), 196 (top), 222 (center left), 224, 264, 266, 267, 273

The White House, Office of the Curator, Washington. DC: 97 (bottom right), 192, 193, 194, 195

Woodrow Wilson House, Washington, DC: 63 (left), 169 (bottom), 170

Winterthur Museums and Gardens, Wilmington, DL: 58 (top right), 240 (bottom left), 257

INDEX

Page numbers in italics refer to illustrations